T0327351

RESEARCH IN MARITIME HISTORY
NO. 6

MANAGEMENT, FINANCE AND INDUSTRIAL RELATIONS IN MARITIME INDUSTRIES: ESSAYS IN INTERNATIONAL MARITIME AND BUSINESS HISTORY

Edited by
Simon P. Ville and David M. Williams

International Maritime Economic History Association

St. John's, Newfoundland
1994

ISSN -1188-3928
ISBN -0-9695885-4-2

Research in Maritime History is available free of charge to members of the International Maritime Economic History Association. The price to others is US$15 per copy.

Back issues of *Research in Maritime History* are available:

No. 1 (1991)   David M. Williams and Andrew P. White (comps.), *A Select Bibliography of British and Irish University Theses about Maritime History, 1792-1990*

No. 2 (1992)   Lewis R. Fischer (ed.), *From Wheel House to Counting House: Essays in Maritime Business History in Honour of Professor Peter Neville Davies*

No. 3 (1992)   Lewis R. Fischer and Walter Minchinton (eds.), *People of the Northern Seas*

No. 4 (1993)   Simon Ville (ed.), *Shipbuilding in the United Kingdom in the Nineteenth Century: A Regional Approach*

No. 5 (1993)   Peter N. Davies (ed.), *The Diary of John Holt*

Research in Maritime History would like to thank Memorial University of Newfoundland for its generous financial assistance in support of this volume.

CONTENTS

CONTRIBUTORS

iii

ABOUT THE EDITORS

SIMON P. VILLE is Senior Lecturer and Head of the Department of Economic History at Australian National University. He has published widely on transport and business history, including *English Shipowning in the Industrial Revolution. Michael Henley and Son, London Shipowners, 1770-1830* (Manchester, 1987) and *Transport and the Development of the European Economy, 1750-1918* (London, 1990). He is also editor of *Shipbuilding in the United Kingdom in the Nineteenth Century: A Regional Approach* (Research in Maritime History No. 4, St. John's, 1993).

DAVID M. WILLIAMS is Senior Lecturer in the Department of Economic and Social History at the University of Leicester, Chair of the Editorial Board of the *International Journal of Maritime History* and Secretary of the British Commission for Maritime History. His writings on nineteenth-century maritime topics have appeared in a variety of international books and journals. He is co-compiler of *A Select Bibliography of British and Irish University Theses about Maritime History, 1792-1990* (Research in Maritime History No. 1, St. John's, 1991).

CONTRIBUTORS

TONY ARNOLD is a Reader and ICAEW Academic Fellow in the Department of Accounting and Financial Management at the University of Essex. He has a particular interest in the relationship between the state and the shipping during the nineteenth and early twentieth centuries.

KUO-TUNG CH'EN received his PhD from Yale University and has been associated with the Institute of Economics at the Academia Sinica in Taiwan since 1982. His main interest is in Chinese economic history, particularly commercial and trading activities. Dr. Ch'en has published several articles on Chinese maritime customs, junk shipping and Spanish and Dutch colonial activities on Taiwan.

GIUSEPPE CONTI is Associate Professor of Economic History at the University of Pisa. His research deals with the evolving relationship between the financial sector and corporate finance. His publications include a book on the history of an Italian mortgage bank in the nineteenth century.

LEWIS R. FISCHER is Professor of History at Memorial University of Newfoundland and Editor-in-Chief of the *International Journal of Maritime History*. He has published widely on various topics in nineteenth- and twentieth-century maritime economic and business history.

MARTIN FRITZ is a Senior Reader in the Department of Economic History at the University of Gothenburg. The author of a number of books and articles on the Swedish iron and steel industry, his research interests currently focus on nineteenth-century economic development in Gothenburg.

ROBERT GREENHILL is a Principal Lecturer in the Department of Business Studies at Guildhall University, London. He has published widely on nineteenth- and twentieth-century shipping firms, especially in the South American trades.

TONY HENDERSON gained his PhD in 1992 with a study of prostitution in Georgian London. He is currently Research Fellow, Port of London Project, in the History Department of Queen Mary and Westfield College, University of London.

YRJÖ KAUKIAINEN is Professor of Economic History at the University of Helsinki. He is a specialist in Finnish and international shipping, especially in the nineteenth century, and has recently published *A History of Finnish Shipping* (London, 1993).

HELGE W. NORDVIK is Professor of Economic History at the Norwegian School of Economics and Business Administration. A specialist on nineteenth- and twentieth-century Norwegian and international maritime history, he has published in a variety of maritime and economic history journals and is Editor of the *International Journal of Maritime History*.

KENT OLSSON is a Senior Reader in the Department of Economic History at the University of Gothenburg. The author of numerous books and articles on income distribution and the Swedish shipbuilding industry, he is currently studying the twentieth-century economic history of Gothenburg.

SARAH PALMER is Senior Lecturer in the Department of History at Queen Mary and Westfield College, University of London. She is the author of *Politics, Shipping and the Repeal of the Navigation Laws* (Manchester, 1990).

JESÚS M. VALDALISO is Lecturer in Economic History at the Universidad del País Vasco in Bilbao. His recent publications include *Los navieros vascos y la marina mercante en España, 1860-1935. Una historia económica* (Bilbao, 1991) and *Desarrollo y declive de la flota mercante española en el siglo XX: Historia de la Compañía Marítima del Nervión (1907-1986)* (Madrid, 1993).

YUKIO YAMASHITA is Professor of Business History at Chuo University in Tokyo. He is a specialist in Japanese maritime business history in both the pre- and post-World War II periods.

Introduction: Studies in Maritime Business History[1]

Simon P. Ville and David M. Williams

Maritime and business history are two fields of economic history that have generated immense scholarly interest in recent decades. While maritime history has a long and distinguished pedigree, the formation of the International Maritime Economic History Association in 1986 and the launch of its specialist journal, the *International Journal of Maritime History*, in 1989, have provided new impetus. That maritime history has taken on a new dimension and embraced novel approaches is clear from a recent historiographic survey by David Williams.[2] Likewise, business history has undergone enormous expansion; its growth and specialist sub-fields are evidenced by new journals, such as *Accounting, Business and Financial History* (1991), together with new societies, including the Association of Business Historians, founded in Britain in 1992.

It is highly appropriate that these two areas should be foci within economic history. Man's relationship to the sea is an established theme, for the sea occupied a crucial position in human history by directly affecting the experiences and lifestyles of communities on or near the coast. Moreover, as inland transport links became more extensive, the hinterland of seaward influence expanded. The sea was not only a means of transport but also an important resource, primarily as a source of food. Significantly, in the context of global development, the sea provided the means to expand horizons and to facilitate contacts with other civilisations. Mankind's knowledge of world resources and opportunities was acquired through this medium. The development of a modern, integrated world economy in the past two centuries is a direct consequence of man's growing skills in traversing the sea and harnessing

[1]The editors would like to express their appreciation to the Centre for Business History in Scotland and the Aggregate Foundation for sponsoring a conference in Glasgow in August 1993 at which early drafts of all these papers were presented and discussed.

[2]D. Williams, "The Progress of Maritime History, 1953-93" *Journal of Transport History*, Third Series, XIV (1993), 126-142.

technology. The increasing mobility of people, goods, ideas, and information underlies the spread of economic development; in global terms, until the beginning of real commercial aviation after World War II, such movements were almost solely functions of maritime acumen.

The growth of big business has been equally seminal to modern historical development. Indeed, Alfred Chandler has suggested that the large-scale companies which have evolved since the mid-nineteenth century are the most efficient means of conducting business. As well, the "visible hand" of corporate decision-making has exercised a major influence on economic development.[3] While Chandler's views are not shared by all scholars, particularly those studying economies other than the United States, his path-breaking work has done much to stimulate the academic study of business history, especially changing organisational structures and strategic decision-making. Business history has also benefited from thought-provoking and accessible advances in industrial economics. The work on entrepreneurship and management by the likes of Frank Knight, Mark Casson, Oliver Williamson, Edith Penrose, William Baumol and Robin Marris has done much to provide an effective and historically relevant set of theories for business historians.[4]

These two realms of scholarly study are linked by an intertwined tradition because maritime industries provide an appropriate focus for business historians. The sector produces a range of goods and services, most obviously the carriage of goods and passengers, which in turn generates a range of ancillary activities, including shipbuilding and repair, broking, insurance, and a plethora of port operations. Besides providing a transport function, the sea is also a resource for extractive industries like fishing and, in recent decades, mineral and oil exploitation. Each generates a diverse range of challenges for the individuals and

---

[3]A.D. Chandler, *The Visible Hand: the Managerial Revolution in American Business* (Cambridge, MA, 1977); Chandler, *Scale and Scope: The Dynamics of Industrial Capitalism* (Cambridge, MA, 1990).

[4]F. Knight, *Risk, Uncertainty and Profit* (Boston, 1921); M. Casson, *The Entrepreneur: An Economic Theory* (Oxford, 1982); O.E. Williamson, *The Economic Institutions of Capitalism* (New York, 1985); E.T. Penrose, *The Theory of the Growth of the Firm* (Oxford, 1959); W.J. Baumol, *Business Behaviour, Value and Growth* (New York, 1959); R. Marris, *The Economic Theory of Managerial Capitalism* (London, 1964).

enterprises involved and provokes a broad spectrum of general issues of interest to business historians, such as the problem of agency; the dilemma of operating under conditions of uncertainty and imperfect information; and the question of strategic response to economic growth. It is also important to remember that maritime industries operate in international markets; while this may today be true of many economic sectors (in part because of the development of sea transportation), maritime enterprise by its nature has for millennia been shaped by trans-national influences. As a result, it is hardly surprising to find an extended tradition of maritime business history. Although this stretches back a considerable time, an important watershed came with the series of company histories produced from the late 1950s by the "Liverpool school" under the aegis of the late Francis Hyde.[5] These works set new standards for careful scholarly research and analysis. Their focus was very much on decision-making, resource allocation, and entrepreneurial behaviour, all central issues to economic historians. Appropriately, the Liverpool historians were responsible for the establishment in 1958 of the highly successful journal, *Business History*. The maritime business history tradition continued to flourish throughout the 1970s and 1980s.[6]

The current volume not only continues but also builds upon this tradition. The themes originally addressed formed the contents for a session on "Management, Finance and Industrial Relations in Maritime Industries" at the Eleventh International Economic History Congress in Milan in September 1994. While the original papers written for the session can be found in the appropriate volume published by the congress

---

[5]See, for example, F.E. Hyde, *Blue Funnel. A History of Alfred Holt and Company of Liverpool, 1865-1914* (Liverpool, 1957); Hyde, *Shipping Enterprise and Management, 1830-1939. Harrisons of Liverpool* (Liverpool, 1967); Hyde, *Cunard* (London, 1975).

[6]Examples include P.N. Davies, *Henry Tyrer: A Liverpool Shipping Agent and his Enterprises, 1879-1979* (London, 1979); E. Green and M. Moss, *A Business of National Importance: the Royal Mail Shipping Group, 1902-37* (London, 1982); A. Porter, *Shipping, Business and Imperial Policy: Donald Currie, the Castle Line and South Africa* (Woodbridge, 1986); S. Jones, *Two Centuries of Overseas Trading: The Origins and Growth of the Inchcape Group* (London, 1986); S. Ville, *English Shipowning during the Industrial Revolution. Michael Henley and Son, London Shipowners, 1770-1830* (Manchester, 1987); M. Falkus, *The Blue Funnel Legend: A History of the Ocean Steam Ship Company, 1865-1973* (London, 1990).

organisers, we also asked the authors to build upon their original essays to investigate key issues in greater detail than was possible in the space allocated by the congress. The current volume contains these more detailed papers, which in some cases have been broadened to address additional questions. They cover a wide range of geographic, temporal and subject areas.

While seeking to embrace a representative sample of maritime business activities, the editors also sought a common focus by requiring contributors to direct their research specifically towards the issues of management, finance and labour. In so doing, the intention was to encourage them to consider the economics of maritime industries and the factors that influenced decision-making. All the papers analyze management policy and decisions, which are functions not only of current and future market prospects but also of past experiences and practices. Industries and their constituent enterprises, like the economies and societies of which they are a part, are conditioned by previous events and behaviour. Decision-making thus has an historic as well as a contemporary dimension.

The importance of the volume, we believe, lies in its attention to relatively neglected areas of maritime business history. Lewis Fischer and Helge Nordvik's current research project on the Norwegian shipbrokers, Fearnley and Eger, is the first scholarly study of the history of a specialist broking firm. Their essay looks at the company's approach to information acquisition and utilisation. The authors engage uncertainty theory to show that, despite its alleged importance for brokers, this company was long inefficient in processing information and that decisions were often made on non-economic grounds. Our knowledge of labour management is limited. Sarah Palmer and Tony Henderson make an important contribution towards filling this lacuna in their chapter on early nineteenth-century London dock companies. Of necessity, these large-scale organisations adopted labour management strategies dealing with recruitment, control, retention, workplace division, rewards, and punishments. If we know little about labour management in port, our knowledge of what went on at sea is not much more advanced. It has long been assumed, for example, that the managerial role of shipmasters was of great importance. Yrjö Kaukiainen's study of Finnish masters in the nineteenth century provides vital evidence to bolster this hypothesis. Jesús Valdaliso's study, like the examination by Martin Fritz and Kent

Olsson of Gothenburg shipbuilders, investigates the managerial strategies of important shipping companies within the context of twentieth-century economic fluctuations. The novelty of Tony Arnold and Robert Greenhill's contribution lies in their revisionist interpretation of a popular topic: mail subsidies. Focusing on the experience of the Royal Mail Company, they argue that British government mail payments did not represent bounties but instead were due consideration for services provided. The issues of ownership and finance – for an entire sector rather than merely an individual company – are the themes of Gelina Harlaftis' paper, which undertakes a detailed statistical analysis of the Greek shipping industry. Given the concentration within maritime business history of studies set in an Atlantic or "northern seas" context, such a survey provides valuable breadth to our understanding of the business of shipping. The rapidly changing fortunes of national shipbuilding industries in the twentieth century is a recognised but limited area of research study. The enormity of Britain's decline has served to divert attention from both the problems and the successes of other nations. The papers by Giuseppe Conti and Yukio Yamashita thus serve to extend considerably our knowledge. The former reveals the complexities of relationships between the banks and industry in interwar Italy, while Professor Yamashita examines the factors underlying the expansion of postwar Japanese shipbuilding. Finally, Kuo-tung Ch'en's survey of Chinese junks and their trades provides a wealth of new information about ownership, technology, manning, and trade routes in the eighteenth and early nineteenth centuries.

This volume thus comprises studies which, while encompassing a common theme, range widely in analytic focus and geographic context. The essays most certainly add to our knowledge and understanding of many facets of entrepreneurial behaviour in maritime industries, often in hitherto little-researched sectors. In so doing, they testify to the current level of scholarly interest in maritime business history and, above all, to its international character.

Economic Theory, Information and Management in Shipbroking: Fearnley and Eger as a Case Study, 1869-1972[1]

Lewis R. Fischer and Helge W. Nordvik

Introduction: Information, Management and Economic Theory

Economic theory until recently has had relatively little to offer business historians interested in decision-making within a particular enterprise. The central dilemma was in effect a lack of congruence between theory and reality. In particular, two assumptions shared to varying degrees by both classical and neo-classical economists ran counter to what many scholars encountered when examining intra-firm behaviour. The first — an insistence upon the concept of perfect competition (or, in another guise, the "perfect market") — has always constrained the utility of economic models for business historians confronted with monopsonies, monopolies or other forms of imperfect markets. According to traditional theory, such conditions could only be transitory, since inflated returns would eventually induce new entrants, thereby restoring competition.[2] Yet even ignoring the vexing problem of defining "transitory" (or its oft-used synonym, "short-term"), the difficulty is that there are many historical cases of companies with sufficiently substantial market shares to enable them to be consistent price makers rather than price takers. Moreover, some enterprises have been able to defy the model's

[1]We would like to thank Anders Martin Fon for research assistance as well as for sharing his insights into Fearnley and Eger. We are also grateful to participants at a preliminary conference in Glasgow for comments and suggestions, and especially to Dr. Gordon Jackson for a stimulating commentary. Funding for this project was provided in part by the the Social Sciences and Humanities Research Council of Canada and Astrup/Fearnley.

[2]See, for example, the discussion in Walter Nicholson, *Microeconomic Theory* (4th ed., Hinsdale, IL, 1988). A particularly glaring statement of this dilemma is contained in Jean Tirole, *The Theory of Industrial Organization* (Cambridge, MA, 1988), 50-51.

Research in Maritime History, No. 6 (June 1994), 1-29.

predictions for much longer than even the most generous construction of "transitory" would permit.[3] Fortunately, the theory of agency and the concept of transaction costs have enabled economic theorists to design models which have largely overcome this difficulty.[4]

But the second assumption has in many ways been more difficult to rationalize. This is the idea that individuals or firms always make decisions based upon perfect knowledge. That this is unlikely to be true is suggested by common sense and practical experience. Since even the most learned economist would be hard-pressed to describe a transaction in which all actors were guided by anything approaching "perfect knowledge," how reasonable is it to incorporate such a concept into economic models? Economists concerned with this conundrum eventually turned to the theory of uncertainty. While this helped to a certain extent, it did not entirely solve the problem for two reasons. First, the so-called "Arrow-Debreu theory" which lay at the heart of this approach was highly mathematical and as such unlikely to meet the needs of most business historians. Perhaps more important, the model was not originally designed as a way of simulating equilibrium under conditions of uncertainty; the elaboration which enabled it to be so used has struck many scholars as only marginally satisfactory.[5]

---

[3]Despite the insistence of traditional theorists that no firm would be able to affect the price of a transaction, the rise of large-scale industrial organizations in the late nineteenth century and the merger movement of the early twentieth produced numerous contradictory examples. For a particularly insightful discussion of this problem, see Daniel M.G. Raff and Peter Temin, "Business History and Recent Economic Theory: Imperfect Information, Incentives and the Internal Organization of Firms," in Peter Temin (ed.), *Inside the Business Enterprise: Historical Perspectives on the Use of Information* (Chicago, 1991), 7-35.

[4]Perhaps the clearest discussion of agency theory is M. Jensen and W. Meckling, "Theory of the Firm: Managerial Behavior, Agency Costs and Ownership Structure," *Journal of Financial Economics*, III (1976), 305-360. On the concept of transaction costs, see George Stigler, "Imperfections in the Capital Market," *Journal of Political Economy*, LXXV (1967), 287-292; and Oliver E. Williamson, "Transaction-Cost Economics: The Governance of Contractual Relations," *Journal of Law and Economics*, XXII (1979), 233-261.

[5]The Arrow-Debreu theory was designed originally to elaborate on the theory of value. The seminal works are K.J. Arrow, "The Role of Securities in the Optimal Allocation of Risk-Bearing," *Review of Economic Studies*, XXXI (1953), 91-96; and G. Debreu, *Theory of Value* (New York, 1959). For a defense of this theory, which we

Fortunately, the real problem for business historians was alleviated (although not cured) in 1961 when George Stigler, later to be honoured as a Nobel laureate in economics, observed that since information is scarce, it is therefore expensive. As a result, he argued, it is highly unlikely that economic actors (or business decision-makers) would wish to incur the costs associated with obtaining the totality of available information in all circumstances. In practical terms, it is clear that few business decisions are likely to be made under the conditions specified by traditional economic theory.[6] Over the past three decades this insight has been generally accepted and has gradually become part of what may be thought of as a new economic theory of the firm.[7]

Stigler's insight was important since it provided business historians with a theoretical perspective from which to analyze those instances in which complete information was not sought. Yet neither he nor his disciples went very far toward explaining why firms often chose to make decisions based upon partial information. If the factors that induced this behaviour were always economic this would not present a problem, since there are a plethora of models that purport to explain such choices. But there is good reason to believe that non-economic

---

believe far overstates its utility, see the eloquent essay by Roy Radner, "Uncertainty and General Equilibrium," in John Eatwell, Murray Milgate and Peter Newman (eds.), *The New Palgrave: A Dictionary of Economics* (4 vols., London, 1987), IV, 734-741. The most useful statement linking the idea of uncertainty to business (and business history) is Jay Galbraith, *Designing Complex Organizations* (Reading, MA, 1973).

[6]George Stigler, "The Economics of Information," *Journal of Political Economy*, LXIX (1961), 432-449.

[7]For summaries of recent developments on this subject, see especially Oliver E. Williamson, *The Economic Institutions of Capitalism* (New York, 1985); Williamson, *Economic Organization: Firms, Markets, and Policy Control* (New York, 1986), xi-xviii; Thomas McCraw, "The Challenge of Alfred D. Chandler," *Reviews in American History*, XIV (1986), 160-178; Daniel Levinthal, "A Survey of Agency Models of Organizations," *Journal of Economic Behavior and Organization*, IX (1988), 153-185; and Bengt R. Holmstrom and Jean Tirole, "The Theory of the Firm," in Richard Schmalansee and Robert Willig (eds.), *Handbook of Industrial Organization* (2 vols., Amsterdam, 1989), I, 61-133.

variables can also influence choice, as Masahiko Aoki has shown clearly in a recent study of Japanese firms.[8]

Lacking a solid theoretical base for understanding why firms at certain times choose to pursue information more assiduously than at others, we are forced to cast our nets more widely. The business historian JoAnne Yates has noted that approaches to the acquisition of information have been discontinuous and uneven in the firms she has studied. Moreover, the choice of when and how to collect and utilize data appears to stem primarily from managerial needs, financial and human investments in the existing system, and the costs (both economic and non-economic) entailed in bringing about change. These factors, she concluded, applied not only to the question of whether to obtain external information but also to the issue of the way it is stored, analyzed and retrieved internally.[9]

The introduction of management into the equation is important because it explicitly sensitizes scholars interested in proceeding from a theoretical perspective to the human dimension. While few managers are likely to value information for its own sake, the great majority will be interested to the degree that it assists them in meeting goals. As Alfred Chandler reminded us thirty years ago, good managers will attempt to design a structure that facilitates goal-attainment, including the management of information flows. While not all managers will be successful, it behooves business historians to begin by attempting to delineate the goals of the firms they study.[10]

In this essay we propose to focus on the issues of management and information in a maritime enterprise. In so doing we want not only to analyze the factors that influenced choices about the collection and utilization of information in a specific company but also to examine the results. From the particular perspective of maritime history, we hope as well to contribute to an understanding of the development of shipping

---

[8]Masahiko Aoki, "Toward an Economic Model of the Japanese Firm," *Journal of Economic Literature*, XXVIII (1990), 1-27.

[9]See JoAnne Yates, *Control through Communication: The Rise of System in American Management* (Baltimore, 1989); and Yates, "Investing in Information: Supply and Demand Forces in the Use of Information in American Firms, 1850-1920," in Temin (ed.), *Inside the Business Enterprise*, 117-154.

[10]Alfred D. Chandler, Jr., *Strategy and Structure* (Cambridge, MA, 1962).

over a 100-year period by shedding some light on the operations of a group of often overlooked middlemen. Our vehicle for attaining these goals is an examination of the Oslo shipbrokers, Fearnley and Eger. It is particularly appropriate to pose such questions about shipbrokers, since information was (and is) particularly important to this profession. Indeed, it is not a great overstatement to suggest that it is virtually all they have to sell. Successful shipbrokers must match a variety of buyers and sellers of shipping services, a process that requires a good deal of knowledge. In chartering, they need to know the needs of shippers and shipowners, the availability of suitable transport, and the price at which a satisfactory deal can be struck. When working in sale and purchase, they require data about world markets in order to link prospective buyers and sellers of tonnage, whether new or second-hand. And if they wish to assist in arranging finance for their deals, a practice which has become more prevalent in recent years, they need information on the state of financial markets as well as interest and exchange rates. Since the conclusion of the First World War, brokers have increasingly become the principal source of information for most of the world's shipowners.[11]

Given these requirements, it might be expected that brokers would spend an inordinate amount of time, effort and money acquiring, analyzing, disseminating and storing information. But an examination of Fearnley and Eger suggests that this was rarely the case. The firm seldom attempted to procure perfect information; had a mixed record of analysis; was poor at disseminating the intelligence it did collect to key actors; and for most of its history had atrocious storage and retrieval systems. Nonetheless, the enterprise has been continuously (although not always equally) profitable. Indeed, at the end of our period it was by most measures the second largest shipbroking firm in the world.[12]

These observations about Fearnley and Eger constitute something of a puzzle, not all of which can be unravelled in this essay. To understand why in the face of a generally poor record in procuring and handling information the firm was so successful would require a

---

[11]For general overviews of the role of shipbrokers within the maritime sector, see J. Bes, *Chartering Practice* (Amsterdam, 1960); and Lars Gorton, Rolf Ihre and Arne Sandevärn, *Shipbroking and Chartering Practice* (London, 1980).

[12]It was certainly the largest shipbroking firm to be completely owned by one man (Hans Rasmus Astrup) and the only major company of its type to refuse to admit its brokers into partnerships.

comparative study which, given our paucity of knowledge about its competitors, is presently impossible.[13] Instead, our goal is more modest: we want to explore why Fearnley and Eger treated information as it did. The burden of our argument is that the explanation was sometimes economic, as might be inferred from Stigler's model. More often, though, the rationale was non-economic, having to do especially with management styles. But regardless of which factor was most important at any given time, it is clear that for this firm the procurement and use of information had limits. Moreover, its high rate of client-retention suggests something that contrary to their protestations, owners have seldom expected brokers to provide perfect data. While this may have facilitated cozy relationships for many decades, it would come back to haunt shipowners during the mid-1970s, when many were lured into costly errors by an overdependence on middlemen dispensing advice based upon incomplete and often flawed information.[14]

The First Half-Century, 1869-1919

Thomas Fearnley founded the firm that bears his name in February 1869.[15] His vision of the future comprised both short- and long-term goals. In the short-run, he was especially interested in profits. Toward this end he engaged not only in broking but also in shipowning and

---

[13]The only scholarly historical studies of brokers are those by the current authors cited throughout the paper. But see also Peter N. Davies, *Henry Tyrer: A Liverpool Shipping Agent and His Enterprises, 1879-1979* (London, 1979), which examines a firm which did some broking.

[14]A more complete discussion of the increasing reliance of shipowners on the advice of brokers may be found in Lewis R. Fischer, "The Shipbroker in History" (unpublished paper presented to the British Commission/ICMH seminar, London, December 1992). This paper, which is currently being revised for publication, shows how from the 1920s onward shipowners often shed costly internal structures for information-gathering in favour of less costly, but often flawed, services offered by brokers.

[15]The "Eger" was Fearnley's cousin, Engelhardt, who joined the firm in 1874 and was a silent partner with no particular role in day-to-day operations. See Lewis R. Fischer and Anders M. Fon, "The Making of a Maritime Firm: The Rise of Fearnley and Eger, 1869-1917," in Fischer (ed.), *From Wheel House to Counting House: Essays in Maritime Business History in Honour of Professor Peter Neville Davies* (St. John's, 1992), 304.

agency work. Yet he was not a pure profit-maximizer because of his approach to the long-term goal of ensuring the stability of his enterprise. This he judged could best be accomplished by forging alliances and finding activities in which he could capitalize on his comparative advantages rather than by extracting all possible profits from a given transaction. From the start Fearnley seemed to be thinking of a company which would far outlive him. As a result, he adopted an exceedingly conservative management style designed to minimize risks. The agencies that the firm assumed, for example, were sufficiently diversified to act as hedges against sectoral fluctuations, while its investments in shipping were spread among a large number of vessels.[16]

But if risk-aversion were a hallmark of his approach to management, it is best to admit that his style was also highly idiosyncratic. As Thomas Johnson and Robert Kaplan have shown, conservative management values are most often related to a reliance upon carefully-planned structures.[17] Yet the structure and organization of Thomas Fearnley's brokerage in its first half-century of operations were in important ways the antithesis of what might have been expected. In particular, decisions and analysis were concentrated at the very top and the owner seldom relied on input from support staff.[18]

The impact of this style on the company's approach to information was mixed. On the one hand, Fearnley always invested in information collection, albeit with an eagle eye on the bottom line. Moreover, he treated the gathering of data in accounting terms as a charge on the company (a practice that would change after World War II), thereby acknowledging its importance to the firm as a whole. Yet on the other hand, he presided over a structure in which information could, at his discretion, flow downward, but less frequently upward and almost never between brokers. As well, his investment in analysis was paltry and the storage and retrieval of information was neglected. These conditions

---

[16]The components of this conservative management strategy are discussed in detail in *ibid.*, 306-308.

[17]H. Thomas Johnson and Robert S. Kaplan, *Relevance Lost: The Rise and Fall of Management Accounting* (Boston, 1987).

[18]Lewis R. Fischer and Helge W. Nordvik, "The Growth of Norwegian Shipbroking: The Practices of Fearnley and Eger as a Case Study, 1869-1914," in Fischer and Walter Minchinton (eds.), *People of the Northern Seas* (St. John's, 1992), 135-155.

existed because it was Thomas Fearnley who was the prime conduit for information coming into the company, its most important analyst, the main repository for its storage, and the principal decision-maker for most of the first half-century. Although the firm employed more than forty people by the outbreak of the First World War, it was still run as though it were a small operation.[19] It is therefore obvious that to comprehend the manner in which Fearnley and Eger handled information requires a focus on the complex man who was at its helm.

When he returned to Christiania (Oslo) after a four and one-half year apprenticeship with a firm of London shipbrokers, Thomas Fearnley entered a relatively stagnant maritime brokerage market. There were only a handful of shipbrokers in the Norwegian capital, in part because of an 1818 law which erected significant barriers to entry into the profession.[20] More important, however, Norwegian shipbrokers suffered from serious locational disadvantages exacerbated by poor communications. Given the need for information, it is hardly surprising that brokers located in or near major shipping centres dominated the profession. Although London's position as a port had been usurped domestically by Liverpool and was being challenged internationally by several continental cities, the British capital remained far and away the most important *market* in which to conclude shipping deals in the second half of the nineteenth century. By comparison, Christiania was very much on the periphery.[21] Norwegian brokers were handicapped by both delays in receiving the latest shipping intelligence and a lack of access to the most important maritime actors.

---

[19]But it was not run like a family firm. Several colleagues have suggested that Fearnley and Eger sounds almost like a "family business" and that we might be advised to situate its experience within that literature. After a good deal of reflection we have chosen to reject this advice, since in important ways this company differed from typical family firms. Perhaps the most obvious was that for most of its history Fearnley and Eger was not undercapitalised.

[20]Norway, Storting (Parliament), Meglerloven, 8 September 1818. The most restrictive provisions of the law were not repealed for Christiania until 1871.

[21]Indeed, it was not until the mid-1860s that the port even became the busiest in Norway. For a discussion of the rise of Christiania as a port, see Lewis R. Fischer and Helge W. Nordvik, "The Evolution of the Norwegian Export Ports, 1850-1910" (Unpublished paper presented to the conference of the North Sea Society, Aberdeen, Scotland, August 1993).

But this situation was on the verge of changing when Fearnley arrived home. Indeed, it is hard to avoid the conclusion that the impending opening of the North Sea telegraph, which went into operation later in the year, convinced him that the decision to return to Norway was timely. More than any other event, the introduction of the cable made it possible for those on the periphery, such as Fearnley in Christiania, to compete with British-based brokers. While it would be inaccurate to assume that this improvement enabled Norwegian brokers to overcome totally the constraints of distance, the new technology certainly alleviated the problem.[22]

Fearnley used the telegraph as part of a strategy to build his brokerage, especially to stay abreast of the latest shipping news from abroad. But he did not use it as much as might have been predicted. During the era that he was actively involved in company affairs – a period which lasted until the First World War – the telegraph was hardly the principal means employed to keep in touch with developments in London or elsewhere. Not all of the firm's correspondence for this period has survived, but from what remains it is possible to chart the relative mix of telegrams and letters. Before 1880, only six percent of the firm's international and less than eight percent of its domestic outgoing correspondence employed the new technology. Between 1880 and 1900, the figures were eight and nine percent, respectively, while in the years from the turn of the century to the outbreak of World War I the proportions were seven and nine percent. In short, despite the potential importance of rapid communications to shipbrokers, Fearnley and Eger used the telegraph sparingly. And while there was a slightly upward

---

[22]Although it would seem logical that the telegraph would play the role outlined above, there is a minor debate in the literature about its impact. For a concise summary of the argument in favour of the positive effect of the telegraph, see JoAnne Yates, "The Telegraph's Effects on Nineteenth Century Markets and Firms," *Business and Economic History*, 2nd ser., XV (1986), 149-163. For a different perspective, see Alexander James Field, "The Magnetic Telegraph, Price and Quantity Data, and the New Management of Capital," *Journal of Economic History*, LII (1992), 401-413. Field, although sceptical of the more traditional interpretation, accepts that in those sectors that depended heavily upon price and financial data the benefits may have been substantial, at least for the transmission of firm-specific information.

secular trend, it appears that the firm's proclivity to use the fastest mode of communication was relatively stagnant over the period.[23]

Why did the firm continue to rely upon slower, more traditional forms of communication both domestically and internationally, despite the high premium that it placed upon speed and up-to-date information? Part of the explanation is obviously economic. The telegraph was expensive relative to the cost of letters transported either by land or sea. In 1869, for example, domestic rates averaged 1.5 kroner for the first twenty words, compared to three øre for a posted letter; the ratio declined relatively little prior to the war.[24] In choosing to utilize letters rather than telegrams, Fearnley and Eger made a conscious decision to accept slower information flows in order to minimize costs.

We have no way of knowing whether competitors in Christiania or elsewhere made greater use of the new technology. But even if they did, Fearnley and Eger was not necessarily at a competitive disadvantage. This is because the firm had alternative methods of gaining information for its clients, a fact which must have entered into its decision calculus. In 1874 the company became the exclusive agent in Norway for H. Clarkson and Co., the largest London shipbroker. This arrangement had two particular advantages for Fearnley. For our purposes the most important was that it guaranteed the Oslo firm access to Clarkson's information network, which was arguably the best in the international broking world. Since Norwegian competitors could not match this source of shipping and market intelligence, it allowed

---

[23]The surviving letters are in various uncatalogued letterbooks and folders in the Norwegian Public Record Office (Riksarkivet), Fearnley and Eger Collection (hereafter F&E). It is also significant that even when he was requesting current shipping intelligence from contacts in Britain the overwhelming tendency was to use the post. While Fearnley's incoming correspondence comprised a slightly higher proportion of telegrams, it is important to note that these did not cost him anything.

[24]See Thorolf Rafto, *Telgrafverkets Historie 1855-1955* (Bergen, 1955), 121. The ratio of the cost of telegrams to letters compares reasonably well with the United States, where in the 1850s the first ten words of a telegram from New York to Chicago cost $1.55 compared to three cents for a first-class letter; see United States, Department of Commerce, Bureau of the Census, *Historical Statistics of the United States from Colonial Times to 1970* (2 vols., Washington, 1975), II, series R-72 and R-190.

Fearnley and Eger to choose to use the costly telegraph less than it might otherwise have done.[25]

But the second part of the agreement also had an effect on Thomas Fearnley's decisions about information. The two firms agreed that in return for acting as an exclusive agent, Fearnley and Eger would receive a share of any commissions deriving from Clarkson's chartering activities to or from Norway, whether or not the Christiania firm actually provided any brokerage services. This relationship thus became a guaranteed source of income and shaped the company's business strategy, allowing it to concentrate on serving a small but select group of clients, the most important of whom was Wilhelm Wilhelmsen, Norway's largest shipowner. With this orientation, rapid access to information became less important, since Fearnley could anticipate reasonably well the likely requests from his customers. This further alleviated the need to incur heavy costs for information.[26]

Not surprisingly, there was a price to be paid for all this. In the case of Fearnley and Eger it was an implicit agreement not to compete with Clarkson outside of Norway. In other words, in order to obtain privileged access to information and a guaranteed commission income the firm accepted voluntary limits upon its activities and growth. This was reflected especially in its chartering operations, which were always focused upon Norwegian ships, shipowners and trades. Indeed, even in the 1890s almost ninety percent of the firm's charter parties involved Norwegian vessels or shippers.[27] Although the company possessed

---

[25]On Clarkson, see *The Clarkson Chronicle 1852-1952* (London, 1952). The nature of the agreement with Clarkson is sketched in Thomas Fearnley to Gunder Aas, 17 April 1872; Fearnley to Clarkson, 18 September 1873; Fearnley to Aas, 10 January 1874, Thomas Fearnley Copy Books, F&E.

[26]Another benefit of the relationship between the two broking firms was that Thomas Fearnley was likely introduced to Wilhelmsen by Henry Benham of Clarkson. The alliance between the Christiania broker and the Tønsberg shipowner eventually led to a partnership in the shipowning firm of Fearnley and Wilhelmsen shortly before the outbreak of World War I. See Gunnar Christie Wasberg and Kaare Petersen, *Fearnley & Eger 1869-1979* (Oslo, 1971), 28. On Wilhelmsen, see Leif B. Lillegaard, *Over alle hav. Wilh. Wilhelmsens rederi* (Oslo, 1986); Kr. Anker Olsen, *Wilh. Wilhelmsen i hundre år* (Oslo, 1961); Jan Petter Syse, *Wilh. Wilhelmsen 1861-1977: A Brief History* (London, 1978).

[27]Derived from an analysis of charter parties in F&E, Box 39.

sufficient information and contacts to enable it to enter other markets, Fearnley and Eger upheld the agreement and steered away from competition with Clarkson.[28]

If Fearnley and Eger was consistently conservative in its approach to external information, it was even more so in its structures for handling this data internally. While it is possible that the surviving records are not representative, what is especially striking is the high proportion of correspondence either to or from Fearnley himself. Not even after the establishment in 1880 of a separate chartering department did the pattern change. Most data entering the company – and all intelligence gathered from the formal links with Clarkson – passed through the owner's hands.

This pattern went hand-in-hand with Thomas Fearnley's proclivity to depend on his own analysis and to keep his own council. There was some logic behind this behaviour; after all, he was the best-trained and most mature broker in the firm. Indeed, when in 1880 he chose Carl O. Lie as the first manager of the chartering department, the new executive was only seventeen years-old and had never been outside Christiania. Yet by monopolizing information Fearnley not only made it difficult for his subordinates to improve their competence but also forced them to search for other sources of intelligence. To exacerbate the situation, he tended to keep what he knew to himself. There were almost no memos to the staff and the filing system through which data could be shared was haphazard at best. In short, Fearnley was the "gatekeeper" of information flows both into and within his company and did little to establish any formal lines of internal communication.[29]

As long as the company was small and the founder came to the office on a regular basis, these flaws might not have been decisive. Indeed, a lack of formal structures was probably common among similar fledgling enterprises elsewhere. But the size of the firm, especially on the

---

[28]Fearnley's sources of information and contacts stretched throughout Europe, Asia and the United States. Only in the last few years before 1914 did the firm begin to diversify slightly, especially into the coal trade from Hampton Roads to Colon during the construction of the Panama Canal. But even in this endeavour there was no serious attempt to breach the agreement with Clarkson, since the economics of the trade made it incumbent to use older sailing vessels. Fearnley could (and did) charter these primarily from his regular core of Norwegian owners.

[29]F&E, letterbooks.

broking side, grew to ten by 1905 and to nineteen by 1914. As it expanded it became more essential to share vital intelligence. Yet it also became increasingly difficult to accomplish this, even had Thomas Fearnley been predisposed to do so. The lack of a filing system, for example, meant that if a broker left the firm, arrangements to look after his clients required a replacement to start virtually from scratch. Moreover, as Thomas Fearnley's interests gradually shifted into land-based investments after the mid-1890s, a new barrier to the flow of information was introduced. The owner began to appear in the office less frequently; as his working habits changed, the flow of information lessened.

This placed a special burden on Carl Lie. While Lie was described by one contemporary as "a born shipbroker," this ironically may have been the source of his problems as a manager. Although by the early 1900s his contract called for him to receive as a commission one-third of the profits of his department, he had what we would characterize as a typical "broker's mentality," which made him loathe to share information with colleagues and predisposed to monopolize the data that came his way, despite the potential impact that such a strategy could have had on his income.[30] Like the owner, Lie established no systematic schemes of communication, reporting to Fearnley orally only when the owner made a specific request. He did not establish a filing system even within the chartering department and wrote few memos to disseminate information. Lie also shared Fearnley's bias against secretaries, perhaps fearing that clerical staff would see it as their responsibility to create and maintain records. Carl Lie, like so many who followed him, was opposed to the existence of too many records.[31]

---

[30]Given the available financial records, it is impossible for us to know for certain whether Lie would have been better off by maximizing his own broking activities or motivating the other brokers. This is because while his commissions were based on revenues, the sums he could earn from the work of others were based on profits. Our suspicion, however, is that he would have earned more from transactions completed by others.

[31]F&E, Box 39. This bias against "writing down too many things" was (and is) endemic in the profession. As part of a parallel project one of the authors has conducted more than fifty interviews with brokers in the United Kingdom; when asked, more than eighty percent mentioned that their firms "frequently" or "always" destroyed records after the consummation of a deal. An even higher percentage indicated that the corporate climate mitigated against the creation of extensive records in the first place. The

Lie also lacked Thomas Fearnley's contacts. While the ties to Clarkson remained a source of information, to be certain of receiving relevant data Lie had to develop his own network. The search for new sources of information led him – and the firm – increasingly into niche trades in which the company had no particular comparative advantage. In 1912, for example, Lie dispatched his son Sverre to Bordeaux, where the young man developed contacts in the West African groundnut trade. While this became a profitable activity in the interwar years, it led away from the mainstream of international broking. Indeed, by the early 1930s the mere mention of the groundnut trade was enough to evoke sardonic smiles in the headquarters in Oslo.[32]

In short, during the first half-century the firm's record on acquiring and managing information was not promising. Although Thomas Fearnley arranged for a superb source of external information, which not only enhanced growth but also enabled the company to keep costs under control, he did not use the data obtained to the best advantage and set several dangerous precedents. He monopolized the information flow to the virtual exclusion of other members of the firm and established no procedures for internal dissemination or retention. While the success of the enterprise (equity rose to 1.7 million kroner by 1914) was largely based on Thomas Fearnley's ability to solicit useful data, information was highly compartmentalized and the structure for using it was shaky. Both the strengths and weaknesses of the system of collecting and handling information that Thomas Fearnley bequeathed to his successors would become glaringly apparent in the years between the two world wars.

The Interwar Years, 1919-1939

The decades between the First and Second World Wars were character-ized by stagnation within the firm. This was especially true for its brokerage operations, which had been separated from shipowning at the

---

treatment of records as anathema to the health of the firm also can make the historical study of shipbrokers exceedingly frustrating.

[32]Interview with Ole Boe, 19 January 1944, F&E.

beginning of 1917.[33] As before the war, a good deal of the success or failure of the firm depended upon information. But from the perspective of the brokers, this reorganization introduced a new set of complications. Although the chartering company was in effect owned by the shipowning firm and shared the same overall management, the leaders who succeeded Thomas Fearnley were much less interested in broking than in shipowning, manufacturing and civic causes. Their main goal appeared only to be that the chartering company should continue to generate what they viewed as "satisfactory returns." Although profits grew slowly during these two decades, the fact that the owners seldom interfered and apparently never complained leads to the inference that they found them acceptable. But the unfortunate result was a lethargy which had a plethora of negative effects on the enterprise. The problem had twin roots. The first was the legacy toward the management of information left by the founder, while the second was a lack of full-time leadership and vision. The latter, of course, exacerbated the former.

The men nominally in charge of the chartering company during the interwar years were Thomas Fearnley, Jr. and Nils Astrup, neither of whom perceived themselves primarily as shipbrokers. Fearnley, the son of the founder, was referred to by employees as "The Shipowner," a generally accurate gauge of his primary interest. Although his father had ensured that he received excellent training as a broker, dispatching him for a three-year apprenticeship with Clarkson, the Shipowner was much more interested in owning and operating vessels. Indeed, in recognition of his contributions in this field he was elected both Vice-President and President of the Norwegian Shipowners Federation. But increasingly his interests turned to matters outside the maritime realm. He invested in a number of companies and eventually sat on the boards of more than twenty Norwegian and international firms. A member of countless civic organizations, for twenty years he was also a member of the International Olympic Committee and played an important role in the selection of Oslo to host the 1952 games. With his wide-ranging

---

[33]Both the shipowning and shipbroking firms were referred to as Fearnley and Eger. To avoid confusion, in any place where the usage might be ambiguous we will hereafter refer to either the "shipowning company" or the "chartering company."

interests, it is little wonder that he had few hours to devote to managing a shipbroking concern.[34]

His principal partner – and the man who became the sole owner when Fearnley died in 1961 – was Nils Astrup, his cousin. Like Fearnley, Astrup had a good grounding in broking, spending time with both Clarkson and a leading New York shipbroker, Winchester and Co. Joining Fearnley and Eger in 1931, he was immediately made a partner and shared responsibility with the Shipowner until Fearnley retired from active involvement in the firm in 1942. The two were remarkably similar. Like Fearnley, Astrup's principal maritime interest was shipowning. Similarly, over time he became more interested in manufacturing and civic duties. Broking for both was a secondary occupation.[35]

The lack of involvement by the owners meant that day-to-day decisions were left in the hands of the managing director, Sverre Lie, who literally inherited the post from his father in 1921. Although a man of some experience, he was ill-equipped for the rigours of management. Many of Lie's foibles were arguably the result of having been trained within Fearnley and Eger. Not surprisingly, his attitudes toward information were shaped by this experience.[36]

As the managing director in a firm in which the two principals showed little interest in broking, Lie became the *de facto* heir to Thomas Fearnley's information system. It was Lie to whom intelligence from the company's "friends" now came. But being a product of the firm's compartmentalized approach to data, he seldom shared it. To make matters worse, Lie had never been well-trained in analysis. While he was arguably the world's leading expert on the peculiarities of the groundnut trade, he knew much less about other facets of broking. Instead of using information to seek out new opportunities, he employed it instead to reinforce preconceived notions. The result was that the major changes in shipping during the interwar years hardly touched the firm.

---

[34]A good overview of his career may be found in *Thomas Fearnley. Utgitt til 75 Års Dagen* (Oslo, 1955).

[35]For an excellent overview of Nils Astrup's career, see *Orkla Informasjon*, No. 3 (1972).

[36]Sverre Lie is discussed in much more detail in Lewis R. Fischer, "Profits and Stagnation: Fearnley and Eger and the Interwar Crises, 1919-1939," in Poul Holm, *et al.* (eds.), *The Northern Seas* (Esbjerg, 1993, forthcoming).

Perhaps the most revealing example of this was the chartering company's failure to become a significant force in the transition to motorships and tankers. Both were major growth areas in the 1920s and 1930s; indeed, by 1939 these types of ships comprised a higher proportion of the Norwegian fleet than in any other national merchant marine.[37] Yet the chartering company was at best a minor participant in this remarkable transformation. In the 1920s only ten percent of the transactions handled by its sales and purchase department involved motorships and less than five percent dealt with tankers. During the next decade, the corresponding figures were twenty-five and nine percent, respectively.[38] Moreover, the firm had no role whatsoever in the twenty-six deals by which most of the Anglo–Saxon tanker fleet was transferred to Norwegian ownership in the largest single infusion of tanker tonnage during the period.[39]

Why was the chartering company so dilatory in becoming involved with tankers and motorships? Part of the explanation may have to do with the conservatism of many of its clients, few of whom were among the pioneers in adopting either technology. Indeed, even Wilhelm Wilhelmsen, a leader in deploying diesel liners, was conspicuous by his absence from the list of owners who invested in motor tankers: although Wilhelmsen owned fifty-three tankers by 1939, all were powered by steam rather than diesel. While for some reason he failed to grasp the potential of motor tankers, the more salient point is that none of the tankers that he did own were purchased through Fearnley and Eger.[40]

---

[37]Norway, Statistisk Sentralbyrå, *Historisk Statistikk 1978* (Oslo, 1978), tables 181 and 191; S.G. Sturmey, *British Shipping and World Competition* (London, 1962), 36-60; Vidar Hole, "The Biggest Gamblers: Structure and Strategy in Norwegian Oil Tanker Shipping during the Era of Growth, 1925-1973" (Unpublished MA thesis, Norwegian School of Economics and Business Administration, 1993), 21-29.

[38]Calculated from F&E, Box 39.

[39]On the Anglo-Saxon deal, see K.U. Kloster, *Perler på en snor. Eventyret om norsk tankfart* (Oslo, 1953); Anders Martin Fon, *Norsk skipsfart i mellomkrigstiden. Kan satsingen på tankfart og motordrevet moderne tonnasje forklare den sterke ekspansjonen?* (Bergen, 1991); L. Nørgård, *Tanksfartens etablerings- og introduksjonsperiode i norsk skipsfart 1912-1913 og 1927-1930* (Bergen, 1991).

[40]Equally significant, the shipowning company was also a laggard in investing in this technology. This point is discussed more fully in Fischer, "Profits and Stagnation."

This suggests that the chartering company was not perceived by even long-time patrons as having much expertise (or interest) in handling the purchase of the most modern vessels.

If shipowners had this perception, they were undoubtedly correct. The evidence available in fact suggests that the major reason for the absence of the chartering company from the tanker and motorship sectors was a belief that they were fads rather than harbingers of the future. To understand why this was so only requires a consideration of the firm's major source of information and the weakness of Sverre Lie as an analyst. Britain was slow to adopt motor vessels and Clarkson, still the principal source of the chartering company's intelligence, shared this view. Indeed, the official history of the British firm does not even mention any interest in the newer vessels until after World War II.[41] Although no communications from Clarkson have survived for this period, it is a reasonable assumption that the British broker would hardly have been counselling its Norwegian contacts to plunge into motorships and tankers if it were not doing so itself. Lacking any independent analytic ability, it seems reasonable to conclude that Lie took this as an affirmation that the firm could ignore these new vessel types, which he had already judged unsuitable for the West African trades. As a result, the brokers did not advise their clients to invest in the new technology. Instead, the company slumbered, basking in the glories of its dominance in groundnuts while the maritime world passed it by.

The attitudes toward information remained in most ways unchanged in the years between the wars. Shipping and market intelligence, generated largely from a single source, remained in the hands of a single man who was not disposed to share or conserve it. Yet there were also three key differences. One was that the source of the firm's international data was becoming increasingly remote from the realities of the non-British market. The second was that the company employed no one with analytic skills comparable to those of the founder. The final difference was that the key decision-makers failed to sense the drift that had captured their company.

It is this last difficulty that was most significant. Had either the Shipowner or Nils Astrup been more involved with the chartering company, they *might* have been able to diagnose the problems. Indeed, the actions initiated by Nils Astrup after World War II underscore this

---

[41]*The Clarkson Chronicle*, 59-70.

possibility. Moreover, there were alternative sources of information that could have been tapped and individuals with reasonable analytic skills who could have been employed. But with their attention focused elsewhere, and apparently satisfied with the contribution that the company continued to make to their personal fortunes, neither sensed the dangers. Although the firm in this era almost never obtained perfect – or even adequate – knowledge, no one in authority seemed to care. The decisions about the provision and use of data were in the interwar years based entirely upon the whims of management rather than economic reasoning.

The Postwar Years, 1945-1972

As shipping in the quarter-century after World War II became increasingly complex, so too did shipbroking. If the 1914-1918 conflict had shaken the structures of the maritime sector, the second set of hostilities rent them almost beyond recognition. Yet, despite the uncertainties in shipping, the chartering company was remarkably successful at adapting to the new environment. What is perhaps most surprising is that it did so with the same cast of characters in command. Although the Shipbroker was now more-or-less retired, Nils Astrup was still very much around, as was Sverre Lie, who remained managing director until 1957. Nor had the principal corporate goal changed – all that Astrup asked was a reasonable annual return. Yet the chartering company underwent some significant alterations. The motivation for this came from the top. The war had provided the owner with a good deal of time to assess the state of his business.[42] He concluded that the erosion of its position in the interwar years had been a function of the poor quality of information. Moreover, as he scanned the horizon he was concerned that in the more uncertain postwar maritime world the company might be unable to generate satisfactory profits without some change. A sharp fall in revenues in 1946 likely exacerbated these fears. Although he had no master strategy – and while none of his reforms worked precisely as he planned – his intervention caused important alterations in the corporate climate that facilitated change. Nothing in the next two and one-half

---

[42]An examination of the firm's records during World War II show that it transacted little business after the spring of 1940 aside from arranging the odd short-sea charter for the Germans.

decades was as central to the revitalization of the firm's fortunes as a new attitude toward the procurement and use of information.

While Astrup's diagnosis was more right than wrong, it was unfortunately incomplete. He apparently saw only indistinctly that a large portion of the weakness stemmed from what happened to information once it entered the firm. Moreover, since he continued to spend little time in his office, he judged the success of his reforms principally by the state of the bottom line. As a result, his interventions were sporadic rather than continuous and were prompted largely by short-term declines in profits. Although his reforms enjoyed some success, they never succeeded in overcoming the totality of Fearnley and Eger's problems in handling information.

Despite these shortcomings, it is important to admit that Nils Astrup created an environment in which change could occur. Once convinced that improvements had to be made in the procedure of procuring information externally, he wasted little time in acting. His choice of cures reflected fairly accurately his understanding of the problem. Had he concluded that the weakness was solely in the source of outside intelligence, he could simply have searched for a supplement to, or replacement for, Clarkson. But he did not do this because he had an intuitive feeling – which he never was able to articulate properly during the next twenty-five years – that part of the problem was also internal. He thus chose another route.

The problem, he judged, was that in a large, modern brokerage operation information could not flow solely from the top. This was especially true if the owner had no intention of participating actively in broking. Instead, he concluded that the brokers had to be induced to assume a far greater responsibility for the collection of intelligence. To try to get them to do so he rescinded a decision made at the time of the company's founding. Believing correctly that information was vital to a successful brokerage, Fearnley and Eger had always treated it in accounting terms as a general charge against the company. While on one level this was sensible, for at least two reasons it was flawed, Astrup reasoned. First, since the owners paid for it, the brokers had correctly come to treat it as a free good. There was thus little incentive for them to be concerned about either its quality or cost. Second, such a policy did nothing to ensure that the brokers received the data necessary for the optimum performance of their tasks. The owner therefore decided to alter decisively the tradition. Rejecting as unfeasible the idea of charging the cost of information to individuals (which would have had the additional benefit of removing it completely from the firm's cost structure), he opted instead to shift it to departments.

To enhance the probability that this policy would be successful, he implemented one additional change. In the past, employee remuneration had comprised both salary and commission. Assuming the motivational power of rewarding performance with enhanced income – and rejecting, as had his predecessors, the tactic of admitting successful brokers into partnership – Astrup proposed to increase the proportion of economic rewards based on performance. Moreover, to induce departments to obtain better information and hence to increase sales, he also implemented a scheme by which commissions were paid not only on an individual's performance but also on a department's results. This, he hoped somewhat optimistically, would provide motivation for brokers to ensure that all data collected was of the highest quality and that it was shared among the staff.

While these reforms were largely administrative and easily implemented, they did not work precisely the way Astrup envisaged. In giving a clear signal of a vague dissatisfaction at the top, they also betrayed the owner's incomplete understanding of the problems, ignoring the very real difficulties of the performance of the managing director, the general ennui within the firm, and the compartmentalization of information. Astrup demonstrated his ignorance of the first by allowing Sverre Lie to remain until his retirement. As for the second, he made the simplistic assumption that more money would lead to better results. But the brokers were already well paid; while none turned down the opportunity for higher remuneration, it did not lead to greater efforts to make the company function better. And if Astrup believed that the reforms would lead to better internal information flows he was to be severely disappointed.[43]

Yet despite such criticisms, Nils Astrup's intervention did have decisive effects. The most important was that by showing his displeasure he weakened the control of the managers, especially Sverre Lie, whose real power derived from a monopoly of information rather than his place on the formal organization chart. By downgrading the importance of

---

[43]This account is derived principally from *Norges Handels og Sjøfarts Tidende*, 11 February 1969; Kjell Halvorsen, Interview, 13 February 1992; Carsten Anker, Interview, 20 February 1992; Erik Dahl-Hansen, Interview, 14 October 1992; Finn Grape, Interview, 7 December 1992; Fearnley and Egers Befragtningsforretning (FEB), Board, Minutes, various dates.

rank, he opened the door for ambitious brokers to take greater initiatives. The result was a classic example of Adam Smith's theory that by pursuing their own best interests individuals would also benefit the larger entity of which they were a part. Freed from virtually all shackles, brokers were able to pursue a variety of new initiatives. And by decreeing that information was no longer to be treated as a free good, he motivated brokers to develop their own sources of intelligence.

Nothing epitomized the new milieu more than the rise within the firm of the tanker department, which by the mid-1950s was routinely generating half of all profits. This was the work primarily of an extraordinarily gifted broker named Birger Gran. Although he joined the chartering company in the late 1920s and became a tanker broker in 1934, it was after the war that his contribution became decisive. The roots of Gran's success lay first of all in cultivating sources of information, an activity in which he had few peers. Because his specialty was tankers, he knew better than most the danger of continuing to depend on the single source of information that Thomas Fearnley had developed back in the 1870s. Fortunately, he was in a position – thanks to his own contacts and Nils Astrup's reforms – to develop alternatives.

During the war Gran had worked for four years in New York at Nortraship, the organization established by the government-in-exile to operate that part of the Norwegian deep-sea fleet that had escaped German seizure.[44] After the conclusion of hostilities he spent two years as a broker at Tankers Company, then the largest American tanker broker. His six years in the US enabled Gran to come into contact with a broad cross-section of the men and companies that would dominate postwar tanker shipping. These included Sigval Bergesen, Jr., who eventually became the chartering company's most important long-term client, and J.M. Ribas, a director of the Cepsa refining company in Madrid that became the largest source of tanker charters for Fearnley and Eger in the 1950s and 1960s.[45] Perhaps even more important, Gran made a plethora of contacts among brokers. These included not only

---

[44]The best study of Nortraship is Atle Thowsen, *Nortraship: Profitt og patriotisme* (Oslo, 1992). For a readable introduction to the dilemmas faced by the operators of the Norwegian fleet, see Tore L. Nilsen and Atle Thowsen, *Handelsflaten i krig 1939-1945* (Bergen, 1990).

[45]On Bergesen, see Tore Jørgen Hanisch and Liv Jorunn Ramskjær, *Firmaet Sigval Bergesen, Stavanger. Under vekslende vilkår 1887-1987* (Stavanger, 1987).

Americans but also young men from around the world who had been drawn to the New York during and after the conflict by the city's new position as the world's most important broking market. After the war these individuals became prime sources of information for Gran, who used them to establish a network that far outstripped any the firm had previously enjoyed.[46]

Birger Gran also had one additional attribute which contributed to his success: he was almost certainly the most insightful analyst the firm had ever employed. While his information sources were vital, they would have meant far less had he lacked the ability to interpret the data. It was Gran, for example, who first saw the potential for improved technology to alter decisively the environment in shipping oil and gas. He acted on this conclusion to ensure that the chartering company's clients invested heavily in standard T-2 tankers disposed of by the American government immediately after the war. More important, he also foresaw as early as 1950 the technological innovations that would eventually lead to VLCCs and ULCCs; as a result, Fearnley and Eger's customers were in the forefront of the movement toward these behemoths. Although the effect of the oil shocks in the 1970s caused many to denigrate the wisdom of these investments, it is important to note the contribution they made to shipping company profits in the 1960s and early 1970s. In 1971, for example, a typical 250,000-ton VLCC, which could be purchased for roughly US $28 million, was capable of generating sufficient earnings to pay for itself within two years. Few of Gran's clients would have been disappointed with such returns.[47]

But if Gran were a key figure in the revitalization of the firm's information collection and analysis, he was in two important respects very much in the Fearnley and Eger tradition. First, he abhorred sharing information. Brokers in sale and purchase, for example, were often astonished to learn that a client such as Bergesen had decided to place a major order for new tonnage without even contacting them. Instead, members of the tanker department would supervise the negotiations personally. While to pacify his outraged colleagues Gran often arranged for the commissions to be credited to sale and purchase, the more

---

[46]Halvorsen, Interview; Grape, Interview.

[47]Grape, Interview; Frank Isachsen, *Crude Oil Shipping* (Bergen, 1992); Ewan Corlett, *The Ship. The Revolution in Merchant Shipping 1950-1980* (London, 1981), 24-27.

important point is that other departments seldom were the recipients of his data collection and analysis. Second, Birger Gran probably represented the ultimate triumph of the traditional bias against adequate record-keeping, no easy accomplishment in a firm with a long history of inadequate information storage and retrieval. One broker, who joined Fearnley just after World War II, reported perhaps the most extreme example. Gran's secretary, he recalled, was forbidden even to write down clients' phone numbers lest they fall into the wrong hands. Instead, she was expected to keep them – and much else – in her head, where presumably they were safe from whatever prying eyes Birger Gran feared.[48]

By the mid-1950s, through the activities of Gran and a group of younger brokers, the chartering company clearly had solved some (but not all) of its information problems.[49] This was reflected in its rapidly-rising profits, which expanded more than seven-fold between 1950 and 1957. While Nils Astrup had reason to be content about the return on his investment, it is clear that he was still vaguely uneasy about the impact that inadequate information flows could have on the future viability of the concern. It is equally clear, however, that he still was uncertain about how deeply-rooted they were. This uncertainty, combined with his satisfaction at the firm's profitability, caused him to miss several opportunities for more thorough reform. When Sverre Lie decided to retire in 1957, Astrup reached outside the company for a new managing director. While Lars Usterud-Svendsen, who was recruited from Fred. Olsen Lines, was a superb administrator, his lack of broking experience deprived him of the clout to tackle the remaining problems with information. And, as if to underscore his lack of insight, Astrup appointed Gran to head the tanker department, replacing the long-serving Tormod Schartum, who stepped down at the same time as Lie. With a relatively impotent managing director and an arch-disciple of information

---

[48]Grape, Interview.

[49]While Gran was the most significant contributor both to the firm's bottom line and to the revitalization of its sources of information, it is important to note that he was but one of a number of younger brokers who developed new information sources. Another was Carsten Anker, who in 1948 became the first European to place an order for a newbuilding in postwar Japan. Space, however, does not permit us to examine the impact of these men in this paper.

compartmentalization in charge of the largest broking department, it was unlikely that the deeper problems would be corrected.[50]

With hindsight, it is not surprising that change rather than continuity characterized the approach to information over the next few years. But as in the immediate postwar period, a decline in income provoked a new response from the owner. A short-term fall in profits in the late 1950s led Astrup once again to focus on insufficient market data as the main culprit. And as before, he demonstrated that while he had a feel for the proper target he had still not located the bullseye. In 1961 he decided to establish an in-house research department.[51] To head it he recruited Birger Nossum, an economist from the Norwegian Shipowners Federation. The mandate Astrup gave to his new employee reflected the fact that he still did not see the deeper problems clearly. "Go away," he instructed his new employee, "and find something to do."[52]

Over the next few years, Nossum found much to do, in the process establishing one of the best research departments in the industry. Yet the impressive output of his efforts had little impact on the brokers, who in general ignored the stream of market intelligence that emerged. This may have been because after having been starved of information for years the brokers did not know how to react when suddenly presented with a surfeit of reliable data. Yet an alternative conclusion seems more logical. Had Gran opened his treasure trove of data, several veteran employees have suggested, brokers would have lined up for access; Birger Gran, after all, knew broking. Birger Nossum, on the other hand, lacked a background in broking, and hence they concluded that his analysis was not to be trusted.[53] Although some customers came to appreciate the fact that they could obtain data virtually upon request, the research department had little impact on internal decision-making.

---

[50]FEB, Board, Minutes, 10 October 1957.

[51]The consistency of Astrup's thought on the matter was shown by his decision to charge the expenses of this new venture to the various departments. That the charges were levied in direct proportion to a department's income explains why the tanker department became a particularly strong opponent of in-house research.

[52]Birger Nossum, Interview, 10 February 1992.

[53]Dahl-Hansen, Interview; Anker, Interview.

Nor did Astrup's final decision before his death in 1972 do anything to enhance information flows. When Usterud-Svendsen retired in 1967, Astrup chose to make Birger Gran the co-managing director.[54] While this doubtless was a fitting reward for his contribution to the bottom line, it also was an admission that Nils Astrup still did not understand fully how much the internal communication, storage and retrieval of information remained the firm's Achilles heel. Indeed, the installation of Birger Gran in a position of great authority exacerbated rather than helped the problem.

During his postwar stewardship, Nils Astrup came to realize that problems with information represented a potential threat to the firm's continuing profitability. Perhaps because of the experiences of the interwar years, he saw that there was a need to acquire more complete data. By altering the internal climate, especially to give more responsibility to the departments and more scope to the younger brokers, and eventually by establishing a research department, he succeeded in improving this condition. Virtually by default, the poor quality of analysis was also upgraded, at least within the tanker department. But it does not appear that the owner ever understood clearly (or if he did, never confronted) the difficulties with internal information flows, storage and retrieval of all this data. While the firm was immeasurably stronger at his death than it had been a quarter-century earlier, problems with information remained the greatest threat to its continued economic health. Although his son, Hans Rasmus Astrup, would more correctly diagnose the problem, he would have no more success in solving it.[55]

Conclusion: Information, Management and Theory in Broking

The continuing success of Fearnley and Eger's shipbroking (now operating under the name Astrup/Fearnley) may amaze some economists, who will find it difficult to believe that a company in a sector so

---

[54]He shared this post with Harald Jakhelln, who was Astrup's nephew. FEB, Board, Minutes, 14 October 1967.

[55]One of the younger Astrup's first decisions after taking charge of the firm was to establish a weekly department head meeting at which information could be shared. According to participants, some heads responded by boycotting these meetings, while those who did attend were largely silent. After a few months Astrup gave up the struggle. Twenty years later the problem remains unresolved.

dependent upon information could for so long defy the predictions of their models. Far from attempting to procure perfect information, the firm relied prior to 1939 on a single source. While they will be comforted by the fact that until World War I this source was unparalleled, they will be puzzled that the concern managed to survive all the errors that this system induced in the interwar years. Moreover, they are likely to be appalled that nothing was done to rectify the problem. The postwar experiences will bring little more comfort. Although the chartering company was much more assiduous in pursuing intelligence, even when it possessed something close to perfect information it often chose to ignore it, as the fate of the reports generated by the research department attests.

Furthermore, economists will not be comforted by the fact that economic considerations were seldom of paramount importance in deciding how assiduously to pursue information. While the first Thomas Fearnley took costs into account in his decision to use the mails rather than the telegraph to procure data, his successors were far less likely to make choices on economic grounds. The stagnation of the interwar years, for example, generated absolutely no change in the pattern of information collection. While after 1945 Nils Astrup did have economic considerations in mind when introducing his reforms, by shifting the burden onto his brokers he in effect abrogated any role in the choice of how much information they would procure. Even when he established a research department, he ensured that the economic considerations would be someone else's concern.

Although their models have little to say about what happens to data once it reaches the firm, it is unlikely that economists would grant Fearnley and Eger their unqualified approbation. While it is possible to rationalize the founder's failure to establish reasonable structures for the dissemination, storage and retrieval of information, it is more difficult to justify the inaction of the Shipowner and Nils Astrup except by recourse to the admission that they were unaware of a problem about which they should have known. The inability to make the use of information more efficient should, the theorists will contend, have doomed the enterprise. Yet the fact that the company survives and prospers is proof that Armageddon has not yet arrived. While it is of course possible that at some point these problems will lead to the kind of denouement that economists would predict, there are no signs of this at present.

Business historians, on the other hand, are less likely to be astounded by any of this. While Fearnley and Eger's procurement and use of information is hardly a textbook example of how such things ought to be done, they will know from their own studies how messy the real world often is. Nor are they likely to be surprised that so much of the motivation behind the collection of information was non-economic. After all, they will recognize that cause and effect do not necessarily have to be identical or even similar. Businessmen, as human beings, are subject to all the foibles, imperfections and clashes of interest that characterize the species. In particular, business historians will accept that decision-making, being the product of imperfect human reasoning, will not necessarily conform to the pristine logic of theory.

Although the management style at this shipbroking firm has been highly idiosyncratic, they will know that privately-owned firms often lack the discipline that, at least in theory, can be brought by pressures from shareholders and the stock market. Business historians are also likely to understand how owners can be seduced by the lures of competing activities and hence lavish neglect rather than attention on an undertaking that they judge to be performing satisfactorily. The owners of Fearnley and Eger are hardly the first to engage in non-maximizing behaviour, nor are they likely to be the last.[56]

Yet the different responses that this case study is likely to evoke illustrate why business historians and economic theorists need each other. As Douglas North has observed, "history without theory is nothing."[57] What he meant by this was the main goal of all history is to explain what can be observed in the significant past. Explanation requires generalization, and to engage in this process requires some basis for deciding what is (and what is not) important. Theory is the best – and, we would argue, the only – guide for making these difficult choices.

Business historians in particular require the assistance of economic theorists. Our observation that much of the behaviour at Fearnley and Eger can be explained by reference to non-economic

---

[56]While economists might argue that even in its seeming disorder the firm was maximizing a utility function, it is hard to discern just what utility might have been maximized by the actions of the owners.

[57]Douglas North, "Conference Summary," in Lewis R. Fischer and Eric W. Sager (eds.), *Merchant Shipping and Economic Development in Atlantic Canada* (St. John's, 1982), 233.

motivations does not change the fact that business is an economic activity. It may have social, cultural or even political consequences, but particularly in a capitalist society it is primarily an economic endeavour. Philanthropic endeavours aside, if a firm does not earn a profit it cannot survive indefinitely. This being the case, economic theory can do much to sharpen the questions that business historians pose.

But to maximize its utility to scholarship, dialogue between business historians and economic theorists must be mutual. Theorists have as much to learn from practitioners as *vice versa*. Too often theorists forget that their only empirical facts are historical. They can ponder the way the world "should be" to their heart's content, but when it comes to finding data to test their models, they must turn to history. If something has not happened, by definition it cannot be evidence. Unfortunately, much economic theorizing about firms has ignored what business history has to teach; in so doing, theorists cut themselves off from a good deal of potential evidence. They also, of course, save themselves from many of the contradictions and imprecisions that litter the historical landscape. This is why so many theories do not seem to fit the conditions that business historians confront.

This study of a shipbroking firm underscores these same points for those interested in shipping and related activities. Maritime economists, to their discredit, are for the most part ignorant of what their historical brethren have learned about the way this industry operated in the past. Yet maritime historians, especially those primarily interested in shipping, are no less guilty of a false sense of exclusivity. Some have justified this myopia by arguing erroneously that theory ought to play no part in explaining the past, while others have tried to deny that shipping has always been essentially an economic activity. We have already expressed our views on the first contention. On the second we would only say that while it can be argued that not all maritime activities are primarily economic – a point we accept – shipping certainly is. Although there are a plethora of non-economic consequences that stem from this industry – and which deserve scholarly attention – the act of moving goods and people over the world's waters is first and foremost an economic activity. So too is shipbroking. If we accept this, then it follows that it would behoove us to pay more attention to what we can learn from economists. It is not only business historians who can benefit from an interchange of ideas. Maritime history would also be better off if its practitioners engaged in more intellectual dialogue with those who can help to sharpen the questions they seek to answer.

The Early Nineteenth-Century Port of London: Management and Labour in Three Dock Companies, 1800-1825[1]

Anthony R. Henderson and Sarah Palmer

Introduction

One of the most challenging issues currently confronting labour historians is the impact of industrialisation on the experience of work. As economic historians increasingly emphasise the slow, uneven and diverse character of British industrial development in the eighteenth and early nineteenth centuries, so the notion of the transformation of the labour process as involving a substitution of time discipline, regular attendance and intensity of work for older modes is being called into question.[2] In addition, even in developed manufacturing sectors, the role of the worker has been identified as closer to that of an active protagonist than a subservient and oppressed factor of production.[3]

---

[1]This research is part of a larger study of the nineteenth-century Port of London supported by a grant from the Economic and Social Research Council. The prime archive is that of the Port of London Authority (PLA) and the authors gratefully acknowledge the encouragement and archival assistance of Bob Aspinall and his colleagues at the Library and Archives, located in the Museum in Docklands.

[2]See E.P. Thompson, "Time, Work Discipline and Industrial Capitalism," *Past and Present*, XXXVIII (1967); E. Hopkins, "Working Hours and Conditions during the Industrial Revolution," *Economic History Review*, Second Series, XXXV (1982); John Rule, *The Labouring Classes in Early Industrial England 1750-1850* (London, 1986).

[3]See J. Zeitlin, "From Labour History to the History of Industrial Relations," *Economic History Review*, Second Series, XL (1987); R. Price, "The Structure of Subordination in Nineteenth-Century Relations in Production," in P. Thane, G. Crossick, and R. Floud (eds.), *The Power of the Past: Essays in Honour of E. J. Hobsbawm* (Cambridge, 1984).

Research in Maritime History, No. 6 (June 1994), 31-50.

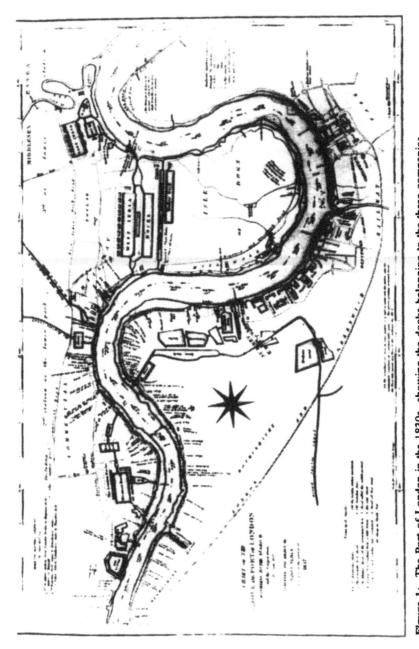

Figure 1: The Port of London in the 1830s, showing the docks belonging to the three companies.

Source: Port of London Authority Collection, Museum of London.

This re-evaluation has led not only to an interest in industrial relations focused less on trade union activity and more on broad labour/management contact but also to a new emphasis within business history, encouraged by a revitalisation of the sociology of work, on the significance of the labour process.[4] It has also resulted in a closer scrutiny of the situation in individual cases.[5] Yet what Berg has termed the "new microeconomics of the industrial revolution" is still firmly rooted in traditional expositions in that the area of concern is primarily manufacturing.[6] The kind of questions asked about conditions in the textile industry, for example, have not been addressed to the management of labour employed in the movement of goods.

As far as port work is concerned, the lack of attention may follow from the perception that in the early nineteenth century this was a traditional business unaffected by mechanisation and dependent on manual labour – a view possibly encouraged unintentionally by studies, from the Webbs onward, of late nineteenth century dock workers which necessarily emphasise the seemingly primitive context of casual work in which many were employed.[7] Ports, from this viewpoint, have little in common with those sections of the economy affected directly by

---

[4]For a summary of recent scholarship, see Patrick Joyce, "Work," in F.M.L. Thompson (ed.), *The Cambridge Social History of Britain 1750-1950* (Cambridge, 1990), II; Joyce (ed.), *The Historical Meanings of Work* (Cambridge, 1987); Paul Thompson, *The Nature of Work: An Introduction to Debates on the Labour Process* (London, 1983).

[5]See, for example, R. Price, *Masters, Unions and Men. Work Control in Building and the Rise of Labour 1830-1914* (Cambridge, 1990); Maxine Berg, *The Age of Manufactures: Industry, Innovation and Work in Britain 1700-1820* (Oxford, 1985); C. Behagg, *Politics and Production in the Early Nineteenth Century* (London, 1990); Dennis Smith, "Paternalism, Craft and Organisational Rationality 1830-1939," *Urban History*, XIX (1992).

[6]Berg, *Age of Manufactures*, 17. One exception is Neil Casey and David Dunkerley, "Technological Work Cultures: Culture and Assimilation Within a Mid-Nineteenth Century Naval Dockyard," in K. Thompson (ed.), *Work, Employment and Unemployment* (Milton Keynes, 1984).

[7]See Sidney and Beatrice Webb, *A History of British Trade Unionism* (London, 1920); John Lovell, *Stevedores and Dockers, A Study of Trade Unionism in the Port of London* (London, 1969); Gareth Stedman-Jones, *Outcast London: A Study in the Relationship between the Classes in Victorian Society* (Oxford, 1971); E.L. Taplin, *Liverpool Dockers and Seamen 1870-1890* (Hull, 1974).

industrialisation. Yet, while at first sight it might appear that their history can shed little light on the issue of proletariatisation, a moment's thought will call this into question.[8] The challenges were presented as forcibly on the quayside or in the warehouse as in the factory or workshop, so issues such as recruitment, timekeeping, labour discipline, the role of trades, and control over the labour process arose as much in this service industry as in manufacturing. If the increased scale of British port business in the late eighteenth and early nineteenth century could be shown to have been accommodated within the pre-industrial pattern of management/labour relations, this would tell us something. But, at least in the case of the Port of London, there is evidence of change.

It is a truism of British labour history that industrialism involved a reshaping of the work experience. As Sidney Pollard observed:

> the modern industrial proletariat was introduced to its
> role not so much by attraction or monetary reward, but
> by compulsion, force and fear. It was not allowed to
> grow as in a sunny garden; it was forged, over a fire, by
> the powerful blows of a hammer.[9]

Whether or not this characterisation is appropriate for the factory system, it bears only intermittent resemblance to the situation in the Port of London in the same period, where "compulsion, force and fear" had limited efficacy for reasons explored below. Yet the dock was no "sunny garden;" employers attempted to create the labour force they desired, although the greenhouse is a better metaphor than the forge.

In the early nineteenth century the Port of London was fundamentally reformed. Riverside quays, wharves and warehouses, which since the sixteenth century had enjoyed a legal monopoly in the landing and storage of dutiable foreign goods, lost this privilege to the newly-constructed enclosed docks owned and managed by three separate joint-stock companies: the West India Dock Company (WIDCO), the East India Dock Company (EIDCO) and the London Dock Company

---

[8]I. Prothero, *Artisans and Politics in the Early Nineteenth Century London* (London, 1979), usefully touches on some aspects of this issue.

[9]Sidney Pollard, *The Genesis of Modern Management: A Study of the Industrial Revolution in Great Britain* (London, 1985), 243.

(LDCO). Under the terms of the Acts of Parliament which established these companies, each was given a twenty-year monopoly over particular categories of cargo, broadly defined by the region from which they were imported.[10]

This paper is concerned with the three companies during the period when they were not, generally speaking, in competition with each other but rather operating as monopolies. Our interest is the relationship between these new enterprises and their workforces, as well as the nature of that association and the forces that conditioned it. Our sources are primarily the minutes of the directors' meetings of the companies, hence discussion focuses on management strategies. We would stress, however, that we do not regard dock labour as passive or without influence in determining the labour process, although the nature of the available information dictates that to a large extent its role has to be inferred. An adversarial model would focus appropriately on our evidence on strikes, but in so doing underestimate the extent to which the underlying conflict of interest between capital and labour must also have been resolved through compromise, co-operation and accommodation.[11]

Viewed from a longer term and wider perspective, it is important to appreciate that since we are dealing with a rather special period, we are not justified in assuming that management/labour relations operated similarly once the monopoly era ended – though to date our research on subsequent periods suggests that they did. Second, our discussion does not include all port work. Nothing is said about practices either in the docks on the South Bank, which handled primarily low-duty, bulky Baltic goods, or in the Thameside wharves and on the river itself, although coasting accounted for much of London's business in the early nineteenth century and it remained in many respects a river port even after the introduction of wet docks. This is therefore an investigation of the labour process in companies handling high-value dutiable goods; it adds to our knowledge of early nineteenth-century London port labour, but by no means completes it.

---

[10]For the general history of the Port of London, see Joseph Broodbank, *History of the Port of London* (2 vols., London, 1921); J.H. Bird, *The Geography of London River* (London, 1957); R. Douglas Brown, *The Port of London* (Lavenham, 1978); R.J.M. Carr (ed.), *Docklands* (London, 1988).

[11]There were strikes by coopers in the London Docks in 1810 and 1812 and in the West India Dock in 1812 and 1821.

Company Objectives

The starting point for understanding the management tasks faced by the Port of London's dock companies is a consideration of why and how they were created in the first place. Although the initiative came first from merchants in the West India trades concerned about delays in loading and unloading vessels and thefts of cargo, it was "the Aid and Authority of Parliament" which made the project possible.[12] As a result, although the finance and management of the companies was in private hands, the amount of capital they could raise, their maximum charges and the dividends payable to shareholders were legally defined. Further practical constraints were placed upon their day-to-day operations by the central role that customs officers necessarily played in the weighing and analysis of goods and, officially at least, in ensuring security.

Parliamentary limitations on the dock companies' freedom of action were the corollary of the monopoly status they were given over particular trades. This represented on the one hand a guarantee of business, but on the other a contractual obligation, in the case of WIDCO, to handle every cargo from the West Indies, or in the case of LDCO, every shipment of wine. Each dock company not only could claim one hundred percent of the market but also was obliged to satisfy it.

In terms both of protection from competitive pressures and scale, these companies can be compared with the large industrial firms that emerged in Britain at the end of the century.[13] Though not without parallels elsewhere, the millions of pounds invested and the numbers employed on a single site certainly made them exceptional within the London economy.[14] But while studies of labour relations within large

---

[12]Preamble, West India Dock Act, 1799, 39 Geo. 3, CLXIX.

[13]Rule, *The Labouring Classes*, notes that Portsmouth dockyard had 2228 workers in 1772 and that the Wheal Alfred copper mine in Cornwall employed over 1000 in 1790. See Pollard, *The Genesis of Modern Management*, for a discussion of structural change in early industrial Britain.

[14]By 1825 the value of fixed capital in these three companies was approximately £5.5 million. The precise size of the workforce (salaried and waged) is difficult to establish because of insufficient information on the size of the casual labour force, but at peak season the numbers certainly were over 1000 on any one day.

monopolistic firms offer some theoretical insights, the constraints placed upon the dock companies created a distinctive environment arguably more analogous to that faced by the much later nationalised public utilities. The degree of public scrutiny to which their operations were subjected – including the submission of their annual accounts to Parliament – reinforces this perception.

The docks and their accompanying warehouses were built to provide a service for two types of clients: merchants and shipowners on the one hand and Customs and Excise on the other. Shareholding interests (predominantly the same merchants and shipowners) were confined by the legal limit on dividends on subscribed capital of ten percent. Nevertheless, while it would be misleading to describe the companies as "profit maximisers," there was an incentive to ensure that income exceeded expenditure. The first calls on this surplus, as laid down in the legislation, were the repayment of loans and the payment of dividends, but thereafter such sums could be applied to further development of facilities, and eventually to the reduction of charges to customers. In the case of LDCO, financial difficulties in the first years of operation lent urgency to ensuring a profit, and in any case, since all the companies faced the prospect of losing their monopoly, it made sense to maximise current gains. The surplus could then be used to build projects to strengthen a company's competitive position in the event of this happening. Alternatively, by permitting the lowering of charges, it could undermine the case for ending their privileged positions. In the event, these were the strategies adopted.

The problem for the companies was that with maximum charges fixed and the amount of business circumscribed by the size of the market, they had little control over their income.[15] Moreover if they could not increase their earnings by encouraging greater custom, neither could they cut marginal costs by restricting output. If there were a demand for warehouse space, the companies had to provide it, even if the additional cost of renting accommodation in the short term or constructing facilities in the longer was not justified by the return.

This economic scenario made control of expenditure the prime issue for dock companies and so put labour, the source of productivity

---

[15]The dock companies did have other sources of income, such as rents and fees for services like packing and bottling. There is also evidence of competition for goods not covered by the original Acts, but their share of total earnings must have been small.

and of costs, at the forefront of their strategy. The size of the workforce, as well as its quality, organization, wages, and output, all had to be confronted. Indeed, the design of the new docks reflected the experience of port employers. As the prominent warehousekeeper Edward Ogle warned the West India Dock Committee in February 1800:

> If a certain number of Labourers *must* necessarily be employed to transact a specific business which must be the case at Dock warehouses, and if those warehouses should be constructed as not to afford them full employment, or on the other hand to surcharge their power, it will in either case operate most injuriously to the Parties interested.[16]

A related concern is identified in the last element of the motto of EIDCO, "Oeconomy, Utility and Efficiency." Most of the directors in all three companies were identified professionally with particular trades handled by their dock and therefore personally sensitive to criticism of the standard of service offered. They were also keenly aware of the influence of their organised captive customers in government circles and of the finite term of dock monopolies. Delay, damage to goods or clerical errors might be the fault of a company's workers, but the blame would be attached to its directors.

In the debates that preceded the decision to build docks, theft was identified as a major problem. Indeed, preventing "loss to the Revenue" was the justification for the state's active promotion of docks to allow large vessels to unload at the quayside rather than mooring in deep water and discharging into lighters, which were easy prey for thieves.[17] While dutiable goods had previously been stored in warehouses in the City, cargoes landed at the docks went into secure warehouses on the premises. Yet despite the emphasis placed by Patrick Colquhoun (a prominent contemporary campaigner for port reform) on the role of organised gangs, it is clear that much appropriation of cargoes was

---

[16]PLA, West India Dock Company (WIDCO), Journal of Proceedings, 10 February 1800.

[17]See P. Colquhoun, *A Treatise on the Commerce and Police of the Thames* (London, 1800); Alex Werner, "The Port of London 1750-1806," in Poul Holm and John Edwards (eds.), *North Sea Ports and Harbours: Adaptations to Change* (Esbjerg, 1992).

carried out by men whose work brought them into direct contact with goods, such as customs officers and wharfside workers. What was judged by employers as theft might be regarded by a casual labourer as a legitimate perquisite, particularly if he was carrying out a task at the behest of another worker in return for, say, "sugar sweepings" as pay.[18]

The design of docks as virtual fortresses, surrounded by high walls with only a few closely guarded entrances, reflected a determination to exert control over the workforce *within* rather than to keep out intruders. Indeed, as EIDCO's Chairman noted in 1808, this novel "accumulation of property within a small compass" at night provided an obvious target for any "determined and enterprizing set of desperadoes...bent on committing serious mischief."[19] But such a disadvantage was more than offset by the facilities docks offered for searching and supervising labour, providing at least a partial answer to a question put by Colquhoun to the West India Committee in June 1799:

> In what manner are from two to three thousand labourers, who must be frequently employed at one time within these docks, and those too of a class that have been accustomed to plunder, and are not refrained by any sense of the turpitude of their actions, to be over-awed and controuled [sic]?[20]

The very location of the docks (in the case of the West and East India Docks, well downriver; in the case of the London Dock, nearer but still some distance from the old port), together with their threatening appearance (enclosed and isolated from the encounters of the street), further testifies to their fundamental nature as disciplinary structures.[21]

---

[18]See Peter d'Sena, "Perquisites and Casual Labour on the London Wharfside in the Eighteenth Century," *London Journal*, XIV (1989).

[19]British Library, Additional Manuscripts, 38191, f. 148. The context was fear both of foreign invasion and civil insurrection.

[20]PLA, West India Merchants Committee, Minutes, 7 June 1799.

[21]This point draws on insights in Anthony Giddens, "Time, Space and Regionalisation," in Derek Gregory and John Urry (eds.), *Social Relations and Spatial Structures* (London, 1987), 265-295.

Our argument thus far has identified economy, efficiency and security as objectives. The new facilities provided a base, but attaining such goals relied only in part on these capital assets; the key ingredient was the day-to-day exploitation of labour. Returns from this required both appropriate managerial structures and labour strategies. We follow Howard Gospel in defining structure as "the various organisational forms and personnel which entrepreneurs have used to recruit and maintain a labour force; to monitor, discipline and reward workers; and to deal with trade unions as they have emerged," while strategy comprises the "plans and policies used to direct work tasks; to evaluate, discipline and reward workers; and to deal with their trade unions."[22]

The basic organisational structure desired by the dock companies is readily identified as providing direct control over waged or salaried employees rather than the task-based subcontracting system which appears to have been the norm previously. The difficulty of exercising direct control led to the adoption of organisational structures which took a very similar form in each case, while within these structures the practices of the three sets of directors in relation to their workers also had common features. This congruence did not owe everything to the fact that the companies had common objectives as businesses. It was also shaped by experience; by the labour market each confronted (where they were in competition); and by the skills and attitudes of those whose labour they needed if their enterprises were to prosper.[23]

Management Strategies: Recruitment and Structure

The first major policy decision which confronted the directors of each new dock company was how the work was to be organised, who should be employed and what each employee should do. The size of operations ruled out personal overseeing of workers by directors; there was

---

[22]Howard F. Gospel, "Managerial Structures and Strategies," in Gospel and Craig R. Littler (eds.), *Managerial Strategies and Industrial Relations: An Historical and Comparative Study* (London, 1983), 6, 11.

[23]Although we have not attempted in this essay to differentiate between companies, contemporaries believed that WIDCO was better managed and more secure than the London Dock (LDCO). The East India Dock (EIDCO) came under much less scrutiny because it was rightly regarded as an adjunct of the EIC and less of a public concern. Despite different management cultures, attitudes towards labour were strikingly similar.

therefore a need to appoint and train supervisory staff. The nature of the business, with the handling of goods matched by the amount of paperwork generated, demanded particular manual and clerical skills on an exceptional scale. The pronounced seasonality of trade meant that demand for labour, both within and without port work, varied over an annual cycle. Moreover, wartime conditions further distorted the flow of business docks had to handle, with convoys exacerbating the tendency of vessels from the West Indies to arrive in fleets.

The most novel features of these new enterprises were the docks themselves, with the entry, mooring and departure of vessels requiring supervision and assistance. The remainder of the work, other than by accountants and clerks in the central office, was concerned with unloading cargo, transferring it into warehouses, providing for its storage, ensuring its security and recording the entire process. In the West India and the London Docks, the warehouses were on-site, owned and generally operated by the companies. The East India Dock, which was in practice an adjunct of the East India Company, provided storage in the EIC's bonded "Town" warehouses in the City. This company thus had much less interest in this aspect of cargo-handling.

Since all these tasks had previously been carried out within the legal quay and sufferance wharf system, there was nothing new about the work required and no functional innovation was involved. What was distinctive about the new docks was organisational: bringing together of all these operations on a single site under unified management. Such horizontal and vertical integration not only resulted in a much greater scale of operations than experienced hitherto but also allowed (except in the case of EIDCO) for the exclusion of categories of workers previously involved in intermediate transport between wharf and warehouse – the porters and carriers.

The three companies adopted broadly similar management patterns, dividing their efforts into separate departments under a general superintendent based on facilities (for example individual warehouses), as well as a service provision by coopers and the Watch.[24] This structure was conservative in reproducing the traditional pattern of port work. Nevertheless, while the treatment of the cooperage is likely to have been dictated by the conditions of the craft, both the hierarchical structure within divisions and their separate treatment as units can be

---

[24]PLA, WIDCO, Minutes, 9 July 1802; EIDCO, Minutes, 25 July 1806.

seen as functional, offering clear lines of authority, enabling comparisons of performance, and introducing a framework for competition within the organisation. There is a strong reflection of military and naval practice, made explicit in the title "captain" initially given by WIDCO to its warehousekeepers, and by the use of the noun "officer" by all three companies to describe those in authority.

In practice the effectiveness of these arrangements relied on the availability, recruitment and retention of suitable "company servants." In the opinion of the Secretary of EIDCO:

> dispatch and efficiency arises more from having active, intelligent persons to direct, inspect & controul [sic], than from an additional number of labourers, or the subordinate Officers attending and working with them.[25]

Impressive salaries,[26] provision of accommodation; promotion by seniority (and eventually, in the case of LDCO, the introduction both of a non-contributory pension scheme), and a structure of salary increases based on length of service, suggest that neither were easy.[27] Evidence cannot be found, but we can assume that the West India and London Docks took on men previously employed on the legal quays, while we know that EIDCO used the EIC as a source of recruits. Demand for "constant and punctual attendance" in the job specifications for salaried employees drawn up by WIDCO hint at a scope for individual laxity which is confirmed by the experience of LDCO with a senior officer whose inefficiency went undetected for several years.[28] At first sight these salaried warehouse keepers, gangsmen and master coopers appear

---

[25]PLA, EIDC, Minutes, 25 July 1818.

[26]The annual salary of warehousekeepers at both LDCO and WIDCO in the 1800s was £200, while weekly wages for casual labourers were eighteen shillings.

[27]PLA, LDCO, Special Wine and Spirit Committee, Minutes, 11 November 1818; Court and Committee, Minutes, 20 December 1825.

[28]On the death of Waistall, the tobacco warehouseman, the directors discovered £1171 unaccounted for, together with 367 unsettled customer accounts, some dating to 1806. PLA, LDCO, Special Wine and Spirit Committee, Minutes, 11 August 1819.

to be a stratum of management, but in relation to the directors (but not their subordinates) they are more accurately seen as a segment of the workforce, themselves subject to supervision and control.

One indication of this is the way in which all three companies' directors had the right to nominate appointed and preferable labourers. Although this may appear to be simply an example of the continuing power of patronage in early nineteenth-century England, it also reflects a concern to avoid any element of labour sub-contracting, although in the case of quayside "gangs" it is not at present clear whether they all broke with this older port practice.

Such control was most difficult to exercise over coopers – a unionised craft in which entry was controlled by apprenticeship – who occupied a strategic role in port operations.[29] Cooperage departments, which mostly repaired casks, operated more-or-less independently. In 1821, at the trial of coopers involved in a strike at West India Dock, the master cooper, a man named Adams, made this distinction between the rum (or wet) and sugar (or dry) coopers: "the men on the rum side are entirely their own masters, under their own directions, there are officers, a particular set of officers for them" whereas sugar coopers "are taken on and placed at the warehouses they belong to, and there are captains of the warehouses who pay them, the rum coopers are separated from them."[30] Even so, there are indications that the companies did impose some conditions on the employment of coopers which were not normal for that trade. The master, for example, was an employee, with apprentices bound to the company rather than to him, and those working under him were waged rather than pieceworkers, employed for an eight-hour day. We can detect a diminution of the status of skilled workers, but one not necessarily detrimental to their interests in that the limited

---

[29]London School of Economics and Political Science, Webb Trade Union Collection A, XLIV, item 1, f. 21 and 28. The London Society of Coopers was founded in 1808. By the early 1820s there seems to have been at least four cooper societies in London: Philanthropic Society of London, Amalgamated Society of London, United Society of London, Hand in Hand Society of Coopers.

[30]Goldsmiths Library, Anon., *Report of the Trial of an Indictment, prosecuted as the instance of the West India Dock Company versus John Smith, Walter Foreman, Samuel Hucks, and Daniel Hall, for an alleged conspiracy which was tried at the Old Bailey on Thursday 13th December 1821* (London, 1821), 18-19.

length of the working day provided an opportunity for dock coopers to take on piecework elsewhere in spare hours.[31]

Among dock employees, coopers were the only formally skilled group.[32] Cargo-handling generally benefitted from experience while tasks like operating cranes, stripping tobacco, crashing sugar and packing cotton required training, but dock workers, whatever their specialty, were differentiated by their terms of employment: permanent (those with guaranteed, though not necessarily continuous, employment), preferable (those eligible for employment and in practice normally given work), or extra workers (those taken on once preferables were employed). These categories, which seem to deny the importance of skill differentiation, were similar to those within the Customs and Revenue services. The value placed by management on experience was acknowledged by a hierarchy within the first two groups, with vacancies for permanent "appointed" men normally filled from the pool of preferables and companies using a numbered card system to signify entitlement. That there were pay differentials between the categories suggest that the greater security of "permanent" or "preferable" employment was not the key distinction; rather these categories were the means of identifying levels of competence and fitness for certain jobs.[33] Throughout our period, both the WIDCO and LDCO directors periodically noted the absence of permanent workers and updated the ticket system, suggesting that it was not as effective at retaining labour as might be supposed.

One problem faced by dock management was to keep a balance between both types of employment; too small an established workforce necessitated the recruitment of suitable additional labour at short notice, while too many permanent workers imposed a heavy fixed burden on earnings. Concern about the size of the workforce surfaced periodically in all the companies, sometimes as a source of disagreement between the

---

[31]Pat Hudson and Lynette Hunter (eds.), "The Autobiography of William Hart, Cooper, 1776-1857: A Respectable Artisan in the Industrial Revolution," *London Journal*, VII (1981), 158.

[32]For a useful discussion of the concept of skill, see Charles More, *Skill and the English Working Class, 1870-1914* (London, 1980), 13-26.

[33]In 1807 LDCO paid its permanent and preferable labourers twenty-four and twenty-one shillings per week, respectively; in 1823 the rates were twenty-one and eighteen shillings; in 1824, 16s 5d and fifteen shillings.

directors and those responsible for daily operations. In February 1808, for example, the Dock Superintendent of LDCO rejected a suggestion from the directors that the labour force was too large with the comment that "as few men are employed as possible considering the machinery in use and the extent of wharf and warehouse" and warned of "delay and dissatisfaction" if the numbers were cut.[34] The problem was compounded by the division of authority over recruitment, with decisions on the creation of permanent posts taken by the directors, while the issue of whether to employ extra labour on a particular day belonged to warehouse keepers or similar middle-ranking employees.

Anxiety to restrain costs by keeping a grip on the size of the workforce has to be set within a wider context. An alternative strategy would have been to reduce wages, but this could only be done when the supply of labour was sufficient to allow recruitment at lower rates of pay. On the basis of admittedly fragmentary evidence from LDCO, it seems that dock labourers' wages fluctuated with general labour market levels, suggesting that the attraction of such work was not sufficient to permit payment below the going rate.

Recruitment and continued retention of workers on an extensive scale required was likely to prove problematic, particularly for WIDCO and EIDCO, both of which were situated in relatively sparsely-populated parishes on the eastern extremity of the metropolis. All the companies added to the difficulties posed by their need for sheer numbers of workers by demonstrating marked preferences, not only in initial recruitment but also in deciding which employees to retain, for men who displayed two essential qualities: competence and respectability.

Controlling the Workforce

Although all the dock companies insisted on the ability and integrity of their employees when these qualities were questioned by outside interests, their various labour management strategies reveal a shared belief in the capacity of employees for idleness, neglect and dishonesty. In the case of salaried workers, this found expression in a deep reluctance to trust even senior officers with anything more than the most routine decision-making functions, while labourers were assumed prone

---

[34]PLA, LDCO, Minutes, 2 February 1808.

to misconduct and theft. This suspicion led to the erection of elaborate systems for ruling the everyday activities of each company's workforce.

At the heart of these systems was a series of detailed regulations prescribing the precise duties, responsibilities, and expected conduct of all employees, with the aim of guaranteeing efficiency, order and homogeneity in operations. As WIDCO's Court of Directors declared, "the expediency of adhering precisely to one plan, when properly organised, in the mode of conducting an extensive business, is universally admitted."[35]

The officers thus had to enter their names and times of arrival in attendance books at the beginning of the day. In LDCO, clerks who arrived late found a line drawn across the page and were fined, while WIDCO's servants mustered for roll-call at the opening and close of each day and no one was allowed to stop work until the ringing of the "Great Bell." In all docks labourers and coopers were searched upon leaving. In the case of those responsible at WIDCO for setting aside samples of imported merchandise, instant dismissal was ordained for anyone who deviated in the least from the methods and instructions laid down by the directors – an especially significant policy as it went to the heart of the coopers' right to retain control over their craft.

Unity

Those who performed their tasks in accordance with the regulations were told by WIDCO that they might expect "some consideration" at the end of the season. A policy of rewards for work well done, or beyond what might be normally expected, was common to all the companies. Aware that external policing of the workforce – whether by strict enforcement of rules or by the close attention of immediate supervisors – was not sufficient to ensure efficiency and honesty, EIDCO's directors tried to imbue even the most menial of their employees with a sense of loyalty. In 1806, Joseph Cotton, the Chairman, expressed his belief that the company's few permanent labourers "being as it were fixtures...have an interest in the Concern." Cotton recommended building upon this supposed mutuality of interest by dispersing the permanent men among the casual labourers "to prevent Idleness or peculation." In his opinion, even the "occasional men...employed only as required" were capable of

---

[35]PLA, WIDCO, Minutes, 8 February 1805.

moral improvement. The payment of a retaining fee, together with a ticket to protect them from the attentions of the press gang, should ensure (when taken together with the company's more punitive regulations) that "they will become, and feel respectable in themselves."[36]

The paternalism indicated here was also expressed in other ways. All three companies on occasion made payments to men unable to work because of sickness or accident. In May 1823, for example, the WIDCO directors considered the cases of three "infirm coopers." Isaac Bedding, who had worked for the company for twenty years, was nearly blind as a result of an accident; unable to work, he was granted £25. At the same time, Michael Curtis and Henry Dearson, "who have been occasionally employed for fifteen years & upwards, but are unfitted by age for further employment," were given £15 each.[37] LDCO routinely paid "subsistence money" to labourers hurt while working and gave gratuities to the dependants of those killed. The same company made no deduction from the wages of permanent "appointed" men for public holidays.[38] These were symbolic gestures, since the sums involved were hardly princely, but they are suggestive of a wish to be seen as sensitive employers, as loyal to their workers as they expected them to be to the company.

Division

This stress on the unity of the company and its workforce, and on the importance of centralised planning and control, ran counter to the divisions evident in each company, whether derived from functional imperatives or cultural and ideological notions. In practice, LDCO and WIDCO were divided vertically by the tendency of the directors to treat each department as semi-autonomous, with the officer in charge responsible for the efficiency, attendance and payment of "his" workforce. In both WIDCO and LDCO, comparative studies of the costs and throughput of each warehouse were made, and at the former the captain of the warehouse with the highest annual productivity was given fifty guineas. According to a former cooper, this reward was "called by the Labourers

---

[36]PLA, EIDCO, Minutes, 25 July 1806.

[37]PLA, WIDCO, Minutes, 16 May 1823.

[38]PLA, LDCO, Court and Committee, Minutes, 2 July 1811.

and others the 'blood money' from the manner of driving the labourers and others at work and the accidents that hapings [sic]."[39] When the first Principal Dock Master at WIDCO resigned over the nature of work expected of him, the directors displayed their faith in this system (and their desire to keep as much direct responsibility as possible for day-to-day management) by delaying the appointment of his replacement, instructing the captains to consider themselves wholly independent of each other and to report directly to the Court of Directors.[40]

This structure reduced the likelihood of any unity of interest developing between departments and hence increased the directors' authority. But if combinations among workers at roughly the same level were viewed with disquiet, anything subversive of formal relations between officers and servants provoked great unease. The information in 1823 that labourers on the Rum Quay at WIDCO had for some years been operating a benefit society to relieve those "as might from sickness be thrown out of work" was mildly alarming; that they had been holding an annual dinner attended by many of the officers was horrifying. "This sort of association," the directors complained, "must break down the pale of distinction, and be subversive of all proper discipline."[41]

Rewards

This incident, which came to light with the discovery that the society was funded by gratuities received (or possibly extorted) by labourers on the quay from the spirit merchants with whom the company dealt, also sheds light on another aspect of management policy. All the dock companies fiercely prohibited the acceptance of any type of personal payment from a customer. Outside gratuities not only reduced a company's claim to have respectable, honest and impartial workers but also undermined one of the chief holds any employer has over its workforce: a monopoly on the scale of material rewards received in return for their labour.

While practical demands eventually led to the devolution of some managerial functions, the types and levels of payments to the workforce,

---

[39]Public Record Office, T92/23, "Evidence of Commission of Inquiry into the Customs," Letter from Henry Forister, "read 26 March 1819."

[40]PLA, WIDCO, Minutes, 24 September 1802.

[41]*Ibid.*, 29 August 1823.

and even to individual employees, were treated as major policy decisions, to be reached only by directors. Promotions (seen by WIDCO as "the strongest inducement to industry and attention"), wage and salary rises, and bonus payments were all used to stimulate exertion, reward assiduity, promote good conduct, indicate approbation, and, ultimately, to place all servants demonstrably under the control of the directors.[42]

Punishments

A more direct method of accomplishing the same thing was found in the punishments instituted by all the companies. The least – and most often used – took the form of fines levied for a variety of offences, including lateness, absenteeism, negligence (especially when it resulted in damage to merchandise and machinery or injury to a fellow employee) or general misconduct (including the failure to achieve a satisfactory work rate). The officers mentioned above who dined with their labourers, for example, were fined amounts ranging from £5 to three shillings per week for six weeks, depending on the level of salary. Temporary suspension without pay (again imposed on these officers) was also common. Even apparently trivial infringements of regulations could result in dismissal, frequently with the rider that the offender never be employed at that dock again.

The most common offence reported to directors was theft, for which dismissal was not the ultimate sanction. Companies' private watch forces and constables co-operated closely with the Revenue watch and Thames Police Magistrates; directors of all the concerns were zealous in pursuing felonious employees through the courts. Trade union activity – the "conspiracy to raise wages" – was also risky. In November 1810 a number of former LDCO workers were "indicted for a riot at the docks" the previous July, when the eighteen-shilling labourers had gone on strike for higher wages. Charges were also laid against the leaders of the WIDCO coopers' strike in 1821.[43] There was a presumption that participation in strikes meant dismissal, but after a coopers' dispute at LDCO in 1812 the directors, having been advised by the master cooper that "the service will feel considerable difficulties without some of these

---

[42]*Ibid.*, 11 May 1813.

[43]PLA, LDCO, Minutes, 6 July and 6 November 1810.

men," felt constrained to reinstate some of the offenders.[44] We can see here a conflict, also evident in some cases where employees were allowed a second chance despite breaking company rules, between the need to maintain discipline and the need to maintain the workforce.

Conclusion

When contemporaries spoke of London's adoption of "the dock system" they were referring to more than simply a revolution in facilities; they also meant a whole new way of dealing with trade. Of necessity this change would be expected to affect the experience of work, but what this essay has sought to demonstrate is that the centrality of labour in the new situation resulted in structures (physical as well as organisational) and strategies (reactive as well as pre-determined) directed at its control.

Within the field of labour history, and still more within labour sociology, the subject of our study in this early period of industrialisation is unfamiliar. Indeed, some of the cruder schematic typologies would suggest that the kind of arrangements we have delineated are associated only with the growth of monopoly capitalism. While we would not want to claim that the dock directors discovered new ways of regulating work, we can suggest that their systematic approach to managing labour has much in common with late nineteenth-century industries. Our account, reflecting as it does the employers' perception, may exaggerate their success in influencing what went on in the warehouse or on the quay. Nevertheless, in the determination of the companies to prevent any increase in artisanal power, and to reduce the independent status of those who already possessed it, we can see the shaping of a workforce that later came to be described not by what it did, but by where it earned its wages: dock workers. For the employers this was a considerable achievement; for their labour, it was something altogether different.

---

[44]PLA, LDCO, Special Wine and Spirits Committee, Minutes, 4 December 1812.

Owners and Masters:
Management and Managerial Skills
in the Finnish Ocean-Going Merchant Fleet,
c. 1840-1880[1]

Yrjö Kaukiainen

Introduction: The Role of Masters in the Age of Sail

> He looked with extreme jealousy at the beautiful and
> well-appointed ships frequenting Newcastle from Russian
> and Swedish Finland: but, he saw that no fairer class of
> merchant ships came to any port; their dimensions, their
> rigging, everything about them was admirable; while
> their commanders and officers inspired respect from
> their general competency. Their log-books were beauti-
> fully kept in English...No doubt, these northern mari-
> time countries could be regarded in no other light than
> that of formidable rivals.[2]

The above quotation is from the evidence of a Tyneside shipowner,
William Richmond, before the 1847 committee examining the future of
the Navigation Acts. Since he was a keen protectionist, the bright picture
he painted of Finnish ships and masters was certainly influenced by his
conscious and unconscious fears.[3] At the same time, the statement

---

[1]The author wishes to thank the participants in the Glasgow pre-conference and
especially the discussant, Frank Broeze, for useful suggestions.

[2]W.S. Lindsay, *History of Merchant Shipping and Ancient Commerce* (4 vols.,
London, 1876), III, 151-152.

[3]That Mr. Richmond singled out Finnish vessels must have been a reflection of the
Reciprocity Treaty signed by Russia and Britain in 1843; *ibid.*, III, 151. On the
committee's work, see Sarah Palmer, *Politics, Shipping and the Repeal of the Navigation*

indirectly emphasizes the importance of the master: his qualities and skills were not only reflected in the outward appearance of the ship but also in many cases decisively affected its economic success.

In the present maritime world, the master may be regarded as a highly-skilled employee, a foreman or a chief of personnel. He may manage everyday work fairly independently but all important business decisions are made by the owners or managers. Yet before the era of the telegraph and liners he had far wider powers and responsibilities, at least in the long-distance trades. Not only did he manage the *ship*, he also had an important say in managing the *business*. Thus, he frequently decided things which today fall outside his province, such as freight contracts and the ship's expenses in foreign ports. Indeed, he was more like a manager than a foreman. This role was particularly important in deep-sea trading, in which a vessel might be away from its home port for several years. In such cases, the entire managerial system was of necessity very different than modern practices.[4]

In this essay I will examine the system of management during the "heyday of sail" using the Finnish merchant marine as a case study. While it can hardly be argued that Finland was a typical maritime country – it was situated too far from the major oceans for that – it was engaged in the cross-trades in faraway waters. Because of this, the bifurcation of powers and responsibilities between owners and masters was well developed. I will focus particularly on the skills required to cope successfully with the challenges of the business and on how well owners and masters possessed them. Since many skills were developed during early modern times and originated in western Europe, their diffusion to a fairly peripheral nation is of special interest.

The Overall Management of Long-Distance Shipping

From the early 1830s to the 1870s, Finnish shipping experienced a period of expansion and prosperity. The total tonnage owned in urban

Laws (Manchester, 1990), 90-105.

[4]The active role of masters was further reinforced by their frequent ownership of shares, sometimes major, of their ships. In addition to a monthly wage, they universally received commissions, (*kapplake*), normally amounting to five percent of gross freights. During "the twilight of sail" from the 1880s, masters tended to increase their ownership in order to secure employment and *kapplake* (which in bad times exceeded net profits).

ports trebled and its geographic range came to span practically the entire world.[5] This growth depended mainly on "cross-trading," that is, the carriage of goods other than Finnish exports and imports. By the 1860s about sixty percent of Finnish shipping income originated from such trades; in fact, the country owned three times more tonnage than was needed to meet its own requirements.[6] Considering the small and relatively stagnant domestic economy, such developments were logical.

Participation in long-distance shipping meant that ships generally sailed on a series of voyages and often were away for three years or more. Even when not involved in such trades, many Finnish vessels wintered far from the frozen Baltic, for example sailing to the Mediterranean in the autumn and returning with salt in the spring. In the mid-nineteenth century, two-thirds to four-fifths of urban tonnage was normally recorded as being away at the end of the year.[7] Such a state of affairs narrowed the control of owners. Once the vessel had left its home port the only means of keeping in contact before the telegraph was by correspondence, and the time-lag could be very large. Often an owner's orders reached a distant port only after relevant decisions had been made.

Of course, this was a dilemma which all early long-distance vessels faced. In the sixteenth century British owners solved the problem by personally leading their expeditions, becoming "merchant adventurers" in the true sense of the phrase.[8] East India companies, on the other hand, recruited strong corps of officers whose responsibilities were divided between the navigational and the commercial; in Swedish ships, for example, a *superkarg* was in charge of all transactions concerning the cargo.[9] But humble merchantmen could not afford such expensive manning, at least not in the competitive nineteenth-century world. As a result, owners adopted various methods to strengthen their control.

---

[5]Yrjö Kaukiainen, *A History of Finnish Shipping* (London, 1993), 69-82.

[6]Yrjö Kaukiainen, *Sailing into Twilight. Finnish Shipping in an Age of Transport Revolution, 1860-1914* (Jyväskylä, 1991), 218-19, 280.

[7]Kaukiainen, *A History*, 71, 80.

[8]See, for example, Ronald Hope, *A New History of British Shipping* (London, 1990), 115-165.

[9]See Eirik Hornborg, *Segelsjöfartens historia* (2nd ed., Helsingfors, 1948), 394-404.

In Finland, as elsewhere, the early cornerstone of this system was a network of foreign representatives and business associates. Since most owners were also engaged in foreign trade, they conducted regular business with customers and suppliers in England, France, Holland and southern Europe. Foreign merchants approached Finnish trading houses via commercial letters or circulars with information on local markets and prices.[10] Regular contacts with shipping and other commercial agents were also common. A special case was Helsingör, where ships had to pay a Sound Toll until 1857. Since a stop had to be made, the opportunity was used to update information on markets and to replenish ships' stores. Most Finnish vessels relied on certain Helsingör agents, such as Julius Schierbeck, who took care of the formalities, delivered information and acted as middlemen in selling cargoes. Another special case was Hamburg, where local bankers like Bauck and Dürkoop, and Salomon Heine, were relied on for short-term credit and for remitting earnings home; ships were also insured by Hamburg underwriters. Later, however, London gained more prominence in credit transactions and insurance. Finally, from the 1840s, shipping agents were also used in the search for freights; in this respect, London was soon predominant and some of the firms, such as Clarkson, specialized in Nordic customers.[11]

Unfortunately, it is not yet possible to present a detailed analysis of the foreign business networks of Finnish merchants, since this would require research that has not been done. But a reasonable estimate might be that a typical merchant or commercial house may have had between half a dozen and twenty regular foreign business contacts, a network spanning the European coasts from Copenhagen to Italy. These men could perform many kinds of services, such as facilitating customs clearances, selling cargoes, searching for profitable freights, and giving

---

[10]Sven-Erik Åström, *From Tar to Timber. Studies in Northeast European Forest Exploitation and Foreign Trade 1660-1860* (Ekenäs, 1988), 138-140. Examples of eighteenth-century business contacts can be found for example in Aulis J. Alanen, *Der Aussenhandel und die Schiffahrt Finnlands im 18. Jahrhundert* (Helsinki, 1957), 353-354.

[11]The description is based on the accounts of several Finnish ships and shipowners. Cf. Kaukiainen, *Sailing into Twilight*, appendix IV; Oscar Nikula, *Malmska handelshuset i Jakobstad* (Helsingfors, 1948); and Christer Norrvik, *Briggen Carl Gustaf* (Helsingfors, 1981). Concerning Clarkson, see Lewis R. Fischer and Helge W. Nordvik, "The Growth of Norwegian Shipbroking: The Practices of Fearnley and Eger as a Case Study, 1869-1914," in L.R. Fischer and W. Minchinton (eds.), *People of the Northern Seas* (St. John's, 1992), 142.

masters all kinds of information. In some cases, decades of collaboration had created personal or family friendships; such friends would be trusted in preference to a newly-employed master.

Since so little is known about these foreign contacts, it is impossible to estimate the accuracy of their knowledge. Doubtless some were better informed than others. Yet it seems that in the Finnish case the majority consisted of importers of wood and/or (in the Mediterranean) exporters of salt and wine whose knowledge was based upon local rather than international commodity markets. On the other hand, they also had their own networks which might include foreign shipping experts. Moreover, until the mid-nineteenth century, foreign trade and shipping were, in practice, opposite sides of the same coin. There are many examples of Finnish ships securing freights to the West Indies, South America or East Asia immediately after delivering wood to an Iberian or Mediterranean port, a phenomenon which suggests that local importers acted as middlemen. In the 1860s and 1870s it appears that shipping agents gradually gained more importance, a development which reflects two significant changes in the business environment. First, there was a gradual separation between trade and shipping; increasingly the owner of a sailing vessel had no personal stake in its cargo. As a result, the demand for first-class shipping information increased. Second, after Britain lowered its tariffs on non-colonial timber products, British ports became the most important destinations for Finnish vessels. To meet the demand for information, specialized shipping agents were soon found not only in London and Liverpool but also in a number of smaller ports. Later, when shipping prospects dimmed and many commercial houses withdrew from the industry, the role of traditional partners ended.[12]

It is clear that since business "friends" and shipping agents could not give orders to a master, a formal agreement on the division of powers between the owner and master was necessary. Normally, the owner gave written instructions to the master, who accepted them by signing two copies, one of which stayed with the ship while the other remained with the owner. Typically, such instructions included detailed orders for the first outward cargo (possibly adding that final instructions

---

[12]Of course, there were always a few exceptions. The traditional "shuttle" trade to Spain remained much the same as ever. The last windjammer in this trade regularly made one winter and one summer trip to Cadiz and Seville until the autumn of 1914. It was later sunk in 1916 by a German submarine while bound from Gulfport to Barcelona.

would be received at Helsingör or Copenhagen); general instructions for the following cargoes (what type of deployment to be preferred); and information on how to remit freight income, which commercial houses and/or agents to contact, how to draw money for expenses, what to do in case of damage or shipwreck, what limitations (if any) to place on money advances to the crew, and what to do in case the master died (a typical order was for the mate to load salt and return home).[13]

After arriving at a port, the master had to notify the owners immediately and, if possible, await their instructions. Moreover, he was expected to keep a detailed account of income and expenses; prior to sailing he was expected to mail these to the owner and remit any surplus from freight or other income, typically using a Hamburg or London bill of exchange. Thus, owners might expect a fairly continual flow of information and even money. Port times being much longer than today, they even had a fair opportunity to make their wishes known by mail, at least if the ship was not on the other side of the globe. Yet it was not uncommon for a master to have the right to sign a freight agreement without consulting the owners if rapid action was needed.

The telegraph, of course, created faster means of communication. Finland obtained its first effective connection with western Europe in 1860, when a cable connection around the Gulf of Bothnia was built to Sweden.[14] But this did not change the system as rapidly as might have been expected, since charges were high enough to keep messages very short and language problems frequently caused confusion. As a result, masters confirmed such messages by repeating them in letters, and correspondence remained the main mode of communication between masters and owners until the end of the century, at least as far as cross-trading windjammers carrying low-paying bulk cargoes were concerned. On the other hand, masters often received telegraphic orders and

---

[13]Arne Engström, *Åbo sjöfarts historia II:1. Segelsjöfarten 1827-1856* (Åbo, 1930), 113-114, 147-148; archives of several Finnish commercial houses (see note 11).

[14]A connection between Helsinki and St. Petersburg was commissioned in 1855, and subsequently the network was extended to many coastal towns. Although it was primarily intended for military purposes, private messages could also be sent, but only on a few lines could languages other than Russian be used. Moreover, the connection with Sweden soon became overloaded. In 1869, Det store nordiske telegrafselskab of Copenhagen laid a cable over the Åland Sea, which vastly improved foreign connections. Einar Risberg, *Suomen lennätinlaitoksen historia 1855-1955* (Helsinki, 1959), 90-187.

information through shippers and agents. Yet as long as the "wireless telegraph" (radio) was uncommon, the traditional system of receiving final orders at a conveniently situated port (such as Falmouth, Queenstown, Hampton Roads, or Galle) prevailed in the tramp trades.[15]

Although owners clearly had primacy, the constraints imposed by time and distance meant that most control over long-distance vessels could only be exercised retrospectively. While the master was bound to follow the general tenor of his instructions, in day-to-day business matters he was the most important decision-maker.

The Skills of Owners

Before 1868, no Finnish citizen could engage in long-haul shipping without being a burgher in a town with so-called "staple rights" (the right to carry on foreign trade), and no one could be admitted as a burgher without certain minimum skills such as writing, arithmetic and basic accounting. Moreover, six to twelve years of practical commercial training were normally expected.[16] Yet such minimum qualifications were insufficient for anyone involved in international shipping. Much, of course, depended on the character of the practical training.

Preserved rolls of burghers (which are to be found for practically all Finnish towns from the 1840s, 1850s and 1860s) reveal that the majority served their apprenticeships as clerks in domestic commercial houses, not infrequently in the family firm.[17] The biggest commercial houses, however, used to send their youngsters for a year or more to be trained in continental or British firms. Of all burghers listed in the foreign trade around 1850, at least two dozen (c. two percent) had such

---

[15]On the development of international telegraphs, see Jorma Ahvenainen, "Telegraphs, Trade and Policy. The Role of International Telegraphs in the Years 1870-1914," in Wolfram Fischer, R. Marvin McInnis and Jürgen Schneider (eds.), *The Emergence of a World Economy, 1500-1914* (2 vols., Weisbaden, 1986), II, 506-507. The use of the telegraph in shipping has not been studied systematically.

[16]Tapani Mauranen, "Porvarista kauppiaaksi – kauppiaan yhteiskunnallinen asema 1800-luvun jälkipuoliskolla," in Y. Kaukiainen, P. Schybergsson and H. Soikkanen (eds.), *När samhället förändras/Kun yhteiskunta muuttuu* (Helsinki, 1981), 202.

[17]Finland, National Archives (FNA), Senate, Finance Department (Finance), series Bj, rolls of burghers.

an apprenticeship; twenty-five years later the corresponding figure was almost forty. Moreover, eleven in 1850 and seventeen in 1875 had studied in German (mainly at G.W. Reys Practisches Handelsinstitut in Lübeck) or Swedish business schools. The first such academy in Finland was founded in Turku (Åbo) in 1839, and similar institutes were later established in Vaasa (1843) and Oulu (1864). Unfortunately, the rolls do not give systematic information on burghers' domestic studies.[18]

Of the top twenty-five Finnish shipowners in 1850 (ranked according to tonnage sailing beyond the Baltic), at least four had studied in a foreign firm and two more had attended the Lübeck institute. Moreover, five had been (or still were) shipmasters, which suggests that it was good training for anyone managing a shipping firm. By 1870 the figures were similar (although the data was less complete): three had foreign commercial education and seven or eight had been masters.[19]

In addition to basic mercantile skills, an ability to acquire current information from abroad was essential in foreign shipping, as was a reasonable knowledge of foreign languages.[20] Fortunately, the mid-nineteenth century rolls of burghers contain data on language skills. Since there were no uniform criteria, different magistrates may have interpreted language ability distinctly.

Nevertheless, the information is still useful. The language skills of shipowners and all Finnish burghers with the right to participate in foreign trade are compared in table 1. Since shipowning was not always carefully recorded, only "samples" comprising the top twenty-five and top forty owners, respectively, were examined.[21] However, since the former controlled about forty-five percent of ocean-going tonnage and the latter almost sixty percent, the figures are representative of the most

---

[18]Nikula, *Malska handelshuset*, 56, 63; Örnulf Tigerstedt, *Kauppahuone Hackman. Erään vanhan Viipurin kauppiassuvun vaiheet 1790-1879* (2 vols., Helsinki, 1940), I, 321-349; Mauranen, "Porvarista kauppiaaksi," 203-204.

[19]FNA, Finance, rolls of burghers, 1850 and 1870.

[20]Practically all foreign-trading burghers were Swedish-speaking and were thus able to communicate easily with Scandinavian colleagues. On the other hand, Russian was spoken only by a small minority and was not an official language; in the following it has, unlike Swedish, been regarded as a foreign language.

[21]The data was also checked by looking at FNA, Finance, series Ef, ship lists.

important owners. There were no dramatic differences between shipowners and other foreign traders: in both groups about one-third did not know any foreign languages. It was equally remarkable that the most common foreign language among shipowners was German: of the top twenty-five, fifteen spoke it, while eight had some ability in English and seven were conversant in French.

Table 1
Language Skills of Finnish Urban Shipowners and Burghers, c. 1850

	1		2		3
	N	%	N	%	%
three or more foreign languages	4	(16)	8	(20)	19
two foreign languages	5	(20)	6	(15)	24
one foreign language	9	(36)	13	(33)	20
no foreign languages	7	(28)	13	(33)	36

Note: 1 = Top 25 shipowners (total tonnage, c. 18,700 lasts); 2 = Top 40 shipowners (total tonnage, c. 24,100 lasts); 3 = All burghers in the foreign trade. Tonnages refer only to ships that sailed outside the Baltic (and normally were away during the winter).

Sources: Finland, National Archives (FNA), Senate, Finance Department (Finance), series Bj 1, rolls of burghers.; Tapani Mauranen, "Porvarista kauppiaaksi – kauppiaan yhteiskunnallinen asema 1800-luvun jälkipuoliskolla," in Y. Kaukiainen, P. Schybergsson and H. Soikkanen (eds.), *När samhället förändras/Kun yhteiskunta muuttuu* (Helsinki, 1981), 203.

Since English was becoming the *lingua franca* of shipping in the second half of the nineteenth century, it might seem that Finnish owners were not particularly qualified. Indeed, three of the top ten knew no foreign languages. But in at least two cases there was a son in the firm with better skills, and it is also possible that some clerks had linguistic abilities. Moreover, many vessels were owned by partnerships in which the *korrespondentredare* (corresponding owner), who tended to have above-average linguistic skills, handled actual management. In 1870 the general picture was similar, although the proportion with no language skills increased slightly. Knowledge of English had increased slightly while French declined. German, however, remained the most common foreign language.[22]

It is also important to understand the degree to which Finnish owners had access to relevant and up-to-date foreign information. As far as public sources are concerned, the flow seems to have been only a trickle. For the most part Finnish burghers did not subscribe to British, French or German commercial journals. Only two Hamburg papers, *Hamburger Correspondent* and *Hamburger Börsenhalle*, were of any importance, but even they had only about a dozen Finnish readers. No British mercantile papers are known to have entered the country before 1860. Stockholm papers, however, were much more common and may have been of some value. One Finnish newspaper, the Swedish-language *Åbo Underrättelser*, frequently published mercantile and shipping news and was popular in coastal towns.[23] In general, newspapers and journals seem to have been of limited importance to Finnish shipowners.

Private sources must therefore have been far more important. In any event, the biggest firms carried on extensive correspondence with business contacts abroad and received letters and printed circulars, often in Swedish, describing local market conditions. Even if a Finnish merchant did not know foreign languages, he was able to communicate with at least some foreigners. German firms often employed Scandina-vian-born clerks and apprentices, as did some English agents and shipbrokers. Indeed, even some southern European houses, such as Torlades and Co. in Lisbon, were able to correspond in Swedish.[24]

It thus seems that the typical Finnish shipowner possessed at least the rudimentary skills and sources to cope with foreign transactions. Yet his ability and contacts were better suited to mercantile pursuits than to the cross-trades. Even had more rapid communication been possible, no more than a half dozen or so of the major owners had sufficient command of English and world freight markets (not to mention good contacts) to be able to manage their ships successfully by themselves, that is, without the help of foreign business associates – and masters. It

---

[22]FNA, Finance, Bj 1; and letter acts: KD 25/75, 15/112, 26/138, 16/152 (1871).

[23]Päiviö Tommila, *Suomen lehdistön levikki ennen vuotta 1860* (Porvoo, 1963), 104-105.

[24]Åström, *Tar to Timber*, 138 ff.; Nikula, *Malmska handelshuset*, 94, 194-195; Fischer and Nordvik, "The Growth of Norwegian Shipbroking," 142.

was thus not only the constraints of time and distance that made masters so critical.

The Skills of Shipmasters

In Sweden, shipmasters' competence was a public concern as early as the eighteenth century. According to a 1748 act, masters had to be burghers in a coastal town (a requirement that subjected them to municipal control), and in 1765 it was decreed that all foreign-going masters and mates had to pass an exam in navigation and other skills before the town magistrate. A navigation school, sponsored jointly by the state and the city, had been operating continuously in Stockholm since 1728 (and its roots can be traced back to the 1650s). During the eighteenth century, at least five more local schools were established, including the Swedish East India Company's academy in Göteborg. Given that British masters were not subject to similar requirements until after 1850, this at first glance seems remarkable. But it is perhaps less startling considering the vital role of shipmasters in long-distance shipping.[25]

Because all eighteenth-century Swedish laws applied to Finland, Finnish ocean-going masters studied either at the Stockholm school or with private navigation teachers. It was only after Finland was separated from Sweden and joined to Russia that state-sponsored navigation schools were founded. The first three were authorized in Turku (Åbo), Helsinki (Helsingfors) and Vaasa, and later more schools were founded in Oulu (Uleåborg, 1863), Mariehamn (1866) and Viipuri (Wiborg, 1874).[26]

---

[25]Olof Traung (ed.), *Navigationsskolornas historia. Minneskrift utgiven med anledning av de statliga skolornas 100-åriga tillvaro* (Göteborg, 1941), 20-61. On the English 1850 reform see Hope, *A New History*, 287. The development of navigation schools and examinations was remarkably similar in Denmark-Norway. The first school was founded in Copenhagen in the seventeenth century and the first in Norway (in Bergen) during the following century. From 1770, masters and mates were required to pass examinations. Proper navigation schools, however, were few and teaching was mainly by private teachers. See Berit Eide Johnsen, *Han sad i prisonen...Sjøfolk i engelsk fangenskap 1807-1814* (Oslo, 1993), 164-171; and Lindsay, *History*, III, 28-35.

[26]Onni Friberg, *Rauman merikoulu ja merenkulkuopisto 1880-1930* (Rauma, 1931), 9-16. By comparison, proper state-sponsored systems were started in Sweden in 1827, in Denmark in 1837 and in Norway in 1840. Johnsen, *Han sad i prisonen*, 171; Traung (ed.), *Navigationsskolornas*, 70.

Although private studies were still possible, the 1813 instructions assumed that teachers rather than magistrates would supervise official exams. Masters sailing within the Baltic might be tested for the "short sea" trade only. At the same time, many magistrates still allowed unexamined masters to sail in these waters until an 1851 law ended such practices by restricting unexamined skippers to coastal waters. The same act created two categories: "Baltic skipper" (*coopvaerdie-skeppare*; from 1864 *Östersjöskeppare*) and "sea-captain" (*coopvaerdie-capitain*; from 1864 *sjökapten*). As far as bluewater masters were concerned the law made little difference: of the roughly 400 *coopvaerdie* masters registered in Finnish towns in 1847 and sailing beyond the Baltic, only a handful had not passed the master's examination from a navigation school.[27]

Table 2
Characteristics of Finnish Shipmasters, 1847 and 1870

	1847			1870		
	1	2	3	1	2	3
Ostrobothnian towns	16	26	36	16	27	41
Southwest towns	17	27	33	16	27	38
Gulf of Finland towns	16	26	33	16	27	42
Whole Finland	16	26	34	16	27	40

Notes: 1 = Median age at the start of the career (first voyage); 2 = Median age when passing master's examination; 3 = Median age of acting shipmasters. Ages were computed by subtracting year of birth from year of the first voyage and examinations, etc. They thus may differ slightly from the precise age of any individual.

Source: FNA, Finance, rolls of shipmasters. 1847: Ef 1; 1870: letter acts, KD 17/62, 21/75, 8/111, 12/136, 20/153 1871; for Oulu, 1872, Ef 3.

The system also required several years of practical training, although this could be performed as a seaman or deck officer; seldom did vessels carry officer apprentices. Compared with other countries, the emphasis on formal schooling and examinations was strong, which likely

---

[27]*Finlands författningssamling*, 21 August 1851, 27 May 1856 and 21 January 1863; Birger Eriksson, *Åbo navigationsskola och navigationsinstitut 1813-1936* (Åbo, 1942), 4-6.

affected the quality of masters and officers.[28] Table 2 presents some basic facts about Finnish masters in 1847 and 1870 (excluding unexamined skippers sailing only in the Baltic). It is clear that the master's exam was typically passed after ten years at sea, but since maritime vocations often started young (a few were less than ten when they first signed-on), new masters were younger on average than might have been expected. Among the 1847 group, a few received their ticket at eighteen, but after 1863 a minimum age (twenty-one) and specified experience were mandated. This may be the explanation for the one-year increase in median age in 1870.

Young masters are not necessarily better than old ones. Indeed, many skills can be learned by experience. Of course, the average age of masters suggests that it was virtually a life-long career.[29] Still, this was not a "learning-by-doing" but rather a "learning-by-schooling" system; its obvious benefit was that those with the necessary talent were recruited relatively young and thus were active for a good number of years.

Practically all Finnish deep-sea masters and mates had reasonable navigational skills on matters such as tidal reckoning and the use of the sextant and chronometer. For masters, it was equally important to possess basic mercantile skills, but the sources reveal much less about this. At first, the navigation schools seem to have concentrated on conventional navigational skills. Gradually, however, more teachers were employed and languages, correspondence and economic geography were added to the curriculum. An 1851 act, which took effect only after the Crimean War, required that future mates be taught the elements of German, French or English, while future masters should learn "mercantile" geography, foreign money and measurements, laws concerning bills of exchange and average (sea damage), plus Swedish correspondence. In 1863, accounting was added and the teaching of English increased.[30]

---

[28]Around the mid-eighteenth century, practical training still seems to have been the norm, since a special Act for apprentices aboard Swedish ships was decreed on 4 November 174; R.G. Modée, *Utdrag utur alle...Publique Handlingar, Placater, Förordningar, Resolutioner och Publicationer* (15 vols., Stockholm, 1742), IV, 2511.

[29]"Virtually" denotes the fact that many masters seem to have left the trade in their late fifties. Although there were masters over sixty-five, a definite "thinning-out" of age groups over fifty-five was observed both in 1847 and 1870.

[30]*Finlands författningssamling*, 21 August 1851 and 21 January 1863.

Preserved ships' accounts suggest that at least since the 1860s masters generally practised a functional and uniform variant of Italian bookkeeping. Whether they learned it at navigation school or elsewhere remains obscure, but it indicates that they must also have possessed other mercantile skills. Surviving correspondence shows that the best masters were able to write perfect English and to make sound cost calculations. As early as the 1850s, some Finnish masters collected weather observations for Captain Maury, and his suggestions for the best routes were printed in *Åbo Underrättelser* in 1861.[31] Since the preserved accounts are mainly from the big commercial houses, it is of course possible that such skills were only common within the top stratum of masters.

Table 3
Language Skills of finnish Urban Shipmasters, 1848 and 1870

| | 1847 | | | | 1870 | | | |
| | 1 | | 2 | | 1 | | 2 | |
	N	%	N	%	N	%	N	%
three or more foreign languages	22	9	16	11	3	2	14	6
two foreign languages	60	26	20	14	50	30	52	23
one foreign language	133	57	39	28	96	59	101	45
no foreign languages	19	8	65	46	15	9	59	26
English-speaking	203	87	47	34	147	90	144	64
German-speaking	73	31	46	33	13	8	51	23

Note: 1 = Ostrobothnian towns; 2 = Other towns

Source: See table 2.

When it comes to knowledge of foreign languages, general levels can be determined with some precision (see table 3). Although the data are as unsystematic as for burghers, some interesting observations can be

---

[31]Oscar Nikula, *Åbo sjöfarts historia II:2. Segelsjöfarten 1856-1926* (Åbo, 1930), 146-147.

made. First, masters on average were as skillful as shipowners; second, knowledge of English was more common. The most striking feature was the great difference between Ostrobothnian and south coast towns: in the former, about ninety percent of masters knew English, while in the latter captains with no knowledge of English or any other foreign language were common in 1847, if not in 1870. This difference reflects shipping patterns. In Ostrobothnia, long-distance tramp trades predominated. Typical voyages began with a leg to England with wood, and many craft depended on English agents to find freights for abroad. South coast towns, on the other hand, usually engaged in the "shuttle" trade to southern Europe; although ships might have carried freight on the Mediterranean during the winter, masters were not in frequent contact with British agents. Yet even their knowledge of English improved between 1847 and 1870, as navigation schools became more effective.

While it seems clear that general skills improved slowly, in 1860 the Board of the Finnish Mutual Maritime Insurance Association (which comprised major shipowners) claimed that there were still too many masters with unacceptable language and other abilities. The Association tried to raise standards by refusing to insure a vessel with such a master. But some foreign observers claimed that British masters were no better and perhaps worse. Given that official approval of testing began in Britain only in the 1850s, this is not unexpected. It appears that the Association's concern reflected high expectations of employers rather than low skill levels among captains. Similarly, the need to improve masters' abilities was also regarded as important in Sweden.[32]

From the 1840s there was a sufficient supply of competent masters in western Finland, the area that concentrated mainly on long-haul shipping. During the late 1860s, the numbers seem to have been even more plentiful, yet because many owners invested in larger and more cost-efficient craft, the demand for masters diminished. In fact, many of the less skilful were now compelled to sign-on as mates.[33] In the following decade, the "golden age" of Finnish shipping came to an end, but this cannot have been due to a lack of competent masters.

---

[32]Nikula, *Segelsjöfarten*, 146-148; Norrvik, *Carl Gustaf*, 20; Eriksson, *Åbo navigationsskola*, 4-5; Kaukiainen, *Sailing into Twilight*, 125-126; Traung (ed.), *Navigationsskolornas*, 91-92.

[33]See the sources for table 2.

Conclusion

The division of responsibilities between owners and masters was quite functional given Finland's geographic position and the nature of cross-trading under sail. This partition was also compatible with the language and other skills of the owners: that burghers knew German better than English is understandable since northern Germany, and Hamburg in particular, was the financial centre for many Finnish merchants. On the other hand, mariners mainly operated within an English-speaking world.

Of course, the Finnish management system was by no means unique – ships were run similarly in Sweden, Norway and elsewhere, although comparisons are difficult because of the lack of relevant studies. Moreover, the basic navigation and commercial skills reflected western European expertise. In fact, the diffusion of navigation schools and techniques was a pan-European phenomenon. The Swedish and Finnish systems of public navigation schools and competence control make an interesting comparison with the pre-1850 British system of *laissez-faire* on such issues. Nordic owners perhaps compensated for the disadvantage of being on the periphery by forcing the diffusion of expertise.

Yet as functional as the system appears, there was a pitfall. The fact that masters could run a ship independently made management less demanding for the owner; it was possible to succeed even with inferior proficiencies and insufficient contacts abroad. Although day-to-day business did not suffer, proper investment decisions required access to good sources of information (such as British journals) and an ability to interpret them. Instead, it seems that tradition was all too often the dominant consideration, a less than satisfactory approach in times of flux. The skills shortage was exacerbated in the last quarter of the century as many large commercial houses, representing above-average competence, withdrew from shipping. At the same time, the transition from sail to steam complicated investment decisions. While the failure to invest in steamers obviously hinged on real economic factors, a shortage of entrepreneurial ability may have contributed. In any case, the weakness in Finnish shipping management was the owner rather than the master, and long-term strategic planning was the most fragile component.

Management, Profitability and Finance in Twentieth-Century Spanish Merchant Shipping: The Compañia Maritima Del Nervion as a Case Study, 1899-1986[1]

Jesús M. Valdaliso

Introduction

In the last decade, the Spanish shipping industry has been severely depressed. According to Lloyd's Register of Shipping, the merchant fleet, which peaked in 1979 at 8,313,658 gross registered tons (grt), declined in the next decade to 3,961,941 grt, a drop of fifty-two percent. A feature of this decline, in the case of Bilbao, has been the dissolution of a number of shipping firms, many of them in business for about a century. The Naviera Aznar (founded in the 1890s) failed in 1982; the Marítima del Nervión (founded in 1907) collapsed in 1986, and the group Naviera Vascongada-Naviera Bilbaína (founded in 1900) came to an end in 1993. Hence, writing about the contemporary Spanish shipping industry is to write of decline and decay. This paper deals precisely with that, for its subject is a shipping firm that has only recently ceased operation, the Compañía Marítima del Nervión (CMN), which had occupied a remarkable position in the Spanish merchant fleet since its foundation at the beginning of the twentieth century.

[1]This paper is part of a larger project on the history of the CMN, supported by the Programa de Historia Económica of the Fundación Empresa Pública (Madrid), which also has published my working paper, *Desarrollo y declive de la flota mercante española en el siglo XX: la Compañía Marítima del Nervión, 1907-1986* (Madrid, 1993), on which much of this paper is based. I would like to thank R. Garamendi and E. Solano, the chairman and manager of the CMN, respectively, and other past employees, especially A. Aizpuru, for generous assistance. A preliminary version of this paper was presented at a pre-conference in Glasgow. I acknowledge the comments of Frank Broeze and other scholars on that occasion and thank Lewis Fischer for his help in editing this paper.

Research in Maritime History, No. 6 (June 1994), 67-90.

In business history, above all in Britain, maritime topics have occupied positions of considerable significance. Although there were valuable studies of shipping firms before the 1950s, the end of that decade represents something of a watershed in maritime business history. In 1957, a year before the British journal *Business History* first appeared, Francis Hyde published his study of the Blue Funnel Line, which pioneered new approaches and set new standards in the field.[2] Under Hyde's influence in the 1960s and 1970s a group of scholars at the University of Liverpool produced a series of major studies of British shipping firms.[3] Doubtless influenced by the "entrepreneurial history" that A.H. Cole and others had undertaken at Harvard since the late 1940s, the Liverpool school was concerned with analysing business strategy. Its focus was on the entrepreneurial capacity of managers to cope with continuous change in markets, technology and other factors, and its effect on the performance and profitability of the firm.[4]

In the 1980s, maritime business history experienced a remarkable growth, not only in Britain but also in other countries.[5] Yet in Spain, literature about shipping companies is far from abundant and the majority of the studies that have appeared, while valuable, can be characterised as descriptive rather than analytic. As in other countries, attention has tended to concentrate on liner companies and many books have been published celebrating firm centenary or other anniversaries. In such vein are volumes on the Compañía Transatlántica, Compañía Transmediterránea, Naviera Ybarra and Naviera Pinillos.[6] In a somewhat broader

---

[2]F. Hyde, *Blue Funnel. A History of Alfred Holt and Company of Liverpool from 1865 to 1914* (Liverpool, 1957).

[3]Ralph Davis, "Maritime History: Progress and Problems," in S. Marriner (ed.), *Business and Businessmen. Studies in Business, Economic and Accounting History* (Liverpool, 1978), 169-197.

[4]See F. Hyde, *Shipping Enterprise and Management 1830-1939. Harrisons of Liverpool* (Liverpool, 1967), vii-x and xviii-xix.

[5]See P.N. Davies and S. Marriner, "Recent Publications and Developments in the Study of Maritime Economic History," *Journal of Transport History*, IX (1988), 93-108.

[6]F. Cossío, *Cien años de vida sobre el mar* (Madrid, 1950); C. Llorca Baus, *La Compañía Transatlántica en las campañas de ultramar* (Madrid, 1990); M. Gómez Santos, *Todo avante. Transmediterránea 1917-1992* (Madrid, 1992); F. Goseascoechea,

vein are two studies of the fleets of Santander and the Balearic islands and González Echegaray's examination of the Spanish merchant fleet during the Civil War.[7] Recent studies utilising an economic history approach include E. Torres on the shipowner Ramón de la Sota and the Compañía Naviera Sota y Aznar and the present author on Basque shipowners.[8]

The origins of the Compañía Marítima del Nervión date from 1899 when Francisco Aldecoa, master mariner, and Tomás Urquijo, merchant, founded the Compañía Anónima de Navegación (CAN). In so doing, they followed a common pattern of finance in the tramp fleet of Bilbao and elsewhere.[9] Aldecoa and Urquijo had gained experience in shipping during the propserity of the late 1890s. Lacking sufficient capital to set up on their own, they appealed to local contacts to finance the company's initial venture, a second-hand steamer to be managed by Aldecoa. Eight years later CAN, with the financial support of shareholders of the Banco de Vizcaya, absorbed part of the fleet of the Compañía Bilbaína de Navegación. The outcome was the creation of the CMN, which continued to operate ships until 1986. For almost a century, the merged CAN-CMN operated largely in the same field despite changes in markets and technology. The firm entered the tramp market with second-hand steamers and in 1919 moved into liners. Later

---

"Historia de la Naviera 'Ybarra' de Sevilla. Años 1846-1957" (unpublished mss., c. 1960); J.C. Díaz Lorenzo, *Naviera Pinillos 1840-1990. 150 años de historia marinera* (Santa Cruz de Tenerife, 1991).

[7]J. Pou Montaner, *La marina en las Baleares. Síntesis histórica* (Palma de Mallorca, 1977); R. González Echegaray, *La marina cántabra. Vol. III: Desde el vapor* (Santander, 1967); and González Echegaray, *La marina mercante y el tráfico marítimo en la Guerra Civil* (Madrid, 1977).

[8]E. Torres, *Ramón de la Sota. Historia económica de un empresario 1857-1936* (Madrid, 1989); Torres, "Barcos, carbón y mineral de hierro. Los vapores de Sota y Aznar y los orígenes de la moderna flota mercante de Bilbao, 1889-1900," *Revista de Historia Económica*, IX (1991), 11-32; J.M. Valdaliso, *Los navieros vascos y la marina mercante en España. Una historia económica* (Bilbao, 1991).

[9]See J.M. Valdaliso, "Spanish Shipowners in the British Mirror: Patterns of Investment, Ownership and Finance in the Bilbao Shipping Industry, 1879-1913," *International Journal of Maritime History*, V, No. 2 (1993), 1-30, esp. 19 ff.

it operated new break-bulk carriers and finally, in 1976, placed multi-purpose ships on time-charters for general and bulk cargo and containers.

If tonnage is taken as an indicator, CMN maintained a remarkable position. From its foundation until the early 1960s, it was always among the top ten Spanish shipping firms. However, from 1960 the rapid growth of the Spanish-flag tanker and bulk cargo fleet relegated liners to a secondary position. CMN thus declined relatively: in 1970 ranking twenty-third and ten years later thirty-third among Spanish shipping firms. But in the Spanish liner sector, CMN was still of significance, particularly on the Atlantic, where there was limited Spanish participation. Until the late 1970s, there were four transatlantic liner services: three mixed cargo and passenger lines between America and Spain (Naviera Aznar, Transatlántica and Ybarra) and one cargo line between US ports in the Gulf of Mexico and Spain, worked by the CMN. Other Spanish lines were deployed until the late 1970s in Spanish coastal traffic or in the carriage of European fresh fruit and general cargo (see table 1).

Table 1
Main Spanish Liner Shipping Companies, 1930-1980
(selected years)

Company	Line	Ships	GRT*	Rank#
1930				
Naviera Sota & Aznar	T-E-C	47	178,129	1
Cía. Transatlántica	T	19	120,583	2
Ybarra & Cía.	T-C	36	107,876	4
Cía. Marítima del Nervión	T	7	33,375	5
Líneas Pinillos	E	8	8,113	>25
Cía. Transmediterránea	C	55	115,079	3
1950				
Naviera Aznar	T	41	168,442	1
Cía. Transatlática	T	5	33,379	6
Ybarra & Cía	T	21	73,927	4
Cía. Marítima del Nervión	T	5	24,607	8
Cía. Marítimo Frutera	E	10	21,048	10
Frutero Valenciana de Navegación	E	6	14,256	15
Naviera de Exportación Agrícola	E	3	8,109	>25
Cía. Transmediterránea	E-C	39	93,078	5
1960				
Naviera Aznar	T-E	34	155,602	3
Cía. Transatlántica	T	8	72,619	5
Ybarra & Cía.	T	16	50,886	7

Cía. Marítima del Nervión	T	7	36,518	9
Naviera Pinillos	E-C	11	23,228	16
Frutero Valenciana de Navegación	E	10	24,226	14
Naviera de Exportación Agrícola	E	6	17,415	18
Cía. Transmediterránea	C-G	42	125,169	4
1970				
Naviera Aznar	E	14	137,287	8
Cía. Transatlántica	T	12	76,109	16
Ybarra & Cía.	T	5	43,290	15
Cía. Marítima del Nervión	T	4	23,140	23
Naviera Marasia	T	2	6,017	>25
Marítima del Norte	E	13	15,017	>25
Naviera Asón	E	7	14,341	>25
Naviera de Canarias	E	9	16,089	>25
Naviera Pinillos	C	7	19,340	25
Naviera de Exportación Agrícola	E	6	11,493	>25
Transportes Fruteros del Mediterráneo	E	9	11,612	>25
Transmediterránea	C	41	172,313	5
1980				
Cía. Transatlántica	T	9	53,689	23
Ybarra & Cía	T-E	3	21,302	38
Naviera Marasia	T	5	34,875	31
Esquimar Marítima	T	4	21,265	39
Naviera García Miñaur	T-E	12	28,025	34
Vasco-Madrileña de Navegación	T	6	39,046	30
Naviera Pinillos	C	4	8,441	>40
Naviera de Exportación Agrícola	E	7	11,691	>40
Naviera de Canarias	E	6	14,539	>40
Transportes Fruteros del Mediterráneo	E	8	11,425	>40
Vapores Suardiaz	E-C	10	20,196	40
Naviera del Atlántico	C	7	15,884	>40
Contenemar	C	19	26,104	36
Cía. Transmediterránea	C	29	131,371	13

Note: T = transatlantic; E = Europe; C = Coastal; G = Spanish line with Guinea. Under GRT each firm's total tonnage is recorded notwithstanding the fact that some companies (for example, Naviera Sota and Aznar, later Naviera Aznar) deployed part of its fleet in other traffic. The Rank for each firm is based on its tonnage registered under the Spanish flag.

Source: *Lista Oficial de Buques* (Madrid, 1931, 1951, 1961 and 1971); Associación de Navieros Españoles (ANAVE), *Empresas navieras asociadas*, 1970 and 1980.

Objectives, Sources and Methodology

The central aim of this paper is to examine over almost a century the
performance of a shipping firm and its managers in a changing technological, institutional and market environment and to explain the factors
that shaped its evolution – not only those linked to business strategies but
also those related to the industry as a whole. According to Barry Supple,
the shape of any business history is determined "not only by its author's
intents but by the amount and quality of surviving business records."[10]
In this instance, the CAN-CMN archive contains the key documents
(Articles of Association, Board minute books, balance sheets, and profit
and loss accounts); other important sources, such as annual reports, are
accessible elsewhere. From this material I have constructed time series
of the main indicators of the firm's shape and performance: its fleet,
balance sheet, profit and loss accounts and financial and profitability
indicators. Unfortunately, documents related to traffic and fleet deployment have not survived and, except for specific years since the 1960s,
it has been impossible to create series on voyages or tons of cargo
carried. Nor can gross earnings be calculated because the extant sources
merely provide data on the net earnings of the voyages – once running
costs had been discounted. Finally, the company's records lack sources
like letterbooks and diaries that would have permitted a deeper insight
into aspects of the firm's life and the character of its managers. Although
some material does exist for the period after 1972, this represents only
a short period and hence its use is problematic.

Nevertheless, the business records available have allowed me to
sketch the broad outlines of the firm's evolution and to analyze the
managers' business strategies, evaluated chiefly by three key variables:
investments, profitability, and financial situation. In this sense, I have
employed the indicators commonly used by modern accountants. But
problems arise from the fact that almost until the last accounts in the
1980s there was no prescribed common format in Spain for balance
sheets or profit and loss accounts. Hence, each firm had considerable
latitude in presenting accounts and sometimes, whether by accident or
design, they appeared in such an obscure manner as to make it very
difficult to assess the exact financial position. The same might also be

---

[10]B. Supple, "The Uses of Business History," *Business History*, IV (1961), 81-90.

said of other countries, including Britain.[11] While it is true that the problem of how to measure entrepreneurial performance has never been successfully resolved, the variables chosen in this study at least permit comparisons with other Spanish and foreign shipping firms.[12] Even so, the limitations of the analysis needs always to be borne in mind.

The analytical framework is thus a specific shipping firm, but the approach endeavours to frame its experience within a global explanation of the development and decline of the Spanish merchant marine during this century. This analysis has been influenced by Nelson and Winter's evolutionary theory of the firm. Their theory views a firm's evolution as a function of six factors.[13] The first is learning, which is conceptualized as a cumulative process undertaken collectively within the firm to produce several kinds of routines, including patterned behaviours and strategies. The second is the firm's previous developmental pattern. This factor subsumes several assumptions: that acquired routines to a great degree determine the future evolution and the possibilities for change; that there are sunk costs that grow from specialisation in a specific technology or service; and that profitability also shapes future behaviour, since if profits satisfy expectations it will strengthen existing routines and *vice versa*. In other words, this approach recognizes that "history matters" in explaining a firm's behavior.[14] The third factor concerns the existing technological in a given period. The fourth is the environment, in which the most efficient firms tend to eliminate the least efficient.[15]

---

[11]See S. Marriner, "Company Financial Statements as Source Material for Business Historians," *Business History*, XXII (1980); and J. Armstrong and S. Jones, *Business Documents. Their Origins, Sources and Uses in Historical Research* (London, 1987), 142-148.

[12]See C.H. Lee, "Corporate Behaviour in Theory and History: II. The Historian's Perspective," *Business History*, XXXII (1990), 168-169.

[13]R. Nelson and S. Winter, *An Evolutionary Theory of Economic Change* (Cambridge, MA, 1982).

[14]See G. Dosi, D. Teece, and S. Winter, "Toward a Theory of Corporate Coherence: Preliminary Remarks," in G. Dosi, R. Gianetti and P.A. Toninelly (eds.), *Technology and Enterprise in Historical Perspective* (Oxford, 1992), 185-211, especially 194.

[15]Many variables, like supply and demand conditions, are exogenous, but others, like the institutional framework, can be influenced by the behaviour of the firm.

The fifth variable is the bounded rationality of businessmen's behaviour. This reminds us that often a firm's behaviour cannot be conceived in terms of deliberate (or maximizing choices) because many decisions are taken mechanically, shaped by previous experience. Finally, there are stochastic elements which are present as much in the decision-making process as its outcome. This last explanatory variable arises specifically from the characteristics of the industry in which the firm operates. In a highly capital-intensive enterprise like shipping, where demand is volatile and slumps are more common than peaks, financial strength (measured most simply by the volume of cash flow) is what matters. This in turn will be shaped by revenues from chartering and operating vessels, the cash cost of operations, and finance charges. These three variables can be combined in several ways – new or second-hand tonnage; tramp, liner or charter markets; or debt or equity financing – to produce a positive outcome. In this sense, financial constraints are some of the clearest determinants of a firm's investment strategy.[16]

The History of CAN-CMN

The long-term evolution of the CAN-CMN fleet shows a moderate growth in total tonnage, a fall in number of ships, and a rise in average ship size (see figure 1). There were two distinct phases of technological change. Between 1900 and 1931 there was a transition from small second-hand steamers (a fleet which reached its peak after World War I) to a mixed fleet of bigger and faster steamers and diesel-propelled vessels which were adapted to the requirements of a liner service. The second transition occurred in the late 1970s when the managers decided to shift to a fleet of multi-purpose ships to operate in the general and bulk cargo (and container) charter market. Between the two phases, there was a period of relative stability based on break-bulk cargo vessels.

Like other Spanish shipping firms, CMN moved from tramp to liners after the First World War.[17] From 1919 to 1976 it ran a line between USA ports on the Gulf of Mexico (New Orleans, Galveston,

---

[16]See M. Stopford, *Maritime Economics* (London, 1988), 93-98. Dosi, Teece and Winter, "Toward a Theory," 200, also argue that "the availability of free cash flow is perhaps the key regulator of selection."

[17]In 1919, Ybarra started its line between New York and Spanish ports; see Goseascoechea, "Historia," 63-64.

Houston, Mobile and Brownsville) and Barcelona, carrying cotton for Catalan textile factories and general cargo. Nonetheless, part of its fleet remained in the tramp trades until the late 1950s.[18] The establishment of liner operations stemmed from three main factors: the United States Shipping Act of 1916, which forbade closed conferences in USA ports; the enormous profits made during the First World War which permitted investment in new ships; and the relationship, which probably commenced during the war years, with Henry Kerr, an American shipowner and shipping agent. The main characteristics of the line did not change until the 1960s when general cargo increasingly displaced cotton, a shift which increased shipping costs. In order to raise revenues CMN endeavoured to find cargoes for the westbound leg, albeit with only moderate results. The near-monopoly it enjoyed over American imports carried by Spanish-flag tonnage from the Gulf of Mexico began to be eroded in the late 1960s when other companies, especially Compañía Transatlántica, tried to enter this trade, an action encouraged by the Spain's partial liberalisation of the rules governing some US imports.[19] Finally, in 1976 Transatlántica displaced CMN in the Gulf trade.

The specialised operations in which the firm engaged for most of its life and the crucial role of the manager, in whose hands information and decision-making was concentrated until 1972, explain the relative

---

[18]The firm's tramp tonnage also met occasional increases in the demand for liner cargo space. There was an element of conscious strategy here – to avoid excess capacity in the liner service, a frequent problem of shipping firms. See J.A. Zerby and R.M. Conlon, "An Analysis of Capacity Utilisation in Liner Shipping," *Journal of Transport Economics and Policy*, XII (1978), 27-46; and J.O. Jansson and D. Shneerson, *Liner Shipping Economics* (London, 1987), particularly 264 ff.

[19]From 1952 the state reserved fifty percent of the imports financed by American loans and half of the commerce between the US and Spain (cotton included) for the Spanish flag (the remainder was carried by American vessels). But from 1963 the government began to liberalise the import of various commodities included under general cargo (but not cotton); see S. Pastor Prieto, *El transporte marítimo en España* (Madrid, 1982), 1014-1020. In practice the CMN which, until the late 1960s, carried all the shipments loaded in Gulf ports under the Spanish flag, saw how the substitution of cotton not only increased its shipping costs but also opened a new era of competition; see Valdaliso, *Desarrollo y declive*.

simplicity of CMN's organization.[20] During the first generation (1900-1937), administrative costs and management charges were based upon net returns plus a fixed sum per ship. Until 1972, the firm was managed by a small administrative staff whose main members comprised the manager, bookkeeper (and an assistant), cashier, ship's inspector and office boy (the traditional criteria of having a man ashore for each ship was followed to the letter!). A similar observation can also be made about its accounting techniques, which did not change noticeably until 1972. There were many opportunities to broaden the company's activities in the 1950s and 1960s, above all by internalizing the agency and ship chandlery functions provided by outside firms. But traditional organizational routines, strengthened during the tenure of F. Aldecoa, Jr., and the appointment to the Board of members with strong interests in these businesses, precluded savings on these transaction costs.[21]

From the beginning, CAN-CMN was a joint-stock, limited-liability company. But its share capital was highly concentrated in the hands of two groups headed by the founders, F. Aldecoa and T. Urquijo. Since the continuity of both groups in the shareholding structure, the Board of Directors and management and chairmanship positions was a constant feature, it is appropiate to regard it as a family firm in which seats on the Board, for example, were passed from fathers to sons or from uncles to nephews. Another clear indication of its family character was the fact that management and ownership went hand in hand; indeed, until 1973 the positions of manager and chairman traditionally were occupied by the same person. From its foundation in 1907 until 1971, CMN developed strong links with the Banco de Vizcaya. Moreover, about half of CMN's directors were also directors of the Bank, which monopolised all the firm's financial operations (issues of shares, payment of dividends, provision of bank drafts, etc.) and provided short-term

---

[20]Fischer and Nordvik, who study the problem of information and management elsewhere in this volume, provide a similar picture of the Norwegian shipbroking firm Fearnley and Eager until 1945.

[21]According to P. Sancho Llerandi, *Transporte marítimo y construcción naval en España* (Madrid, 1979), 22-25, the chief interest of the majority of Spanish owners was not shipping but other activities like consignments or brokerage. For a theoretical approach to vertical integration in shipping based on transaction cost theory, see M. Casson, "The Role of Vertical Integration in the Shipping Industry," *Journal of Transport Economics and Policy*, XX (1986), 7-29.

credits to meet the need for working capital. Sometimes it also provided funds for long-term investments, especially in the early 1910s and the late 1960s, but fixed capital usually was raised by other means. This close relationship ceased in 1972 following a bitter argument between CMN's chairman and the Bank.

Figure 1
The CAN-CMN Fleet, 1900-1986

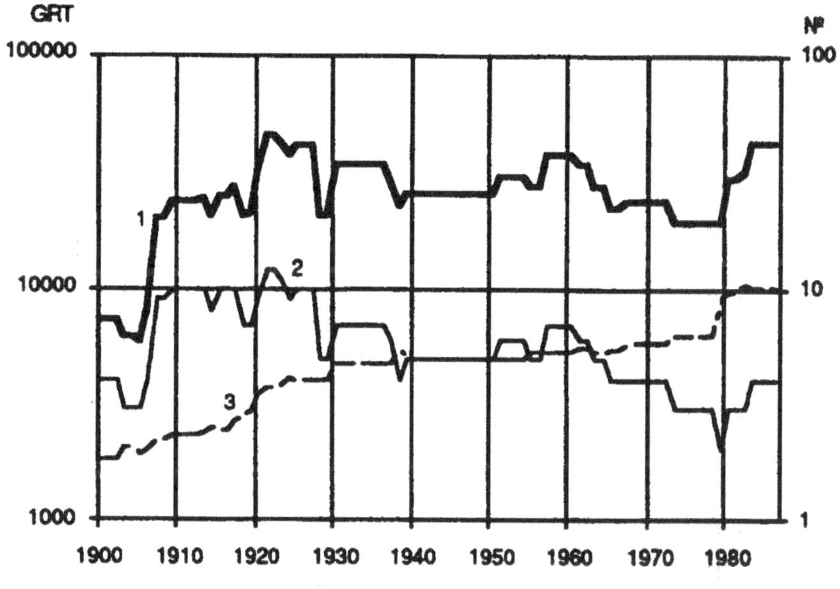

Notes: 1 = GRT; 2 = Number of Ships; 3 = Average Tonnage per Vessel.

Source: CMN Archive, Annual Reports and Board Minute Books for both companies.

The pattern of finance altered as shipping became increasingly capital intensive and other factors, such as technology and institutional arrangements, became more expensive. The chronology of this change is representative of the entire Spanish shipping industry. Until the mid-1950s, CAN-CMN was financed by equity because second-hand tonnage was inexpensive and reserve funds were sufficient for the purchase of more modern vessels (see figure 2). From the mid-1950s, external capital became indispensable. While there were various causes for this shift, all were linked to institutional changes that followed the Spanish Civil War. In the new environment, shipowners were forced to acquire all their tonnage in the Spanish market, a limitation that not only narrowed technological opportunities (and, given the shortages until the end of the 1950s, restricted investment in new tonnage) but also increased costs significantly. To compensate, the state reserved domestic markets for Spanish shipowners and encouraged the shift to external funding. This pattern was strengthened from the 1970s due to a sharp increase in the price of tonnage and widespread under-capitalization in Spanish shipping, including CMN. Finally, in 1986 the state, which was CMN's main creditor, seized its fleet in order to meet the accumulated debts.

Figure 2
Financial Ratios of CAN-CMN, 1900-1986

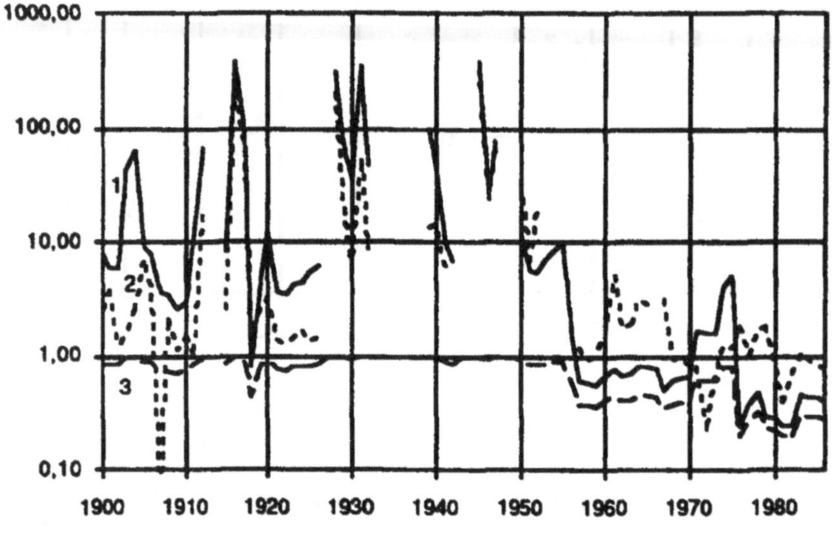

Notes: 1 = Equity/Debt Ratio; 2 = Solvency; 3 = Equity/Assets Ratio. Solvency measures the firm's capacity to cope with its short-term debt by means of its current assets; it is the ratio between current assets and short-term debts (i.e., current liabilities).

Source: CMN Archive, Balance Sheets of CAN-CMN, various years.

The main profitability indicators clearly show three periods of high returns broadly related to peaks in international shipping. These eras coincided with the First and Second World Wars and the Korean War. Although profits decreased thereafter, returns until the early 1970s were still higher than in the interwar period. From 1971 all indicators show negative trends, except in 1974-1975 and 1980-1981 (see figure 3). In constant *pesetas*, returns during World War I were highest: total earnings between 1915 and 1920 were higher than the total earned in either 1907-1914 or 1921-1970. In the highly profitable years 1915-1920, shareholders enjoyed a thirteen-fold return on each *peseta* invested. During both World Wars, CMN plowed a significant portion of its profits into portfolio investments, such as bank deposits, industry and property.[22]

Figure 3
Profitability Ratios of CAN-CNM, 1900-1986

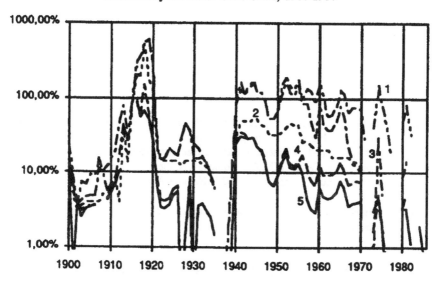

Notes: 1 = Cash Flow/Paid-up Capital; 2 = Dividends; 3 = Net Benefits (Operating Income/Assets)/Paid-up Capital; 4 = Net Benefits (Pre-Tax Profits)/Equity; 5 = Net Benefits (Gross Income/Expenses)/Assets.

Souce: CMN Archive, Balance Sheets and Profit and Loss Accounts of CAN-CMN, various years.

---

[22]The firm's portfolio accounted for more than forty percent of total assets between 1916-1918, and more than seventy percent between 1942-1945; see Valdaliso, *Desarrollo y declive*.

Table 2
Dividends (as Percentages of Paid-up Capital)
Paid by CAN-CMN and Other Spanish and
British Shipping Firms, 1904-1951
(five-year averages)

Years	British			Spanish	
	(1)	(2)	(3)	(4)	(5)
1904-1908	n/a	3.7	4.2	2.6	5.7
1909-1913	6.8	5.7	12.8	8.2	10.1
1914-1918	11.3	14.6	198.6	87.0	58.4
1919-1923	9.4	7.9	69.6	39.6	37.2
1924-1928	5.7	4.8	13.6	9.0	12.6
1929-1933	3.5	2.6	13.2	7.2	9.1
1934-1938	3.0	3.7	2.8	1.4	6.4
1939-1943	5.7	6.6	37.0	n/a	33.4
1944-1948	7.3	10.2	44.2	n/a	67.1
1949-1951	5.4	7.7	20.0	16.7	46.7

Notes: 1949-1951 period comprises only three years because of lack of data thereafter. Figures for Compañía Naviera Sota y Aznar exclude 1936. n/a = not available. 1 = Liner and Cargo Liner Companies; 2 = Cargo Boat Companies; 3 = CAN-CMN; 4 = Compañía Naviera Vascongada; 5 = Compañía Naviera Sota y Aznar (from 1937, Naviera Aznar).

Source: British Firms: *Fair Play*, various years; Spanish Firms: Annual Reports, various years.

In terms of dividends paid to shareholders, CAN-CMN's profitability, except for Naviera Aznar from the mid-1930s, was higher than other Spanish or British shipping companies. From 1909 to 1934, and again from 1939 to 1951, dividends paid by Spanish firms were larger than the premiums paid by their British counterparts (see table 2). Whether this was due to superior Spanish management is difficult to ascertain since other factors must be considered. For example, Spain granted navigation subsidies to shipping companies from 1909 to 1915 and from 1925 to 1936; in CMN's case, these accounted for between twenty-one and thirty-two percent of gross profits. Spanish shipowners gained from the nation's neutrality during both World Wars, and unlike their competitors in Britain and elsewhere experienced no excess profits tax during World War I.[23] Finally, when comparing profits attention must be paid to the institutional framework of Spanish shipping built by the new regime after 1939.

In the course of its life, CAN-CMN operated within two distinct institutional frameworks. Until 1936 a relatively liberal environment permitted unfettered access to international markets for ships, repairs, maintenance, insurance and fuel. Other than granting navigation subsidies, the state interfered little. After the Civil War a protectionist policy with a good deal of intervention ensued.[24] The government confined shipowners to the domestic market and supported a non-competitive, technologically-backward sector with generous subsidies and artifically inflated freight rates. From the mid-1970s, as international shipping sunk into depression, a process of liberalisation began. Unfortunately, this did not lead to increased opportunities. Indeed, in a depressed market with a serious tonnage glut, high-cost Spanish firms suffered from steep drops in income. Together with heavy financial commitments worsened by the slump, this ruined many companies.

An Evolutionary Explanation of the Rise and Decline of CAN-CMN

Utilising Nelson and Winter's evolutionary theory of the firm, a preliminary explanation of the historical pattern experienced by CAN-CMN can be advanced. Such an exercise, using analytical tools drawn from evolutionary and maritime economics, is valuable as a case study. But it also has wider relevance, for CMN's experience was not unique and an understanding of it can contribute to a fuller appreciation of Spanish merchant shipping in the twentieth century.

Phase I: Birth and Expansion, 1899-1945

Company Origins: Learning and Specialisation, 1899-1918

There are two basic processes in the creation of any firm: investment in specialized assets (in this case ships) and mastery of sufficient skills and knowledge to operate in a given environment. For CAN-CMN, the

---

[23]See S.G. Sturmey, *British Shipping and World Competition* (London, 1962), 42-52.

[24]See Pastor Prieto, *El transporte marítimo*, especially 709-711 and 1014-1040.

learning curve was relatively steep because the managers already possessed skills. Through repetition, these became routines which shaped the future course of the firm. The main aim of a company is to generate a positive cash, to achieve financial autonomy and to make profits. In CAN-CMN's case this learning occurred within a favourable institutional framework in a period of technological continuity, albeit with the handicap of changing markets (boom in 1899-1901 and 1915-1918, and crisis and recovery between 1902 and 1914).

The Learning of New Routines, 1919-1945

During this stage CMN partially changed its focus, a process character-ized by the establishment of liner services between the US Gulf and Spain based largely on the carriage of American cotton. Although the firm's basic structure remained the same, as new skills were learned to control liner costs and traffic organization, these became routines. Learning was rapid because the company essentially operated in just one direction (eastbound, carrying an easily stowed bulk commodity); moreover, much of the organisation was the responsibility of CMN's agents in New Orleans and Barcelona. The partial shift in activity entailed investment in specialised ships that were hard to deploy in other trades and hence fixed the choice of technology in a era of obvious discontinuities (diesel and oil vs. steam and coal). Operations were affected by several factors, including the policy of the US Shipping Board in the mid-1920s, the Spanish Civil War and World War II.

Phase II: Consolidation, Decline and Extinction, 1946-1986

"Routine as a Target," 1946-1970

In the quarter-century after 1945 the firm's dynamics and organizational routines did not change since the manager, F. Aldecoa, Jr., had been trained within the company. There was also continuity in administrative staff. The objectives of the enterprise remained unaltered and, because returns met expectations, immutable routines became normal. This created considerable inertia and made it more difficult to adapt in the 1960s when cotton was replaced by general cargo, which involved completely different cost structures and traffic management techniques.

The institutional framework reinforced a strategy based upon continuity because it weakened the selection process (CMN worked in a market protected not only by conferences but also until the late 1960s by the cargo reserve policy), provided high returns, and imposed rigidities on the supply of tonnage by prohibiting access to foreign markets. The growing dependence on externally-generated debt financing and the increasingly capital-intensive nature of the industry heightened the impact of capital costs, notwithstanding generally positive cash-flow figures.

The Years of Crisis, 1971-1973

Decline, which had taken root in the previous period and was exacerbated by a strong inertia, became endemic in the early 1970s. Difficulties mounted as liner income dropped, the transition from cotton to general cargo became painful, capital costs increased, and the selection process in the market was aggravated by falling traffic, intensified competition, and unfavourable exchange movements. The falling returns endangered financial autonomy and, in the last resort, the firm's survival. Some members of the Board of Directors tried to initiate a series of changes, but only to finance existing routines. Troubles inside the firm and within the Board increased, especially during 1972, thereby retarding the implementation of new strategies.[25]

The Search for a New Approach and the Final Collapse, 1973-1986

After changes in management, shareholders and the Board of Directors, attempts were made to change routines. This involved both its dynamic and organization, but the process was nonetheless shaped by previous experience.[26] The new team, with no background in shipping, attempted to remain in the same market but to change existing routines. Optimistically, CMN in the late 1970s invested heavily to update its fleet in an era of technological discontinuity and uncertainty over both the market

---

[25]Faced with the strong opposition of the Banco de Vizcaya and the majority of the Board of Directors, F. Aldecoa, Jr., resigned as CMN's chairman in February 1973.

[26]After his resignation, Aldecoa sold his shares to his nephews (who opposed him in 1972 and from 1973 began to manage the firm). Change took place, but only within the Aldecoa family.

and institutional frameworks.[27] The choice of a new technique (the multi-purpose ship) was the outcome of a number of factors, including doubts over the diffusion of container technology, the likely pattern of market behaviour, and above all constraints imposed by finance. In the latter case, it was almost impossible to obtain sufficient external funds to buy a container fleet, while recourse to a state loan required that the vessels be built in Spain, where yards lacked the necessary technology.

Unfortunately, at the very time such vital decisions had to be made, pressures within the market were very strong. The severe shipping depression since the mid-1970s intensified competition, particularly in Spanish liner traffic. Technological change in liner shipping and its organizational consequences increased concentration through mergers or pools (sometimes with state encouragement) and diminished the power of conferences.[28] The crisis in Spanish liner shipping was acute due to its backwardness in container technology, competition from foreign shipping lines, the small volume of general cargo, the institutional framework, and the absence of a policy that encouraged maritime concentration or cooperation. A final significant factor was the small size and limited business capability of most Spanish liner firms during Franco's regime.[29] The outcome was that many liner companies disappeared and others were sold to the state (like Transatlántica and Transmediterránea). In 1986, the Spanish liner fleet accounted for twelve percent of total tonnage (six points less than the global figure) and its market share in liner trades to Spain was around ten percent.[30]

---

[27]The same strategy was followed by the Swedish Broström firm during the late 1970s and early 1980s; this is examined elsewhere in this volume by Fritz and Olsson.

[28]See J.C. Pujana Madariaga, *Structural Change in the Liner Shipping Industry. The Spanish Liner Trades and Liner Shipping Industry* (Plymouth, 1987).

[29]See Pastor Prieto, *El transporte marítimo*, 1290 ff; J. Membrado Martínez, *Las líneas regulares de navegación y su influencia en la balanza de fletes de España* (Madrid, 1984), 164-170; and Pujana, *Structural Change*, 88-89. The last attribute also applies to the entire Spanish fleet during the Franco period. In a situation of scant competition with markets reserved by the state and controlled by Spanish shipowners through the Oficina Central Marítima, and no risk (the money to invest came almost entirely from the state), it is difficult to talk of either entrpreneurs or entrepreneurship!

[30]Pujana, *Structural Change*, 83-87.

Technical change, increasing competition, shrinking traffic, and financial constraints forced CMN from the Gulf of Mexico in 1976. These factors also led to an organizational shift: CMN became a charter firm, like Naviera Aznar or Naviera Vascongada.[31] This was feasible because the firm had a relatively modern fleet much in demand in the charter market. The strategy to survive the slump was no longer to manage its ships but rather to obtain good charters and assure a positive cash flow. The directors hoped that given the high rate of inflation, a future appreciation in ship prices would enable the sale of the fleet at a profit. But when a series of problems with charterers reduced income and made it impossible to pay capital costs the state, through the Sociedad de Gestión de Buques (which became the main Spanish shipowner in the mid-1980s), seized the fleet and the company ceased operations.[32]

---

[31]See Sancho Llerandi, *Transporte marítimo*, 31.

[32]J.R. Fernández Antonio, *Planes de Viabilidad de la Marina Mercante: La reordenación del sector ante el mercado único* (Madrid, 1991).

Appendices

Table 1
Financial Ratios of the CAN-CMN, 1900-1986

	Equity/Debt Ratio	Solvency	Equity/Assets Ratio
1900	8.12	2.65	0.88
1901	5.84	3.77	0.85
1902	5.98	1.28	0.86
1903	42.75	1.59	0.98
1904	63.52	2.64	0.98
1905	9.14	7.13	0.90
1906	8.16	3.99	0.89
1907	3.68	0.06	0.76
1908	3.51	2.30	0.75
1909	2.64	1.18	0.70
1910	3.10	1.54	0.73
1911	10.59	0.98	0.88
1912	68.13	17.49	0.95
1913	n/a	n/a	n/a
1914	n/a	n/a	n/a
1915	8.57	2.68	0.88
1916	379.94	237.29	0.99
1917	105.68	68.17	0.99
1918	0.81	1.22	0.45
1919	4.71	2.79	0.82
1920	12.33	3.39	0.92
1921	3.67	1.39	0.78
1922	3.53	1.32	0.76
1923	4.18	1.44	0.80
1924	4.55	1.72	0.81
1925	5.40	1.41	0.84
1926	6.12	1.49	0.85
1927	n/a	n/a	0.99
1928	323.19	203.70	0.99
1929	59.64	16.41	0.98
1930	35.17	5.96	0.96
1931	351.27	55.96	0.99
1932	47.28	8.81	0.97
1933	n/a	n/a	0.99

1934	n/a	n/a	0.99
1935	n/a	n/a	0.99
1936	n/a	n/a	0.99
1937	87.68	7.10	0.98
1938	n/a	n/a	0.99
1939	96.89	13.65	0.98
1940	41.13	14.21	0.97
1941	9.87	6.05	0.90
1942	7.06	5.46	0.87
1943	n/a	n/a	1.00
1944	n/a	n/a	1.00
1945	390.36	337.26	1.00
1946	27.05	24.59	0.96
1947	78.91	70.24	0.99
1948	n/a	n/a	1.00
1949	n/a	n/a	1.00
1950	11.63	32.08	0.92
1951	5.68	6.79	0.85
1952	5.41	21.66	0.84
1953	7.41	n/a	0.88
1954	8.52	n/a	0.89
1955	10.33	n/a	0.91
1956	1.44	n/a	0.59
1957	0.63	1.19	0.38
1958	0.58	0.93	0.37
1959	0.55	1.02	0.36
1960	0.69	1.65	0.41
1961	0.77	5.04	0.43
1962	0.68	1.75	0.41
1963	0.70	2.00	0.41
1964	0.81	3.18	0.45
1965	0.84	2.85	0.46
1966	0.80	n/a	0.44
1967	0.52	3.15	0.34
1968	0.60	0.93	0.38
1969	0.64	1.01	0.39
1970	0.67	0.82	0.40
1971	1.69	0.83	0.63
1972	1.61	0.22	0.62
1973	1.60	0.73	0.62
1974	4.04	1.27	0.80

1975	5.11	1.19	0.83
1976	0.25	1.98	0.20
1977	0.39	1.02	0.28
1978	0.47	1.76	0.32
1979	0.30	1.90	0.23
1980	0.28	0.82	0.22
1981	0.24	0.40	0.20
1982	0.24	0.72	0.20
1983	0.46	1.07	0.32
1984	0.43	0.96	0.30
1985	0.43	0.86	0.30
1986	0.40	0.80	0.29

Note: N/A = not available. See also the explanatory notes for figure 2.

Source: See figure 2.

Table 2
Ratios of Profitability of CAN-CMN,
1900-1986

Years	Net Profits/ Assets	Net Bene- fits/Equity	Dividends	Net Benefits/ Paid-up Capital	Cash-flow/ Paid-up Capital
1900	11.28%	12.84%	13.55%	14.92%	23.05%
1901	5.14	5.29	4.50	5.26	7.53
1902	4.09	4.01	3.00	3.67	3.67
1903	2.53	3.02	3.50	4.16	7.31
1904	3.34	3.48	4.00	4.65	6.92
1905	3.43	3.55	4.00	4.82	9.35
1906	3.76	3.55	4.00	4.85	8.95
1907	n/a	n/a	4.00	11.11	15.23
1908	n/a	n/a	5.00	9.97	20.78
1909	4.41	4.33	5.00	5.60	12.17
1910	5.31	5.21	6.00	6.76	15.42
1911	7.30	6.80	8.00	9.03	20.66
1912	10.40	10.28	4.00	18.45	49.08
1913	n/a	n/a	41.00	43.67	78.45
1914	n/a	n/a	13.00	26.66	26.66
1915	n/a	n/a	70.00	77.12	77.12
1916	99.73	88.93	210.00	301.73	302.93
1917	56.08	56.61	180.00	368.93	368.93

1918	65.93	147.53	520.00	541.91	542.92
1919	51.56	62.51	170.00	607.03	609.11
1920	27.78	30.03	130.00	270.52	270.52
1921	6.11	7.77	20.00	21.17	579.49
1922	3.35	4.38	14.00	14.75	14.95
1923	3.34	4.14	14.00	15.59	15.59
1924	3.67	4.47	14.00	21.29	21.29
1925	4.86	5.77	14.00	18.97	18.97
1926	5.56	6.47	· 14.00	16.53	16.53
1927	0.17	1.17	12.00	29.42	29.42
1928	1.20	1.21	14.00	45.80	45.80
1929	8.43	8.57	14.00	34.75	34.75
1930	0.19	0.20	14.00	15.68	24.66
1931	3.58	3.59	14.00	15.18	21.18
1932	3.82	3.90	12.00	15.72	15.72
1933	3.19	3.19	12.00	13.61	13.61
1934	2.53	2.53	8.00	9.02	9.02
1935	1.47	1.47	6.00	6.38	6.38
1936	-5.17	-5.17	0.00	-15.36	-15.36
1937	-1.88	-1.90	0.00	-6.75	-6.75
1938	0.32	0.32	0.00	0.78	0.78
1939	1.06	1.07	10.00	11.83	11.83
1940	24.22	24.81	30.00	84.84	92.09
1941	31.18	34.34	48.00	126.60	159.60
1942	30.10	33.65	49.33	114.26	114.26
1943	28.45	28.45	48.00	127.82	138.72
1944	29.58	29.58	52.00	167.04	177.95
1945	22.83	22.58	53.00	118.45	118.45
1946	19.55	20.27	44.00	117.84	117.84
1947	13.84	14.01	40.00	86.37	86.37
1948	7.76	7.76	32.00	53.97	53.97
1949	6.60	6.60	32.00	52.72	52.72
1950	8.57	9.30	32.00	64.79	64.79
1951	14.17	16.66	36.00	130.40	154.83
1952	17.66	20.93	40.00	164.92	189.36
1953	11.74	13.32	45.20	118.63	143.07
1954	11.13	12.44	44.00	108.58	133.01
1955	13.14	14.41	44.00	149.82	174.25
1956	10.19	17.28	25.00	83.27	95.49
1957	4.45	11.56	26.00	83.56	135.32
1958	3.28	7.95	24.00	50.36	122.24

1959	2.88	6.66	20.00	29.37	84.90
1960	6.45	14.14	20.00	81.00	161.52
1961	4.81	9.37	20.00	43.70	104.02
1962	4.41	9.24	20.00	37.74	57.81
1963	4.62	9.29	16.00	37.53	60.10
1964	5.50	10.35	16.00	49.38	79.44
1965	7.64	14.28	16.00	79.09	130.18
1966	6.27	11.01	16.00	57.67	112.84
1967	3.51	6.80	16.00	22.17	64.55
1968	3.79	7.15	13.33	14.65	75.30
1969	4.05	7.57	12.00	13.96	75.70
1970	4.09	7.39	10.00	11.33	68.14
1971	-0.45	-3.30	0.00	0.00	29.04
1972	-3.63	-7.46	0.00	-52.85	-12.81
1973	2.98	1.63	0.00	0.66	41.17
1974	4.62	4.26	5.00	30.06	147.98
1975	2.09	1.82	2.50	5.09	79.28
1976	0.40	0.88	0.00	-0.22	45.90
1977	0.32	0.24	0.00	-0.26	18.28
1978	-0.82	-3.80	0.00	-12.13	-2.65
1979	-0.70	-5.08	0.00	-10.25	-10.25
1980	3.28	3.36	0.00	8.59	49.36
1981	3.31	5.18	0.00	14.13	79.57
1982	1.10	-9.26	0.00	-15.68	32.22
1983	-1.75	-13.47	0.00	-83.34	-43.63
1984	1.89	-8.97	0.00	-60.95	-60.95
1985	0.87	-10.25	0.00	-71.45	-71.45
1986	-0.32	-18.17	0.00	-110.61	-110.56

Note: N/A = not available.

Source: See figure 3.

Twentieth-Century Shipping Strategies: Broström and Transatlantic, Gothenburg's Leading Shipping Companies

Martin Fritz and Kent Olsson

Introduction

The factors underlying Gothenburg's rise to become the leading Swedish shipping town are found in the increasing concentration of exports through the port in the late nineteenth century. Such growth not only assured national pre-eminence but also led to opportunities for international specialization which went far beyond the original connection to Swedish exports. The town's large, export-oriented shipyards provide one example, while another is found within shipping.

In twentieth-century Gothenburg shipping, three companies stand out: the two long-established firms, Broström and Transatlantic, and the more recent Stena Line, with its concentration on ferries, tramps and offshore activities. This study focuses on the two older firms and examines how they adapted to sudden exogenous changes associated with international economic developments and technological innovations. The essay looks at a variety of situations in which the two interpreted external signals (which could be viewed as threats or opportunities) differently. Because they drew different conclusions, each reacted uniquely, chose distinct solutions and achieved divergent results. Yet if this is primarily a case study of two firms, it also provides insights into the transformation of shipping during this century.

The business of a shipping company is a complex combination of two different activities: carrying freight and buying and selling capital assets. Vessels, unlike industrial fixed assets, are easily transferred within a world economy. Owners must thus constantly consider movements in two fundamentally different markets. The fortunes of firms are determined within these markets, which constantly impinge upon each other. Whether vessels are bought dearly in boom years or purchased cheaply during a recession has a significant influence on profits. The

Research in Maritime History, No. 6 (June 1994), 91-109.

normal pattern in shipping is long periods of low freights interrupted by short booms associated with seasonal fluctuations in primary product trades or political events which dramatically increase the demand for cargo and hence the price that can be charged. The ability to optimize the purchase of new or second-hand tonnage is an important factor in the survival of shipping firms. Moreover, this has become progressively more significant during the twentieth century as increased vessel size has led to fewer occasions on which orders are placed.[1]

In the twentieth century, two particular periods presented crucial tests: the early 1920s, when an era of growth gave way to stagnation, and a similar turning point in 1974. The importance of adjusting to new conditions has been noted in studies of shipping firms elsewhere. A good example is Royal Mail, the sad fate of which in the interwar years stemmed in part from orders for expensive ships during the postwar boom that were only delivered after the slump had set in.[2] The Norwegian shipowner Arthur H. Mathiesen had a similar experience. He recalled in 1939 that "just after the previous World War I ordered three vessels which, when they were ready to be delivered, were worth a maximum 25% of the amount in the contract. We may hope that developments this time will not go in the same direction, but who knows?"[3]

This paper explores the relationship within Broström and Transatlantic of capital management and production (carrying goods and earning freights). Evaluating management decisions is not easy and the temptation to engage in *post facto* criticism must be avoided. There are major difficulties in trying to intuit the realities of decision-making. Moreover, what seems in retrospect to have been competent management may well have been pure luck, particularly regarding timing.

Broström and Transatlantic

Broström and Transatlantic in this century have dominated not only Gothenburg but also Swedish shipping. Broström was the elder. In the

---

[1] Martin Stopford, *Maritime Economics* (London, 1988), 36, 175, 213.

[2] Edwin Green and Michael Moss, *A Business of National Importance: The Royal Mail Shipping Group 1902-1937* (London, 1982), 41.

[3] Göteborg Landsarkivet (GLA), Götaverkens Archives (GA), Arthur H. Mathiesen to Ernst A. Hedén, 27 December 1939.

1860s Axel Broström started a traditional shipping business to transport iron and forest products on Lake Vänern and the Göta Canal. Early in the 1880s he moved to Gothenburg, where the firm expanded. In the next decade Broström founded ÅngfartygsAB Tirfing to ship Russian corn and Swedish iron ore. Tirfing was the parent, owning its own vessels and shares in daughter companies. For the new iron ore trade from Oxelösund and Luleå to Britain and the continent, Tirfing acquired SS *Stanton* from the UK. As this trade, especially to supply industries in the Ruhr and Silesia, expanded, more second-hand ships were purchased. At the turn of the century Broström had become the largest shipping company in Sweden, owning twenty vessels of 28,000 tons – almost one-third of the steam tonnage in Gothenburg. Broström during the 1890s grew through purchases of second-hand vessels in Britain. Britain's earlier investment in steamers created a large market in older and cheaper vessels suitable for operations in the North Sea; Broström was very active in exploiting this opportunity. In the first decade of the twentieth century the firm purchased more newly-built British ships, this time bigger vessels of 5000-6000 tons, chiefly for shipping iron ore from the port of Narvik, which opened in 1903. In 1910 Broström owned thirty ships totalling 124,000 tons, which represented two-thirds of Gothenburg's steam tonnage. The tonnage figures for Broström also include the assets of a new daughter company, Svenska Ostasiatiska Kompaniet, which operated deep-sea liners, a sector Gothenburg first entered around 1900.

During the late nineteenth century, Swedish trans-oceanic exports went through merchant houses in London, Hamburg and Bremen. Earlier direct traffic from Sweden using sailing ships had now largely ceased. In 1904, Wilhelm R. Lundgren, a captain with a small shipping company, saw new possibilities and, together with some Gothenburg merchants, started the Transatlantic Shipping Company to operate liners to South Africa with return cargoes from India. At the start, Transatlantic experienced financial problems, but the transport of timber and other forest products was successful and the firm eventually extended operations to Australia.[4] Three years later, Broström entered deep-sea shipping with a line to east Asia in collaboration with Danish interests. In contrast to Transatlantic, Broström's early deep-sea traffic could rely on earnings

---

[4]Göteborgs Sjöfartsmuseum (GS), Transatlantic Archive (TA), Board, Minutes, 1904-1914.

from the iron ore trade. In 1911 Broström also started a line to North America.[5] Thus, on the eve of World War I both firms were expanding. Broström, led since 1905 by Axel's son Dan, was by far the larger: its 124,000 tons of shipping were twice those of Transatlantic.

The two companies shared common features: both were far superior to other Gothenburg shipping firms and operated in the same local and national markets under the same institutional conditions. Both were involved in world-wide liner trades and were familiar with each other's business. Yet from the very beginning there were also important differences which help to explain their subsequent divergent behaviour. One of these areas was leadership – Transatlantic was managed by employed directors, while Broström was administered by its owners, a significant distinction since owners tend to be more interested in capital assets while directors focus more on operations.[6] The two commenced business at different times, and Broström, established twenty years earlier, enjoyed the advantages and expertise of an early starter. Dan Broström had experienced both the tough conditions of the early 1890s and the better years after 1896. Transatlantic's management, on the other hand, had no similar background. Finally, while Transatlantic was a pure liner company, Broström was foremost a tramp company. This gave Broström certain advantages. Liner companies, with their obligations to maintain regular traffic, require a certain number of vessels of similar tonnage, a requirement that constrains a firm's ability to choose an optimal time to order new ships. Broström's tramp interests not only provided alternative income but also gave it greater flexibility in the timing of purchases. Broström further widened its operations by diversifying into shipyards and engineering during the First World War.

The First World War and After

The period 1910-1920 was characterized by expansion and good returns for Swedish shipping, especially during the war. Despite its small capital base, Transatlantic continued to amass a large liner fleet. The liner traffic

---

[5]Kent Olsson, *Från pansarbåtsvarv till tankfartygsvarv, de svenska storvarens utveckling till exportindustri 1880-1936* (Kungälv, 1983), 40.

[6]Alfred D. Chandler, Jr., *The Visible Hand: The Managerial Revolution in American Business* (Cambridge, MA, 1977); Chandler, *Scale and Scope: The Dynamics of Industrial Capitalism* (Cambridge, MA, 1990).

was organized in collaboration with the Norwegian Wilh. Wilhelmsen Company and the Danish ØK. Transatlantic's early activity concentrated on South Africa and later was extended to Australia, but the traffic was further augmented by the addition of minor lines that complemented its main business, such as a Pacific line between Australia and the American west coast. In the Australian and Pacific liner trades, vessels of around 10,000 tons were used, while the feeder lines employed smaller ships.

Figure 1
The Fleets of Broström and Transatlantic, 1915-1985
(000 tons)

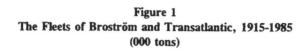

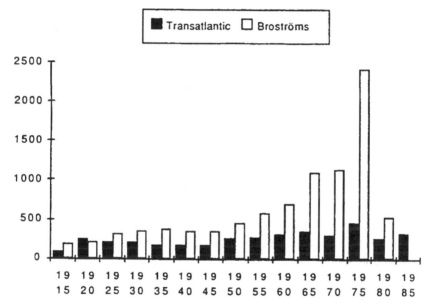

Source: A. Attman, *Göteborgs Stadsfullmäktige 1863-1962* (Göteborg, 1963), I, Part 2; Göteborgs Sjöfartsmuseum (GS), Transatlantic Archive (TA), *Annual Reports*, various years; Broström, *Annual Reports*, various years.

Transatlantic's activity was based on exports of Swedish wood supplemented successively by paper and growing volumes of engineering products. Return cargoes consisted primarily of Australian wool and corn. While Transatlantic's development of different lines wisely spread the risks, its heavy reliance on Australia was a potential weakness. Ultimately, the serious crisis in the Australian economy during the early

1930s was a major contributor to Transatlantic's liquidation in 1932.[7] During the First World War the firm ordered many new vessels from Swedish yards, especially from Götaverken in Gothenburg. The outcome was that in 1918 Transatlantic's total fleet amounted to over 200,000 tons. The wartime boom encouraged expansion and Transatlantic's management, led by Gunnar Carlsson, who took over after Lundgren's death in 1914, seemingly had unlimited optimism in the intrinsic strength and promising future of liners. Indeed, management had no hesitation in accumulating substantial debts. At the same time, shareholders were favoured with bonus shares and dividends of fifty percent in both 1918 and 1919.[8]

Broström provides a sharp contrast to Transatlantic. While the latter was committed to liners with new vessels and high debt loads, the various companies within the Broström orbit used second-hand tonnage and operated chiefly in tramping and iron ore traffic. Returns were constantly reinvested and the business was solid financially, as it had been from the start. The purchasing policy was extremely cautious. Dan Broström's view on investments was that although it was "the most important aspect for the shipowner," it was imperative "that he obtain a vessel which can give the highest possible return on invested capital."[9]

Tramp shipping was extraordinarily profitable during the First World War. This can be seen clearly in table 1, which shows Tirfings' profits on a per vessel basis for the years 1913-1920. Broström, like Transatlantic, earned good profits as well as high returns from insurance. Yet Broström recognised the unusual nature of the wartime situation. Commenting on the good profits of 1916, it admitted that these would "in all probability will not be repeated."[10] In consequence Broström followed a cautious policy; while Transatlantic expanded, Broström retained all financial surpluses and ordered only one new vessel during

---

[7]GS, TA, *Annual Report*, 1932.

[8]*Ibid.*, 1914-1920.

[9]Artur Attman and Martin Fritz, "Dan Broström," in Algot Mattsson (ed.), *From Lake and River to Distant Oceans* (Göteborg, 1965), 59.

[10]*Ferms årsberättelse*, 1916.

the war (which was ultimately delivered in 1922).[11] Dan Broström foresaw a downturn and falling prices after the conflict and this influenced his policy about replacing ships lost during the war: the Board did not feel able to recommend replacements because of high prices. Instead, it followed a "wait-and-see" policy until a suitable occasion arose to enlarge the firm's fleet.[12]

Figure 2
Transatlantic's Capital, 1920-1936

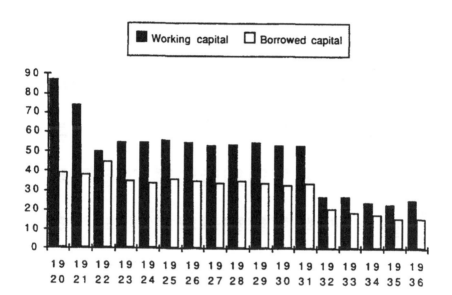

Source: *Svenska aktiebolag*, various years.

---

[11]During these years Dan Broström made one "mistake." In 1919 he ordered a large motorship, MS *Canton*, in order to enhance the competitive power of his daughter company, Svenska Östasiatiska Kompaniet. The price agreed was 12,000,000 kronor. In 1922, when the vessel was delivered, that sum would have purchased three or four similar ships. Broström was reported to be in an extraordinarily bad mood during the sea trials! See Celsius Centralarkiv, Göteborg (CCG), Öresundsvarvets Arkiv (ÖA), Correspondence.

[12]*Ferms årsberättelse*, 1915.

Table 1
Tirfings' Profits, 1913-1920
(000 kroner, current prices)

Ship	1913	1914	1915	1916	1917	1918	1919	1920	bought	price	sold	sec. h.
Sagoland	50	163	720	2542	398	1881	3441	2791	1913	1135	1935	Earls
Hogland	36	146	251	951	219	2601	2368	1225	1914	560	1924	sec.h.
Österland	130	189	394	829	573	530	1597	1151	1905	749	1932	Dox.
Nordland	95	90	313	16	329	935	1221	543	1905	690	1930	Dox.
Götaland	118	96	438	1333	26	1671	976	37	1904	525	1933	sec.h.
Nyland	91	152	608	662	344	606	2016	704	1909	565	1939	Dox.
Jemtland	164	0	0	304	166	920	1366	699	1906	388	1920	sec.h.
Smaland 1	52	39	0	0	0	0	0	0	1901	252	1915	sec.h.
Roland 1	26	106	494	14	0	0	0	0	1913	579	1916	sec.h.
England	59	0	237	20	0	0	0	0	1900		1915	sec.h.
Gretland	105	0	0	675	1056	1913	12	59	1912	450	1918	sec.h.
Hemland	77	46	305	449	1070	1643	710	503	1901	160	1921	sec.h.
Aaland	180	207	503	2313	1060	2566	2619	697	1910	883	1943	Dox.
Inland	99	30	374	1217	20	1233	611	680	1909	449	1934	Dox.
Uppland	89	0	6	0	110	1581	612	1126	1899	351	1915	sec.h.
Daland 1	132	0	0	23	396	1825	340	0	1907	477	1916	sec.h.
Sydland 1	182	0	261	1472	248	859	24	0	1905	624	1918	Green
Fridland	282	179	257	18	139	0	0	172	1910	879	1918	Gray
Vesterland	139	87	531	1339	362	57	0	11	1907	650	1917	Dox.
Malmland	42	127	220	732	0	0	0	12	1904	705	1915	Dox.
Smaland 2	0	0	0	0	236	632	803	850	1917	2000	1924	sec.h.
Roland 2	0	0	0	0	32	458	135	45	1917	2000	1918	sec.h.
Daland 2	0	0	0	0	396	1825	340	0	1917	3080	1918	sec.h.
Upland 2	0	0	0	0	110	1581	612	1126	1917	531	1924	sec.h.
Erland	0	0	0	0	0	639	19	14	1918		1919	sec.h.
Sydland 2	0	0	0	0	0	0	0	1321	1920		1923	Dox.
Profits	2148	1657	5912	14727	6668	22540	18870	12640				
Index 1	100	100	145	185	244	339	330	347				
Index 2	100	108	142	182	240	334	325	342				

Source: Göteborgs Landsarkiv (GLA), Tirfing, Journals, 1899-1920.

For these reasons the Broström fleet contracted after 1914. The company maintained a high level of liquidity: of the total capital in the 1920 balance sheet of Tirfing and Ferm, Broström's two leading firms, only 3.5% was borrowed. The surpluses went partly to invest in two shipyards in Gothenburg, Götaverken and Eriksberg, which were renovated and enlarged, partly through bank loans and partly through debenture and share issues in different companies outside the concern.

The very different strategies of the two companies during the war years had consequences for the patterns of behaviour during the depressions of the 1920s and 1930s. Transatlantic, with its heavy indebtedness, faced major problems in the early 1920s (see figure 2). The collapse of the freight market after 1920 and the consequent fall in ship prices were the root causes, but the Swedish government's prohibition on the sale of old steamers abroad and the company's delayed tax payments on wartime profits compounded matters. Both the value of the fleet and share capital had to be written down in 1922. Later in the decade there was some modernisation of the fleet but debts were not curtailed. In the crisis of the early 1930s Transatlantic's difficulties multiplied. The potential for freight earnings decreased and ship prices fell further. Management observed in 1932 that the "value of the tonnage had fallen to an earlier unthinkable level" and that the need for depreciation exceeded the share capital "quite considerably." Between 1932 and 1933 the value of the company's fleet was reduced from 47,000,000 to 23,000,000 kronor. Liquidation was the only possible course, and in 1933 Transatlantic came under bank administration, which introduced a far-reaching consolidation policy. The over-optimistic management of the war period thus determined the company's future up to the late 1930s, limiting new initiatives and ultimately necessitating retrenchment. From 1932, Transatlantic's management appeared to have learned from past experience. In the improved years of the late 1930s a more realistic view of depreciation prevailed and during the Second World War the company was well known for the low valuation of its vessels – one krona per ship!

For Broström the interwar experience was quite different. It emerged from the war in a strong financial position and subsequently drew on this to diversify (thereby spreading its risks) and to weld the different branches into a consolidated business. The parent company, Tirfing, retained its old tonnage and operated mainly within Europe. This was a stagnating sector in this period and expansion came in the iron ore traffic between South America and the US. Broström's financial strength enabled it to cash in on low ship prices. In 1922, for example, it ordered two 25,000-ton motorships for the iron ore trade to Deutsche Werft in Hamburg. The timing of this order also allowed it to profit from German hyperinflation. The vessels were put into the Chilean iron ore trade for Bethlehem steel, in which long charters assured stable profits during the changeable interwar years. Another development within the Tirfing group was a growing liner traffic to the Orient, built in collaboration with Baltic shipowners and Greek businessmen.

> Dan Broström was very keen to start this liner traffic
> and through it achieve a certain balance and stability for
> Tirfing. Tramp shipping company may encounter severe
> difficulties in finding employment in times of severe
> economic fluctuations. Liner traffic serves to counter-
> balance this.[13]

Tirfing also increased its shares in the Swedish-American Line and the Ostasiat. At the same time interests in engineering works were developed not merely through Götaverken and Eriksberg (though interests in the former were settled in the early 1930s), but through involvement in ESAB, a welding company, and NOHAB. Broström's financial position thus enabled it to operate from a position of strength. Purchases throughout the interwar years were on favourable terms and borrowed capital continued to be very small (see figure 3).

The experience of the two companies in the years from 1914 to 1939 makes it clear that their different appraisals during the war years of likely long-term developments in international shipping resulted in different strategic decisions. These, in turn, significantly influenced the companies' fortunes in the period before 1939. Transatlantic encountered major problems arising from its over-ambitious, debt-financed expansion and only survived because of the favourable long-term conditions for transoceanic liners. Broström, by contrast, gained from its prudent strategy during the wartime boom and accumulated great reserves, which could be used with considerable effectiveness during the following period of depression.

---

[13]GLA, Svenska Orientlinjen archives (SOA), E. Mellander, Memorial. In a series of interviews in the 1950s, Mellander supplied considerable information and personal reminiscences about the foundation and growth of the Swedish Orient Line.

Figure 3
Svenska Ostasitaiska Kompaniet, Capital, 1920-1936

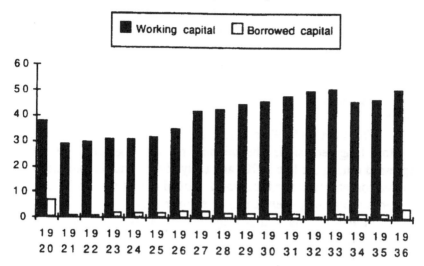

Source: See figure 2.

Reversed Roles: The Crisis of the 1970s

The period from 1945 to the mid-1970s has been characterised as the "golden years" by Swedish economic historians because of the unbroken record of economic growth. It was also a time of continuous progress for Swedish shipping. Broström and Transatlantic maintained their positions within the shipping hierarchy and reacted to this period of expansion similarly. Both emerged from the Second World War with a reinforced transport capacity and new tonnage, having enjoyed access to a large domestic shipbuilding capacity during the war. Within Broström, Tirfing was engaged in iron ore and tramp traffic, while the more important daughter companies operated transoceanic liners and plunged into the expanding oil trade. Broström also totally dominated the prestigious passenger traffic to North America. In 1950, Broström's fleet comprised nearly 500,000 tons and more than 700,000 tons by 1960. The Eriksberg shipyard was retained and considerably enlarged. The company was well and cautiously managed, still dominated by the Broström family even though Tirfing was listed on the Stockholm stock exchange in 1957. For Transatlantic, the severe experiences of the interwar period influenced management's strategy in the postwar era. The dangers of high debts and the ensuing limits on freedom of action were remembered. From 1940, good trading conditions and inflation made it possible to write-off assets and to achieve high liquidity. During the decade after the Second World War Transatlantic's total fleet was renewed but also almost totally written-off. By 1960 the fleet amounted to over 300,000 tons. Transatlantic's position had also been strengthened through the leading role in Swedish shipping during the war of its managing director, Gunnar Carlsson.[14]

From the mid-1970s, however, Sweden's "golden period" gave way to a long recession. The shipping market in general was severely depressed during the late 1970s and early 1980s, with numerous failures of large companies around the world. How did Broström and Transatlantic react to this completely changed environment?

If management and strategy had been relatively similar for the two firms during the "golden years," the subsequent recession elicited contrasting patterns of behaviour. But compared to the World War I years, the roles were now reversed. This time Transatlantic was the cautious company, for in a tenacious struggle to survive, it consolidated. By contrast, Broström pursued ambitious plans which, sadly, went wrong. How is it possible to explain this role reversal?

Transatlantic had concentrated on shipping while Broström had diversified, amassing large interests, especially in shipbuilding. Sweden in the early 1970s was the world's second leading shipbuilding nation, and Eriksberg was Sweden's leading yard. Broström also managed the state-owned Uddevalla shipyard. The huge investments and credit commitments needed for supertankers brought strains. During the boom shipbuilding had come to represent the most expansive part of Broström while the role of shipping was relatively reduced. The international crisis in shipping and shipbuilding hit Eriksberg and Broström hard. The yard experienced major difficulties and after tough negotiations – which in a broad context can be viewed as a trial of strength between the social democratic government and private capitalists – the government took over the yard on favourable terms. As a result, Broström's financial strength was greatly reduced.

Despite this serious setback, Broström's management tried to lift the firm out of the general shipping depression through optimistic invest-

---

[14]*Transbladet*, 1945-1960, especially annual surveys and accounts.

ments. In the same year as the Eriksberg crisis, Broström bought the Holland-America Line using borrowed money.[15] During the late 1970s and early 1980s Broström also embarked on a far-reaching modernization and rationalization programme. But in a depressed shipping market, the business as a whole generated at best small profits. Investments therefore had to be amortized with borrowed money at high interest rates. At the same time, the firm periodically experienced losses on foreign exchange both from Eriksberg and the shipping companies.[16] The outcome was fatal. Between 1975 and 1984 the total number of employees was reduced from 9000 to 700. Profits were small or non-existent, and 1978 and 1983 were especially disastrous. The year 1984 witnessed the final demise of this leading Swedish shipping concern. The sound policy that had characterized the firm during the interwar period thus was not followed during the crises of the 1970s and 1980s; in retrospect, the alternatives proved unsuitable and ultimately disastrous.

One result of Broström's demise was that its Atlantic traffic was engrossed by its great rival, Transatlantic. Transatlantic preserved its concentration on traditional liner traffic, which was modernized to include ro-ro vessels, oil tankers and refrigerated ships in collaboration with other companies, Swedish as well as foreign. When the bad times began in 1974 Transatlantic's old liner traffic had in most cases been replaced by new ro-ro lines. Hence, when Broström was struck by the Eriksberg losses and opted for expensive investments in new shipping companies, Transatlantic consolidated its business and prudently switched from conventional liners to ro-ro vessels.[17] While Transatlantic, along with other firms, earned lower profits during the recession, operating revenues in general covered losses. In 1979, which proved to be Transatlantic's worst year, losses reached 84,000,000 kronor compared with Broström's deficit of 462,000,000 kronor the previous year.[18]

The difference between the two firms boiled down to how to manage a business in a recession. Transatlantic tried to minimize costs and investments and consolidated its position. By contrast Broström,

---

[15]ÅngfartygsAB Tirfing, *Annual Report*, 1974.

[16]*Ibid.*, 1978 and 1979.

[17]GS, TA, Transatlantic, *Annual Reports*, 1971-1979.

[18]*Ibid.*, 1979.

following the Eriksberg crisis, tried to transform its liner activities much more radically. Broström also had wider interests in the bulk cargo and tanker trades which were far more vulnerable to market changes. In a sense Broström suffered because it had become over-extended, while Transatlantic benefited from never having moved outside its traditional liner niche. The old adage of staying within one's area of competence may have some relevance here, but it is also obvious that survival is only possible in a long recession through cost-cutting, liquidating debts and keeping a low profile. During the crisis years of the 1970s and 1980s, Broström did not follow these precepts and acted in a fashion totally alien to its prudent policy in the depression of the 1920s. Consequently, the firm disappeared.

The Transition to Motor Vessels

The two important technological innovations in shipping during this century were the introduction of the motorship and the transition to container traffic. In the first instance the decision lay solely in the hands of the shipping companies; in the case of containerisation, which involved all links in the transport chain, decisions were often made by land-based concerns. The strategic responses of Gothenburg's two leading shipping companies to these innovations differed considerably.

The motorship was developed by the Danish firm of Burmeister and Wain; from 1912, it was an alternative to steam. In Scandinavia, the Danish Östasiatiske Kompagni and later the Nordstjernan Shipping Company in Stockholm were the first to adopt the innovation. While Dan Broström also realized the advantages of motorships, at the same time he recognized that much of his fleet operated in Europe, where oil was expensive while coal was abundant and relatively cheap. Yet there was scope for introducing motor vessels in the liner trades to east Asia and in the Latin American-US iron ore traffic. In spite of this, up to 1920 Broström only ordered two motor vessels. Later it cautiously ordered further motor vessels, notably for the Atlantic passenger trade, but in relation to its large financial resources, Broström made a rather slow shift into motor power. Transatlantic, on the other hand, actively tried to execute a rapid transition to motor vessels during the boom years of the First World War. Significantly, the company never purchased a steam vessel after 1918, but its purchase of new motorships also slowed in the interwar period. Financial difficulties meant that a desirable technological transformation had to be phased in slowly. Even so, by

1939 Transatlantic's fleet was comprised mostly of motor vessels, while for Gothenburg as a whole the transition came comparatively late.

The Introduction of Containers

In the 1960s two factors significantly affected the port of Gothenburg. One was that the long-term transformation of Swedish industry led to exports that consisted less of bulk products and more of refined goods. The other development was more international and involved the introduction of unitization, particularly containers. Container traffic came to be seen as the solution to the demands of increasing international transport volumes and the threat to established liners caused by costly lay-days in port. The outcome in Gothenburg was a run-down of the old harbour and a move to a new container port at the mouth of the river.

Broström and Transatlantic were comparatively late in responding to container traffic. When they did react it was in the form of a collaboration with Atlantic Container Line (ACL). Both Broström and Transatlantic participated with one vessel each, but this involvement was relatively small compared to others. Still, short-term profits were weakened by a lengthy freight war initiated by US operators.[19] A different response occurred in the Australian trades in which Transatlantic had long had a presence. Here return freights were largely comprised of raw materials, notably wool. The homogeneity of freights encouraged the development of particular types of ships. One such was the so-called "Skandia-ship," which had exceptionally large cargo hatches to avoid horizontal movements in the holds. Twelve such vessels were ordered at Eriksberg in 1963 by a consortium of Scandinavian owners; the ships were delivered between 1967 and 1969. Transatlantic took four of these vessels, putting them into the Australian trade. Compared with conventional tonnage these vessels were particularly profitable (see table 2).[20]

---

[19]GLA, Swedish-American Line (SAL), Board, Minutes, 1963-1973. It is possible to follow the development of ACL from its conception through to its time as an operating company. A freight war with Seatrain and Sealand, American companies that sought to engross around sixty-five percent of the market, led to a reduction of income per round trip to only $425,000 while costs were $550,000. The price war ended by July 1973 and profits then recovered.

[20]*Transbladet*, April 1966; April 1967; and January 1968.

Table 2
Transatlantic Australia Line:
Daily Profits for Skandia-ships and Liners,
1967-1969 (000 kronor, current prices)

	Outbound Profit after indirect costs	Profit after direct costs	Homebound Profit after indirect costs	Profit after direct costs
1967				
Total	8	10	8	10
Skandia-ships	10	12	9	10
Liners	5	7	7	9
1968				
Total	5	7	7	9
Skandia-ships	8	10	8	10
Liners	2	5	5	7
1969				
Total	7	10	5	8
Skandia-ships	10	13	8	10

Notes: Figures for liners are missing for 1969. This strange combination of "container ships" and conventional liners was unplanned. The closure of the Suez Canal locked in M/S *Killara*, one of Transatlantic's four Skandia-ships, and forced the company to combine different ships and cargo systems.

Source: GLA, Transatlantic Archive, Seglationsböcker, 1967-1969.

Improved operating profits, however, were only achieved at a cost. New vessels built to handle unitised cargoes were extremely expensive. The price of a new liner in 1950 was 10,000,000 kronor and in 1960, 20,000,000 kronor, but the Skandia-ships cost 35,000,000 kronor each. Container vessels were even more costly; Transatlantic's first container vessel in the ACL collaboration amounted to 43,000,000 kronor and the ro-ro vessel *Bullaren*, acquired in 1979, carried a price tag of 125,000,000 kronor.[21] Such huge investments made it difficult to operate a traditional liner service. The solution was a collaboration

---

[21]GS, TA, Transatlantic, *Annual Reports*, 1969, 1973 and 1981.

between companies, with their joint traffic managed by a separate entity.[22] In the long run, the huge cost of vessels forced the liner companies into a position where they became mere suppliers of vessels rather than operators of shipping services. Ultimately, the large liner concerns were effectively transformed into investment companies.

From the beginning of the recession in 1974 liner traffic appeared the only possible resort for both Gothenburg shipping companies. There were parallels with conditions during the interwar depressions. Then liner traffic had been vital to Transatlantic's survival, while for Broström it had also been significant because of the purchase of shares in the Swedish-American Line and the East Asia Company, as well as the expansion of the Orient Line under Tirfing. Liners were favoured in the early 1970s as the only transport mode in which it was possible both to improve efficiency and reduce costs by introducing containers and ro-ro vessels.

Broström's huge investments during the recession were therefore directed toward liners. Management sought to meet the crisis through a variety of measures, including the purchase of Incotrans (a Dutch container company) with access to LASH vessels and increased partnership in ACL, which it was hoped might lead to a foothold in the EEC. Large orders of ro-ro vessels were placed with Japanese shipyards. The extended crisis, insufficient economic resources and misplaced investments all caused the situation to become a burden that dragged the concern into extinction. In retrospect, perhaps an earlier technological transition or a better outcome to the Eriksberg negotiations might have saved the firm once known as "the pride of Gothenburg."

The experience of Transatlantic was different. In part this was because the enterprise was too small to survive in the long-run. More positively, the company's activities were concentrated in the less vulnerable liner sector. Transatlantic did not experience a financial crisis when the shipbuilding yards crashed nor did the firm, like Broström, place huge orders abroad. Moreover, when vessels were ordered they had diesel engines. Given these factors, the technological and economic opportunities associated with containerization might well have permitted a long-term salvage plan for Transatlantic. A further possibility occurred in 1983 when Transatlantic succeeded in taking-over Broström's expensive liner traffic. In so doing it reached the capacity needed to

---

[22]*Transbladet*, October 1969 and January 1970.

sustain operations in the 1980s. Yet the era in which liner shipping was a separate business had come to an end, and Transatlantic was thus incorporated into the large integrated transport company, Bilspedition.

Conclusion

What explanations can be advanced for the different management responses of Broström and Transatlantic to external economic changes and decisive technological innovations? One significant factor may be that the companies, given their different dates of formation, grew up in different contexts both in terms of international markets and the structural transformation of the Swedish economy.

In historical perspective, Broström's early start meant that it was well-established at the turn of the century and was in a position to participate in Gothenburg's expansion and industrial development. Its experience thus enabled it to emerge from the First World War in a position of strength. These factors proved the prerequisites for the construction of a business empire. Broström enjoyed considerable power with a range of interests in many companies. But the huge expansion of Gothenburg shipbuilding, led by Eriksberg during the post-World War II years, produced some imbalance. This became only too evident in the great economic swing of 1974, when the large shipyard's problems imparted major difficulties to the whole concern.

The contrast with Transatlantic's experience is obvious. Transatlantic started later and was always in Broström's shadow. Its over-expansion during the First World War and the climate of the interwar years meant that it never acquired the resources to develop activities beyond its traditional operations. The firm therefore continued as a "pure" shipping company. Moreover, it was a firm which had learned the value of prudence from its experience in the 1920s and early 1930s. In consequence, it entered the crisis of the 1970s with accumulated reserves and a focus on a sector of shipping that offered the best possibility of survival — liner traffic based upon unitization with ro-ro and container vessels. Broström, on the other hand, entered the crisis with diminished resources after the Eriksberg failure and with an extensive bulk cargo and tanker tonnage.

The two elements of shipping emphasised at the outset of the essay underwent enormous changes during this century. Developments in cargo handling, particularly unitization, required that goods transport be conceived of in larger and more coherent terms with co-operation between sea and land carriers. At the same time the escalating size and cost of vessels forced shipowners to collaborate in larger operating groups. In the end, these pressures proved too much for Gothenburg's principal shipping companies: Broström collapsed and Transatlantic ceased to be a separate entity. The era of separate liner shipping companies had clearly come to an end.

Contractors' Bounties or Due Consideration?: Evidence on the Commercial Nature of The Royal Mail Steam Packet Company's Mail Contracts, 1842-1905[1]

A.J. Arnold and Robert G. Greenhill

Introduction

It is a curious feature of British economic history that in the mid-nineteenth century, traditionally the high-water mark of *laissez-faire*, the government negotiated a series of postal contracts with the private sector. At first through the Admiralty and later through the Post Office, officials placed the carriage of mails on overseas routes with commercial shipping companies. The north Atlantic route was granted to Samuel Cunard and his associates in 1839; the Peninsular Company undertook to carry mails to the Mediterranean; and the Royal Mail Steam Packet Company was in 1840 awarded a contract for a service to the West Indies.[2] By the 1850s British shipowners operated contracts to Africa, Australia, the Far East and South America. Among the original firms, the Peninsular and Oriental Company (P&O) extended its mail line from the Mediterranean

[1]The authors gratefully acknowledge the contributions of participants at the Glasgow pre-conference, at which an earlier version of this paper was presented. They particularly thank Professor Edward Sloan for his comments and Professor John Armstrong, who read an earlier version of the paper. They would also like to thank the archivist of the DMS Watson Library, University College, London, for permission to use its holdings on the Royal Mail Steam Packet Company.

[2]The first mail contract, to Rotterdam and Hamburg, was awarded to the General Steam Navigation Company in 1832 (S. Palmer, "'The Most Indefatigable Activity;' The General Steam Navigation Company 1824-50," *Journal of Transport History*, Third Series, III, No. 2 [September 1982], 11), but "it was the three long-distance contracts that were the most momentous for British maritime history" (F. Harcourt, "British Oceanic Mail Contracts in the Age of Steam, 1838-1914," *Journal of Transport History*, Third Series, IX, No. 1 [March 1988], 2).

Research in Maritime History, No. 6 (June 1994), 111-137.

and Royal Mail (RM) added Brazil and the River Plate to its Caribbean services. New contractors, like the Union Company and the Pacific Steam Navigation Company, began mail services to South Africa and the Pacific coast, respectively.

These agreements typically provided fees well in excess of anticipated postal revenues, a practice which contradicted all that extreme free traders and supporters of *laissez-faire* represented. Historians have seen these payments not as part of a commercial contract but, particularly when paid by the Admiralty, as a deliberate subsidy to shipowners, in part to further the state's imperial and naval objectives. Jesse Saugstad regarded Britain's nineteenth-century postal contracts as state aid to shipping, while Sidney Pollard argued that the British merchant marine has never been left entirely to competition, although Britain granted subsidies less openly than France, hiding them in postal subventions, payments for auxiliary cruisers, loans, Admiralty contracts and the hire of troop transports.[3] Similarly, Freda Harcourt has recently referred to oceanic mail contracts (and the contracting companies) as "subsidised."[4]

A subsidy is a "grant of public money in aid of some enterprise or industry, or to keep down the price of a commodity;" within this meaning, overseas mail services involved subsidies because, given the state's pricing policy, postal revenues could not cover the capital and operating costs of a dedicated fleet, whether operated by the Post Office, as in the period 1832-1836, or by another contractor. Although costs had been much lower when the mails were delivered irregularly by passing ships of the merchant or Royal navies, receipts also had been smaller.

At first, questions of service quality, pricing and cost concerning overseas mail had been left to the market, but difficulties with wartime deliveries led to the establishment of a Ship Letter Office in 1798. Bags had been hung in "every coffee house in London" for merchants' letters

---

[3]J. Saugstad, *Shipping and Shipbuilding Subsidies* (Washington, 1932); S. Pollard, "The Economic History of British Shipbuilding, 1870-1914" (Unpublished PhD thesis, University of London, 1950), 28. The case for modifying the operation of market forces on the shipping industry is still under discussion. The recent contraction of Britain's shipping industry may be optimal in terms of transport costs and the size of her overseas trade but sub-optimal with regard to the country's defence needs. See M. Asteris, "British Merchant Shipping: Market Forces and the Defence of the Realm," *Royal Bank of Scotland Review*, No. 171 (September 1991), 32-45.

[4]Harcourt, "British Oceanic Mail Contracts," 5.

bound for abroad and from 1798 the Post Office arranged for their collection and transfer to suitable ships.[5] There were considerable problems with "contraband mail" (shipowners taking the mail of business friends without charge), which encouraged the Post Office to upgrade the official packet services. As marine steam technology improved, an opportunity arose to make overseas mails more regular, to the benefit of both traders and those administering the Empire, and to promote the development of steam technology for commercial exploitation.

Extravagance in government departments was at that time a "lively political issue."[6] As the Royal Navy was in no position to operate a steam fleet or to provide the necessary bunkering facilities, overseas mail contracts were awarded to private companies. These firms were empowered simultaneously to conduct other business, thus enabling the state to pay a lower fee than for an exclusive mail service, although questions of cost identification and control were more complex. While a majority of businessmen, even in the age of *laissez-faire*, might have accepted that the state was responsible for the mails, they could not agree on which system (private contract or another alternative) was optimal.

State agencies have often been given monopolies in return for the provision of relatively comprehensive services. Under this arrangement, pricing tends to be relatively uniform and the overall return to the operator is a compromise between the rates obtainable from the more and less lucrative services. Thus, some routes of a "common carrier" railway system, or the individual parts of a postal service, may fail to make a surplus or even cover costs. When such services are provided abroad it becomes very difficult to segregate commercial factors from state policy considerations; the existence of the market and the ability to reach it safely depend upon the political, military and naval power of the state. More specifically, the failure of postal revenues to cover costs on overseas routes becomes an amalgam of pricing policy, geo-politics *vis-a-vis* the Empire, naval strategy and the ability of the state to negotiate an appropriate contract price with private sector shipping companies.

---

[5]F.G. Kay, *Royal Mail* (London, 1951), 98.

[6]Harcourt, "British Oceanic Mail Contracts," 1.

The benefits of mail subsidies to the state and the British merchant marine have been extensively discussed in the literature.[7] At the time, however, there were allegations that the prices were over-generous. The General Shipowners Society, for example, complained to the Select Committee on Steam Communications with India in 1851 that mail contracts had "become to a considerable degree bounties in favour of contractors, enabling them to defy the competition of less favoured individuals," although interested parties, such as Arthur Anderson of P&O, denied that they were subsidies, bonuses, or premiums given to establish steam navigation, but rather "consideration for performing a valuable public service."[8] The commercial returns on mail contracts alone cannot, however, be properly identified because the agreements enabled private sector firms to invest in ships and other assets that would provide a joint product of mail revenues and passenger and freight earnings. The contracts produced a fee and some prestige, but the fixed schedules provided their own pressures (on costs and safety standards) and restrictions (on commercial freight, which might take too long to load), while ship specifications and other Admiralty requirements also meant additional costs. Moreover, the need to have spare capacity in case of accident or loss added further costs to the running of a liner service.

This paper is focused not on general issues that concern state subsidies but on the more specific question of whether the state provided private sector shipping companies with excess returns. Clearly, Royal Mail's proceeds were higher than without such fees, if the same routes were operated. But were they higher than commercial revenues available elsewhere? If not, the existence of this element of the subsidy is difficult to sustain. In order to provide data for an initial analysis, the Royal Mail Steam Packet Company has been selected. This enterprise received the largest contract payments and generated the biggest deficits during a period in which its West Indian mail contract was unbroken and in

---

[7]See, for example, H. Robinson, *Britain's Post Office* (London, 1953); Robinson, *Carrying British Mail Overseas* (London, 1964); M.J. Daunton, *Royal Mail: The Post Office since 1840* (London, 1985); Harcourt, "British Oceanic Mail Contracts," 1-18.

[8]Daunton, *Royal Mail*, 156-157. As late as 1901, the point was made before the Select Committee on Steamship Subsidies that P&O saw the "large subsidy which is supposed to be paid to the company" as "no subsidy at all" but instead as merely a "payment for postal services;" National Maritime Museum (NMM), P&O Archives, 6/18.

which, successively, the Admiralty and the Post Office had responsibility for managing oceanic mail services.[9] RM's experiences should therefore provide evidence on the nature of the contractual relationship between the state and the private sector to carry mail to overseas destinations.

The company's archives provided most of the information on the mail contracts and commercial returns. Since the published accounting data does not provide a reliable indication of commercial success, RM's returns have here been calculated and appraised using its internal records, supplemented by trade and commercial data. The second part of the paper describes the operation of RM's mail contracts and the development of its non-contract revenues; the third analyses its commercial returns; and the fourth compares its results with available information on financial returns in the second half of the century. The final section discusses RM's results and draws some conclusions.

Contractual Obligations and Commercial Operations

In 1839 John Irving, MP and partner in a City merchant house, and several other businessmen from the influential West India Committee approached the Treasury with a plan for a company to provide a steam mail service to the Caribbean for an initial ten-year period at a cost of £240,000 per annum, an enormous sum for the times. Steam navigation, still in its infancy, was not cheaper or even faster than sail — although it was less at the mercy of the elements — but the existing Admiralty-operated packet service had a poor reputation. Since the Admiralty was not in a position to operate a steam fleet or to provide the necessary bunkering facilities, a contract was signed in March 1840 for a twice-monthly main line from England, which divided into branches to serve the many ports in the West Indies and along the Spanish Main.

The operation was beset with initial difficulties due to delays in the construction of ships and the despatch of sufficient coal and support vessels to the West Indies. Indeed, even after the first sailings in 1842, RM could not keep to the timetable. The service was almost certainly too

---

[9]In 1852-1853 the West Indies/Brazil contract absorbed 32.8% of mail contract payments, provided 17.8% of postal revenues and caused 53.8% of contract deficits; Great Britain, Parliament, House of Commons, *Parliamentary Papers* [*BPP*] (1852-1853), XCV, 235. Similarly in 1863, the West Indies/Brazil was still the largest contract (32.8% of total payments) but provided only modest revenues (20.2% of total) and the largest deficit (£180,000, or 47.7% of total); *BPP* (1863), XXXI, 195.

ambitious, encompassing numerous ports in the Caribbean and Central America from the Gulf of Mexico in the north to Colombia in the south. It was the route, *The Times* argued, rather than "any inefficiency in the speed of the vessels or disorganisation in the working of the company's fleet," which delayed the mails.[10] To maintain schedules, masters ignored safety procedures; the losses of *Isis*, *Medina* and *Solway* might not have occurred "had not the plan...embraced too wide a sphere of operations in too short a time."[11] Some of the operating problems, although they might have been anticipated, were largely beyond the company's control; narrow channels, unknown currents, ill-informed local pilots and sudden changes of weather all posed serious risks.

While many of these difficulties were the teething problems of a new and complex enterprise, longer-term issues were more intractable. Among these were RM's relations with the British government. During the 1830s, government extravagance had become an important issue and losses on mail packet stations were substantial.[12] The Commissioners who enquired into this recommended a "rational division of responsibility" under which the Post Office and Treasury would agree on the service needed and inform the Admiralty, which would enter into and supervise contracts with private sector firms (if they provided the "best means of securing economy and simplicity of arrangement") or carry the mails itself.[13] But the Admiralty, charged with supervising the new companies, saw things from a naval rather than a postal perspective. The mail ships were regarded partly as naval reserves and the Admiralty was empowered to hire the company ships during national emergencies. Construction costs escalated because of the Admiralty's insistence on designs which would allow the accommodation of guns and each vessel carried a naval officer or Admiralty agent who could over-rule the captain. The Admiralty selected Dartmouth as Royal Mail's UK departure port while

---

[10]*The Times*, 22 October 1849 and 28 November 1849.

[11]*BPP* (1843), IX, q. 684.

[12]Harcourt, "British Oceanic Mail Contracts," 1. Losses on overseas mails in the four years from January 1832 totalled £155,000 (receipts £207,000, expenses £362,000) before inclusion of the prime and outfit costs of the ships of £273,000; *BPP* (1836), XXVIII, appendix A, 27-29.

[13]Daunton, *Royal Mail*, 154.

the company, on business grounds, preferred Southampton. Even more serious was the Navy's influence on technology; as late as 1850 officials refused Royal Mail's application to build iron steamers, insisting on "the number of wooden ones specified in contract being kept up."[14]

Despite these problems the firm continued with the mail contract. Indeed, in many respects Royal Mail benefitted from generous treatment by successive governments. Officials permitted the postponement of services in 1841, allowed the curtailment of the route both before operations started and again in 1843, and exacted only modest penalties for lateness. Moreover, the Admiralty and subsequently the Post Office awarded the company further contracts in 1846 and at roughly five-year intervals until the turn of the century. The cost to the government, however, fell sharply. During the early 1860s, when the Post Office replaced the Admiralty as supervisor of oceanic mails, annual payments were reduced by £70,000; by the end of the century the contract was worth only about £85,000 per year to RM, a third of the original sum.[15]

At first the contract was central to RM's operations, giving it the opportunity to establish a base for its operations and to plan ahead. In 1842 mail payments comprised nearly seventy percent of total income; by the late 1850s, when annual fees were increased by £30,000 to compensate for the extension to Brazil and the River Plate, they still accounted for about thirty-five percent of earnings. Critics argued that such payments gave RM a substantial competitive advantage. The West India and Pacific Company, for example, complained in 1873 that "large subsidies are no longer necessary...in the West Indian trade [and] enable the Royal Mail Company to carry goods at lower rates than will pay."[16] As late as 1898 Lucas, head of the Colonial Office's West Indian Department, thought that RM, spoiled by its monopoly, "would not take any trouble...to develop traffic."[17]

---

[14]*BPP* (1849), XVII, qq. 895-896; see also R.G. Greenhill, "British Shipping and Latin America 1840-1930: The Royal Mail Steam Packet Company" (Unpublished PhD thesis, University of Exeter, 1971), 25.

[15]For further details on Royal Mail's contracts and the calculation of payments, see Greenhill, "British Shipping," 13-54.

[16]Post Office Archives, Post 29, 193/4002 (1874).

[17]Great Britain, Colonial Office (CO), 318/293, Minute 5889, March 1898.

In fact, during the second half of the century, commercial prospects in the undeveloped economies of Central America and the Caribbean, where communities were small and scattered, were poor. The population of Jamaica, the largest of the British islands in the West Indies, increased slowly because of emigration, high mortality and the difficulty of attracting fresh labour. Per capita income and domestic purchasing power were low and exploitable resources few. The sugar industry had already entered a period of secular decline, although up to 1860 Britain's West Indian islands supplied the mother country with more goods than any colony except India. In any case sugar producers could not afford steamship rates as long as the design of early steamers and their huge bunkering needs left little room for freight.[18]

Nevertheless, commercial traffic did develop. Passenger traffic soon picked up and a specialist trade in specie and other high-value, low-bulk commodities like spices evolved. Passenger and freight receipts increased by forty-two percent between 1852 and 1860 and in 1864, a peak year, totalled £620,000, three-quarters of all income. By this time the Brazilian route had been added; while some Caribbean trades were remunerative, others continued to lose money. Freight and passenger business was gradually extended, particularly during the 1870s when the Post Office successfully lowered mail payments, an action which likely encouraged RM to seek competitive commercial work. The company also occasionally derived substantial windfall earnings from hiring its fast mail steamers as government transports. In 1855, during the Crimean War, earnings from this source equalled total revenues from freight and passenger traffic, although running costs were also increased by the heavy wear and tear of transport work and the rising price of coal.

Royal Mail's Commercial Returns, 1842-1905

As a limited liability company, Royal Mail furnished annual accounts to its shareholders.[19] These were quite detailed, particularly compared with those of the notorious Kylsant era, but suffered from a number of

---

[18]See R.W. Beachey, *The British West Indian Sugar Industry in the Nineteenth Century* (Oxford, 1957) and G. Eisner, *Jamaica 1830-1930: A Study in Economic Growth* (Manchester, 1961).

[19]University College, London (UCL), Royal Mail Steam Packet Company Archives (RMSPCA), boxes 13 and 14.

deficiencies regarding classification, disclosure and investment.[20] These flaws mean that published profits cannot be used as indicators of commercial returns without adjustment. Indeed, even today such statements are poor guides to performance, partly because of the impact of post-war inflation but also because they attempt simultaneously to meet both market demands for performance measurement and shareholder wishes for information on the activities of management. The tension between the two can be illustrated by reference to the pervasive accounting concept of "conservatism," which represents an asymmetry that distorts performance measurement (the measurement of how well funds have been used in an economic or commercial sense) but is reasonably appropriate to the more limited notion of stewardship (reporting on the actual usages of the funds by managers).

Royal Mail's accounting practices during the period under examination appear to relate primarily to aspects of the agency relationship. Its profit and loss account, for example, contained information relevant to managers' dividend decisions rather than calculations of financial performance. The dividend decision requires managers to balance the encouragement of dividend payments against safety and prudence, but in shipping there are additional uncertainties arising from the irregular incidence of accidents, losses, repairs, refits and replacements. These doubts were increased when the company decided (despite the loss of *Isis* and *Medina* in the first year of operations) that insurance rates were uneconomic for companies large enough to spread risks through a policy of self-insurance. This strategy appears to have been successful, as savings provided regular bonuses to supplement dividend payments from normal commercial operations.

The operating surplus in 1845 was sufficient for management to declare the first dividend (and to receive a vote of thanks and remuneration for past services), although nothing was set aside in that or earlier

---

[20]For details on the Kylsant era, see E. Green and M. Moss, *A Business of National Importance: The Royal Mail Shipping Group 1902-1937* (London, 1982); P.N. Davies and A.M. Bourn, "Lord Kylsant and the Royal Mail," *Business History*, XIV (1972), 103-123; A.J. Arnold, "'No Substitute for Hard Cash?' An Analysis of Returns on Investment in the Royal Mail Steam Packet Company, 1903-29," *Accounting, Business and Financial History*, I, No. 3 (1991), 335-353; Arnold, "Secret Reserves or Special Credits: A Reappraisal of the Reserve and Provision Accounting Policies of the Royal Mail Steam Packet Company," *Accounting and Business Research*, XXI (Summer 1991), 203-214.

years to provide for depreciation. The rather simple listings used in the first workings and profit and loss account (and balance sheet) were soon succeeded by a more structured approach and by the establishment in 1845 of an insurance fund, which enabled the company to charge constant annual sums against operations to cover inherently irregular misfortunes. As long as such sums were adequate this was a prudent way of defining, through the profit and loss account, the operating surplus available for distribution, but it meant that profit figures less accurately reflected the actual events of individual years. Similarly, in 1846 a general reserve fund was set up and was used explicitly in 1851 to reduce balance sheet asset values, in partial compensation for the absence of depreciation charges in previous years. In 1852 and 1853 the fund also provided a less obtrusive means of absorbing repair costs of £43,900 and £160,900, respectively. In 1855 a statement of changes in the insurance fund and general reserves was included in the annual report, although only by combining and adjusting the profit and loss, insurance and repair funds and the general reserve could a single figure be produced which reveals profit or loss in any modern or commercial sense.

As operations became more profitable, accounting disclosures became more explicit. Following the receipt of substantial government monies for transporting troops to the Crimea, RM felt able to establish depreciation as a regular charge although, in the absence of any generally established accounting criteria for depreciation, it is hardly surprising that the size of the charge was a function more of commercial well-being than any notion of asset deterioration.[21]

The published accounts thus provide a basis on which to calculate RM's commercial returns, once the information is reformatted and standardised, and movements on various funds can be analyzed to reveal unspecified expenses. More important, RM's archives contain sufficient unpublished information to appraise the reliability (which appears quite high) of the published accounts.[22] The archives also provide the means to disaggregate several composite headings on the balance sheet and give detailed evidence on the composition and cost of fixed assets. This means

---

[21]R.C.O Matthews, *et al.*, *British Economic Growth 1856-1973* (Oxford, 1982), shows a surprisingly modest decline from the mid-1870s, given the cyclical downturn in the economy. This does not have any major impact on our argument, although it may serve to exaggerate the poverty of RM's returns from the mid-1870s.

[22]UCL, RMSPCA, 26.

that a major limitation of the published data for performance measurement – the variability of depreciation charges – could be overcome.

The published accounts typically gave the opening balance, added the cost of assets acquired during the year, and deducted depreciation for two main classes of fixed assets – property, plant and equipment; and ships – but did not reveal original costs, which are necessary to appraise and recalculate the yearly provisions. In sub-dividing the annual net figure for property, plant and equipment into its cost and accumulated depreciation components, some figures had to be estimated because of insufficient detail regarding the sale or expiry dates of some assets. This process thus did not permit the estimation of a more consistent depreciation rate for property, plant and equipment with any real confidence, although, since the firm's investment in such assets was modest, any inaccuracies are unlikely to have a noticeable impact on the subsequent analysis. On the other hand, RM's investment in its major asset, ships, was on a very different scale. Fortunately, here the available information is far more complete. The published accounts provided details of ship purchases and losses, which could be checked against the company's internal list of about 120 ships owned between 1842 and 1905.[23] These sources meant that the cost of fleet assets owned at each year-end could be computed, as could a standardised annual depreciation charge.

We decided to use an annual depreciation rate of five percent on a straight-line basis, which would amortise a ship over an expected twenty-year life, although the wear and tear on the fleet, the pace of technological change, and frequent breakdowns all suggest a shorter life of fourteen or fifteen years, which would require a seven percent straight-line depreciation. We opted, however, to stay with five percent because there is evidence that RM often kept its ships for more than fifteen years and because of Napier's selection of this rate for P&O. But we should emphasise that the use of a higher depreciation rate, at least until the 1880s when steel hulls and compound engines were well established, would strengthen rather than weaken our argument about RM's commercial returns.[24] The firm's actual policy was less consistent

---

[23]*Ibid.*, 15.

[24]J.B. Tabb and C.B. Frankham, "The Northern Steamship Company: The Depreciation Problem in the Nineteenth Century," *Accounting Historians Journal*, XIII, No. 2 (Fall 1986), 38, use a seven percent depreciation rate for steamships during the nineteenth century. P&O, however, used a five percent rate, initially on the reducing

or generous than the five percent straight-line approach and there is some evidence that this reflected under-charging, particularly from 1885, rather than proof that five percent was too high.[25]

The use of annual provisions for repairs and insurance, rather than actual annual costs, had relatively minor and temporary effects, since they were sufficient to meet long-term costs and since the information was generally disclosed. But RM's depreciation policy had a much more important and less explicit impact on reported annual profits and cumulatively, from 1875, on retained profits. The actual and standardised depreciation charges, together with the effects on profits, are shown in appendix table 1; the cumulative depreciation undercharge by 1905 of £723,000 indicates the extent to which RM's published reserves of £267,000 were a function of its depreciation policy.

The profits of joint-stock companies represent a return on the capital employed. Definitions of this term range from "all funds" to "equity sources," although it is usual to focus on funds that require a financial return, whether fixed or variable. Returns to shareholders are, however, partly a function of the levels of business and financial risks. Modigliani and Miller have argued that while individuals can borrow or lend at the same market rate of interest, and while there are no barriers to the free flow of information in security markets, firms cannot gain from leverage in a world without taxes, as the value of the firm is a

---

balance system, then supplemented on an *ad hoc* basis and, from 1875, on the straight-line system. C.J. Napier, "Fixed Asset Accounting in the Shipping Industry: P & O 1840-1914," *Accounting, Business and Financial History*, I, No. 1 (1990), 37, found this "realistic given that ships tended to be disposed of after about 20 years for very small residual amounts." In the case of RM, the five percent straight-line basis over an extended period appears appropriate, since it writes costs down to an approximation of residual value at the date of sale.

[25]Despite annual variations and an initial shortfall, RM did charge depreciation at this rate over the period 1842-1875, a time of relatively high commercial returns. Thereafter, in broad terms, returns fell and so did depreciation charges. This was not unusual; the Northern Steamship Company, which at first treated depreciation as a "discretionary allocation of distributable profits needing the sanction of the shareholders" (Tabb and Frankham, "Northern Steamship," 38) had a depreciation deficiency, albeit relative to a seven percent annual charge, of ninety-two percent of reported net profits over the period 1882-1889 (*ibid.*, 52). By 1905, accumulated depreciation on RM's fleet was twenty-three percent of cost which, with an unweighted average age of about nine years, implies an average cost recovery period, and shipping asset life, of about thirty-eight years!

function of its net operating income or, in our case, its profit before interest and taxation.[26] The restrictive assumptions are not entirely appropriate to RM between 1842 and 1905 – although taxation levels were extremely low – but such an approach does mean that a more contemporary market-based return can be calculated alongside yields on historical inputs of equity and debt capital derived from annual accounts.[27] The various returns, with supporting definitions, have been set out on two bases, using actual and standardised depreciation, in appendix table 2. But since shipping is a high-risk business, prone to irregular costs, the returns in this table have been converted to smoothed, five-year moving averages, shown graphically in figure 1.

It is apparent that the six series of returns on capital employed, whether based on after-tax profit as a percentage of equity capital (including reserves) or profits before interest and tax as a percentage of equity and debt capital (with or without allowances for standardised depreciation), provide a fairly uniform view of returns over the period 1842-1905. The rates vary but the orders of magnitude and directions of change are remarkably consistent. Each series is negative for 1842-1843 but positive (as high as fifteen or twenty percent) for 1844-1850. In most years between 1851 and 1873, RM achieved reasonable returns on capital, peaking in 1862-1864.[28] Returns recovered sharply in 1871-1873, but were much lower throughout between 1874 and 1905, following the substantial reductions in mail contract fees made by the Post Office. From 1900, returns were negative if proper allowance is made for depreciation.

---

[26]Although F. Modigliani and M.H. Miller's seminal article, "The Cost of Capital, Corporation Finance and the Theory of Investment," *American Economic Review*, XLVIII (June 1958), 261-297, listed a more restrictive set of assumptions, it is now generally accepted that those identified above are sufficient to derive their main proposition. See, e.g., H. Levy and M. Sarnat, *Capital Investment and Financial Decisions* (3rd ed., Englewood Cliffs, NJ, 1986), 400. A similar "composite measure" is described as superior to earnings yield in Matthews, *et al.*, *British Economic Growth*, 344.

[27]RM's debt was not in the form of securities during the period. We have assumed that the contract rate of interest was a market rate and that debt can therefore be valued at par. The company did not issue preferred shares until October 1906.

[28]The one apparent contradiction between the time series is in 1851 and can be explained by RM's substantial asset write-offs in the published accounts (following several years of no depreciation charges), which artificially depress unadjusted returns.

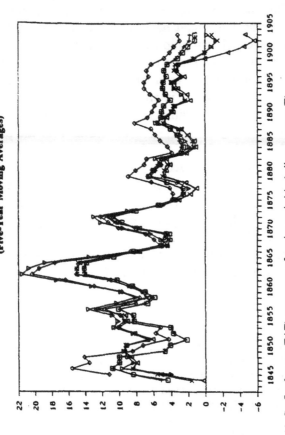

Figure 1
Returns on Capital Employed
(Five-Year Moving Averages)

Key:

□　Profit after tax (PAT) as percent of equity capital including reserves (E).

+◇　Profit before interest and tax (PBIT) as percent of equity and debt capital (E + D).
　　PBIT as percent of market value of equity and debt capital (MV).

◁　As □ except based upon standardised depreciation.

✗　As + except based upon standardised depreciation.

▼　As ◇ except based upon standardised depreciation.

Source:　Calculations as set out in Table 2, columns (1) to (6), based on University College, London (UCL), Royal Mail Steam Packet Company Archives (RMSPCA), boxes 13, 14, 15 and 26.

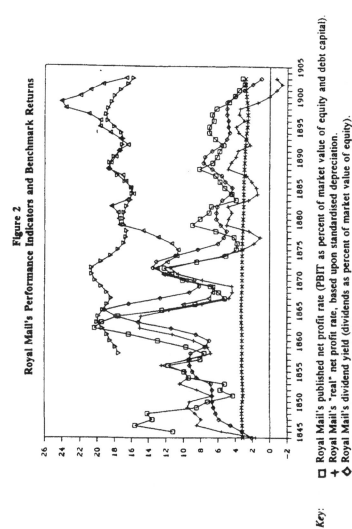

Figure 2
Royal Mail's Performance Indicators and Benchmark Returns

Key:

□ Royal Mail's published net profit rate (PBIT as percent of market value of equity and debt capital).

+ Royal Mail's "real" net profit rate, based upon standardised depreciation.

◇ Royal Mail's dividend yield (dividends as percent of market value of equity).

◁ Royal Mail's real net profit rate (recomputed as if mail contract revenues had remained at £240,000 p.a.).

✕ Yield on government consols.

▼ General net profit rate.

Source: Calculations of RM rates and yields based on UCL, RMSPCA, boxes 13, 14, 15, and 26; B.R. Mitchell and P. Deane (comps.), *Abstract of British Historical Statistics* (Cambridge, 1962), 455, for yields on government consols; R.C.O. Matthews, *et al.*, *British Economic Growth 1856-1973* (Oxford, 1982), 185 and 346 for the general net profit rate.

Benchmark Returns

The conclusion that RM's return on capital employed peaked in 1862-1864, were highly positive in most years before 1873, but were much lower thereafter (and even negative towards the end of the period) can be set against established benchmarks for the second half of the nineteenth century. One is the risk-free rate, indicated by the annual yield on government consols, which fell slowly over the period from 3.4% to 2.8%, with only slight variations around this negative trend.[29] Comparing these rates with the figures in table 2, it is clear that RM achieved considerably higher returns on capital employed for most of the period than did holders of consols. Only from the 1890s were its returns equalled or eclipsed, a phenomenon masked by low depreciation charges.

A further benchmark is provided by the bank rate, which reflects returns on interest-bearing deposits in the main clearing banks. No clear pattern is discernible in this rate, as frequent changes, often several in a single year, complicate calculations.[30] Highs of eight percent in 1847 and 1861, nine percent in 1864 and 1873, and ten percent in 1857 and 1866 do not match peaks in RM's performance very well, although the rate around 1900 seems more in line with (and even in excess of) the firm's returns. If so, bearing in mind their relatively risk-free nature, interest-bearing deposits might from the 1890s have been a sounder investment than Royal Mail shares.

Long-run time series of returns on commercial investments, which would provide a clearer comparison with RM, are surprisingly scarce. For the period 1880-1905, Capie and Webber calculated annual profits (published net profits relative to capital and reserves) for a set of British banks and provided further details which allow an alternative (published net profits to the market value of equity capital) to be calculated.[31] These remained consistently within the range of eight to 11.5%, and 3.4% to 4.8%, respectively, although the lack of variation

---

[29]B.R. Mitchell and P. Deane (comps.), *Abstract of British Historical Statistics* (Cambridge, 1962), 455.

[30]*Ibid.*, 456-459.

[31]F. Capie and A. Webber, "Truth and Fiction: Actual and Published Profits in British Banking, 1870-1939" (Unpublished paper presented to the Institute of Commonwealth Studies' Seminar on "The City and Empire," November 1985), table 1.

and the rather moderate level of returns probably reflect the relatively low risk attaching to investment in British banks and their unusually conservative accounting practices.

Railways are another sector where profit rates have been computed. Terry Gourvish's series for the years from 1870 show gross returns of 9.3% in 1870, falling to 8.5% in 1885 and rising to 9.1% in 1905, while net returns of 4.6% in 1870 fell to 3.4% by 1905.[32] Such moderate profits reflect a lower level of risk and suggest that if railways did not enjoy RM's high rates of return in the peak years around 1870, neither did they experience the same slump from the 1890s.

Data published by Francis Hyde on Harrisons of Liverpool for the period 1884-1905 enable profit rates (five-year moving averages, net of costs including an imputed five percent straight-line depreciation charge, to capital and reserves) to be computed.[33] These averaged 11.8% and varied quite considerably within the range 6.5-17.5%. Direct comparisons between RM and Harrisons are difficult, as the two operated in different markets with distinct cost structures; moreover, Harrisons had no mail contracts. Still, there is little to suggest that RM in the years of reduced mail revenues was able to match Harrisons' high returns.

Instead, Royal Mail's returns are broadly consistent with realised returns on UK shipping equities between 1870 and 1913 as computed by Michael Edelstein. These show that shipping was a low-return industry with a geometric mean return over the period of 5.1%. By comparison, manufacturing and commercial equities averaged about six to nine percent per annum, with preference returns of the order of 5.3% and debentures (in the period 1888-1913) averaging four percent. On a risk-adjusted basis, shipping equities achieved negative returns of 1.9%.[34]

---

[32]T. Gourvish, *Railways and the British Economy 1830-1914* (London, 1980), 42. The failure of railways' net returns to rise after the 1880s in line with gross returns – in fact, the former continued falling – is explained by the onset of diminishing returns, whereby every additional unit of revenue was obtained at an increasing cost.

[33]F.E. Hyde, *Shipping Enterprise and Management, 1830-1939: Harrisons of Liverpool* (Liverpool, 1967), 114 and appendices.

[34]Only domestic electricity, domestic canals and domestic, Eastern European and Indian railways provided lower returns to equity investors; M. Edelstein, *Overseas Investment in the Age of High Imperialism* (London, 1982), 123. Similarly, only domestic canals and domestic, Eastern European and Indian railways provided a poorer, risk-adjusted return; *ibid.*, 122.

Edelstein also calculated the allocation of shipping returns (not risk-adjusted) over shorter periods: 1870-1876, 6.6%; 1877-1886, 3.5%; 1887-1896, 5.8%; and 1897-1909, 2.7%.[35] It is also possible to compare RM's returns with established freight rate series, especially after 1870 (although there are difficulties with this approach since Royal Mail's revenues – mails, passengers and high-value freight – were not included in the standard time series, which tended to concentrate on bulk cargoes). The correlation was low and insignificant.[36]

Perhaps the best indicator of the return on risk-bearing investment is the net profit rate (after depreciation to net capital stock, or gross investment less depreciation) series provided by R.C.O. Matthews and his colleagues for the period 1855-1905.[37] This fell gradually from about nineteen to sixteen percent, with annual variations within the range of fourteen to twenty-three percent. Figure 2 brings together three important indicators of RM's performance – the published profit rate (before interest and tax to the market value of capital), the equivalent rate based upon standardised depreciation charges and a dividend rate (related to equity capital) – and three benchmark returns – a recomputed "real" profit rate for RM (the rate that could have been earned had mail revenues not been reduced from the £240,000 per annum level of 1864),[38] the annual yield on government consols according to Mitchell and Deane (approximating the risk-free rate), and the general net profit rate from Matthews, *et al*. In order to remove short-term fluctuations, each series has been computed as a five-year moving average.

Discussion of Results and Conclusions

It is of course probable that profit-maximisation was not the only, or even at times the principal, objective of the Royal Mail Steam Packet

---

[35]M. Edelstein, "Realised Rates of Return on UK Home and Overseas Portfolio Investments in the Age of High Imperialism," *Explorations in Economic History*, XIII (1976), 318.

[36]The authors thank Professor Lewis Fischer for this point.

[37]Matthews, *et al.*, *British Economic Growth*, 185-186 and 346.

[38]Based on profits before interest and taxation as a percentage return on debt and equity capital, assuming that all the extra notional profits had been distributed.

Company. Its creation owed much to the West Indian lobby, which was almost certainly more interested in the speed and efficiency of communications than simple profit-maximisation. Moreover, as the century came to an end the fleet continued to call at islands and ports which did not pay, while in the early 1900s, even under Owen Phillips' management, a notion of public service may well have modified the primacy of profits. Nevertheless, to assume that over several decades RM's owners and shareholders were indifferent to the rate of return their equity earned is implausible. Conceptually, therefore, RM's returns can be disaggregated into a normal return, a risk-premium appropriate to the shipping industry and a more specific (positive or negative) rate that reflects the company's managerial competence and pursuit of non-commercial objectives. The calculations above of RM's returns have been based upon relatively objective data, but the disaggregation of these revenues necessarily involves far more estimation and judgement.

A first approach might be to set RM's results against the known performance of the British economy during the nineteenth century. Modern research makes historians cautious of such labels as the "mid-Victorian boom" or the "Great Depression" and wary of identifying sharp breaks in economic behaviour, although prices and business confidence were generally higher at mid-century than during its final quarter. Nonetheless it would appear from appendix table 2 and figure 1 that the overall pattern of RM's return on capital employed conforms well with the cyclical performance of the British economy during the second half of the century. Royal Mail's returns during the 1840s were surprisingly high, given the company's difficult beginning and popular impressions of the "hungry forties," but returns from 1848-1850, sometimes seen as the turning point between the more difficult 1840s and the mid-Victorian boom up to 1873, indicate a highly profitable period. Within this span there were exceptional years of low returns, such as 1853, 1859 and 1867-1869, when special circumstances prevailed outside the company's control.[39] The years after 1873 provided much lower returns, an estimate which conforms well with general impressions of the economy in the last quarter of the century, while the weak results after

---

[39]The year 1867 appears to have been particularly bad for shipowners, with P&O passing its dividend for the only time until 1932; Napier, "Fixed Asset Accounting," 27.

1900 are in line with Derek Aldcroft's findings about the shipping depression from the turn of the century until 1913.[40]

The more specific effects of declining revenues from the mail contracts from 1872-1873 can be derived from figure 2 by comparing RM's achieved returns with those obtainable had mail revenues not been reduced. Without the reductions, returns would have risen, with the generation of other business and declines in operating costs, to the same level as the Matthews series and even above it from 1895; with the decreases, returns fell to levels below the risk-free return from investment in government consols, and certainly to levels no better than in the shipping industry as a whole.[41]

The more interesting comparisons are probably in the period to 1872-1873, when mail revenues were at their height. During this era, returns were higher than later, but only in 1862-1863 did they reach the levels of the general series. Moreover, a careful comparison of figures 1 and 2 reveals that this can be said only of the two market-based returns and not of the four historical-input measures. A relatively high return on capital employed is to be expected in the decades immediately after the company's formation in 1840, once initial teething problems had been solved, if only to cover the high risks involved in steam operations in the first two-thirds of the century. Steam was far more expensive than sail to operate and may have been viable only where "some form of regular and high-value income could be guaranteed."[42] Steam operations required considerable investments in ships, coaling stations, drydocks, engineering works and working capital. Yet as RM's early years showed, the threat of maritime loss was never far away.

By the end of the nineteenth century, however, the situation had changed. Improvements in marine engineering and ship construction, as well as better navigational aids, removed some of the risks of maritime disaster and lowered real capital costs. Furthermore, improved designs reduced fuel consumption and increased carrying capacity, allowing

---

[40]D.H. Aldcroft, "The Depression in British Shipping 1901-11," *Journal of Transport History*, VII (1965), 14-23.

[41]Matthews *et al*, *British Economic Growth*.

[42]Palmer, "General Steam Navigation Company," 7; Napier, "Fixed Asset Accounting," 25. General Steam's 1839 annual report doubted that any steam company had been able to maintain average dividends of five percent over the previous ten years.

shipowners to transport higher payloads on each voyage. New entrants into the world of steam, as RM found in both the Caribbean and South America, drove down rates and margins, thus lowering what might be regarded as the normal return. Royal Mail's lower returns after 1873 therefore reflected not only the prevailing economic situation and the more commercial approach of the Post Office but also the lower risks associated with steam operations. During this period, comparisons with two notoriously conservative and relatively low-risk sectors, railways and banking, are not particularly favourable to RM, especially after 1890, while the more general returns on equities suggest that shipping in general, and RM in particular, was a low-yield investment in which the level of returns did not match the risks born by equity-holders.

This implies that the extent to which mail payments permitted RM to earn an excess return may be fairly limited. Given the risks inherent in steam before 1870, as well as the need to provide a contract service in the Caribbean where commercial traffic was scarce, and taking what comparative returns on capital are available for other sectors, RM's returns do not appear exceptional. Any mail subsidies in the early years undoubtedly would have helped the company to compete, but the real benefits in terms of excess returns, at least in the context of trading conditions in the West Indies, seem relatively modest.

But such conclusions are hindered by the probable impact of the third element in the company's returns: the effects of managerial competence. If, for example, RM had been more efficient, this return element would have been greater and total revenues higher, perhaps attaining levels of excess commercial returns. There are, however, obvious difficulties with counterfactual propositions about returns given hypothetical levels of managerial expertise, particularly since the question of Britain's managerial and entrepreneurial performance in the last quarter of the century is highly controversial. Moreover, an acceptance that profit-maximisation was not the sole aim (with directors and managers perhaps merely satisficing as far as shareholder returns were concerned) also modifies any view of managerial competence.

Nevertheless it should be noted that British shipowners have not emerged unscathed by historical judgements. S.G. Sturmey, for example, blamed Britain's long-term decline as a shipowning nation in part on the employment of managers "remote from ships and the smell of salt."[43]

---

[43]S.G. Sturmey, *British Shipping and World Competition* (London, 1962), 396-398.

More specifically, the business performance of RM's directors has attracted criticism. From the start, it seemed that the Board lacked experience of *merchant* shipping unlike, for example, Anderson and Willcox, the managers of P&O. Royal Mail's first directors were closely associated with the West Indian trading lobby rather than shipowning and were subsequently reinforced by superannuated naval officers and MPs. The suspicion was that the Board was resistant to change and lacked enterprise; throughout the nineteenth century critics condemned the retired Admirals "whose knowledge of practical business matters was commensurate with their old sea prejudices."[44] Furthermore, the speed with which Owen Phillips, later Lord Kylsant, was able to revive the firm's fortunes immediately prior to the First World War is perhaps salutary. Any evaluation of RM's management must rely on qualitative, even anecdotal, evidence which, however thin or unreliable, suggests that managerial incompetence was likely to have depressed returns during our period, although we would hesitate to quantify this effect.

Considerable allowances should be made for the limited evidence concerning benchmark returns, for definitional inconsistencies between the differing measures and for the uncertainties involved in questions of managerial competence. But it appears from the information available on RM that payments by the state in its formative years allowed returns broadly appropriate to the risks involved. When RM's depreciation is put on a consistent basis, it seems that profits generally fluctuated in line with general movements in the British economy, once some allowance is made for high initial risks. Available benchmarks do not suggest that the returns were at any time particularly excessive, although this conclusion is heavily dependent upon the reliability of the Matthews' series, which is "less firmly based than many statistics".[45] The reductions in mail fees mandated by the Post Office were difficult for the firm to avoid, given its investments in fixed plant, and severely deflated

---

[44]*Demerara Argosy*, 29 July 1905.

[45]See also Tabb and Frankham, "Northern Steamship;" H. Pollins, "Aspects of Railway Accounting before 1868," in A.C. Littleton and B.S. Yamey (eds.), *Studies in the History of Accounting* (Homewood, IL, 1956), 343; and R.P. Brief, *Nineteenth Century Capital Accounting and Business Investment* (New York, 1976), 66. There was no legal necessity to charge depreciation on fixed assets before paying dividends; see R.P. Brief, *The Continuing Debate over Depreciation, Capital and Income* (New York, 1993), 26-28.

returns from relatively unexceptional to levels more typical of shipping in the late nineteenth century. This might be taken as firm evidence of the Admiralty's failure to negotiate an appropriate fee, although there are indications that the more commercial stance adopted by the Post Office merely reflected technological and risk changes in shipping.

More evidence is needed before any firm conclusions can be drawn about the company's rates of return. Clearly there is a fine line between profits acceptable to the public (as a return on the various costs of mail services) and one which constitutes a satisfactory rate of return for shareholders (who tend to relate this to market share prices). It would nevertheless appear from the affairs of the Royal Mail Steam Packet Company that oceanic mail contract payments probably represented due consideration for the performance of a valuable public service. Rather less, it appears, were they "contractors' bounties" or "excess returns" paid by state agencies to favoured organisations in the private sector.

Appendices

Table 1
Shipping Depreciation Adjustments

	(1) Ds £000	(2) Da £000	(3) Pr £000	(4) RP £000
1842	43.3	0.0	-43.3	-43.3
1843	40.0	0.0	-40.0	-83.3
1844	38.4	0.0	-38.4	-121.7
1845	39.2	0.0	-39.2	-160.9
1846	40.2	0.0	-40.2	-201.1
1847	42.0	0.0	-42.0	-243.1
1848	40.9	0.0	-40.9	-284.0
1849	37.0	0.0	-37.0	-321.1
1850	39.1	0.0	-39.1	-360.2
1851	40.0	329.2	289.2	-71.0
1852	59.3	51.4	-7.9	-78.9
1853	63.0	0.0	-63.0	-141.9
1854	74.8	53.6	-21.2	-163.1
1855	78.3	171.4	93.1	-70.0
1856	67.5	94.6	27.1	-42.8
1857	67.5	67.5	0.0	-42.8
1858	70.7	71.4	0.7	-42.2
1859	70.4	68.5	-1.9	-44.0
1860	76.6	78.5	1.9	-42.1
1861	79.0	84.6	5.6	-36.5
1862	71.4	79.0	7.6	-28.9
1863	71.4	105.2	33.8	5.0
1864	68.4	74.0	5.6	10.6
1865	68.4	72.1	3.7	14.3
1866	71.9	79.6	7.7	22.0
1867	66.4	72.6	6.2	28.2
1868	71.3	10.8	-60.5	-32.3
1869	67.7	74.9	7.2	-25.1
1870	69.6	75.7	6.1	-18.9
1871	63.4	78.4	15.0	-4.0
1872	70.3	76.9	6.6	2.7
1873	76.2	81.2	5.0	7.6
1874	78.2	86.2	8.0	15.7
1875	78.4	72.1	-6.3	9.4

1876	69.4	55.7	-13.7	-4.3
1877	73.7	55.9	-17.8	-22.0
1878	75.9	57.7	-18.2	-40.2
1879	78.2	40.0	-38.2	-78.4
1880	84.2	40.0	-44.2	-122.6
1881	80.4	81.9	1.5	-121.1
1882	80.2	75.2	-5.0	-126.0
1883	82.9	78.4	-4.5	-130.5
1884	80.5	82.4	2.0	-128.6
1885	75.2	40.0	-35.2	-163.8
1886	80.9	40.0	-40.9	-204.7
1887	80.9	65.3	-15.6	-220.2
1888	76.0	72.5	-3.5	-223.8
1889	82.2	70.5	-11.7	-235.5
1890	87.2	70.0	-17.2	-252.7
1891	83.6	45.0	-38.6	-291.3
1892	84.7	40.0	-44.7	-336.0
1893	88.9	82.1	-6.8	-342.8
1894	95.6	50.0	-45.6	-388.4
1895	95.6	60.0	-35.6	-424.1
1896	105.5	80.0	-25.5	-449.6
1897	95.2	65.0	-30.2	-479.8
1898	98.6	63.0	-35.6	-515.3
1899	100.8	70.0	-30.8	-546.2
1900	104.3	80.0	-24.3	-570.5
1901	102.3	55.0	-47.3	-617.8
1902	102.2	45.0	-57.2	-674.9
1903	93.8	52.0	-41.8	-716.8
1904	105.1	84.0	-21.1	-737.9
1905	126.3	141.4	15.1	-722.9

Notes: (1) Depreciation on five percent per annum, straight-line basis.
(2) Depreciation actually charged against annual profits.
(3) Effect on annual profit of charging standardised depreciation.
(4) Effect on retained profits of charging standardised depreciation.

Source: UCL, RMSPCA, 15 and 26.

Table 2
Returns on Capital Employed

	(1) PATa:E %	(2) PBITa: E&D %	(3) PBITa: MV %	(4) PATs:E %	(5) PBITs: E&D %	(6) PBITs:MV %
1842	-10.6	-7.8		-17.4	-13.0	
1843	-4.3	-3.0	-8.4	-10.7	-8.3	-20.9
1844	9.8	9.6	18.7	6.1	6.1	10.3
1845	14.1	14.1	17.8	12.0	12.0	12.5
1846	13.0	13.0	16.0	11.3	11.3	11.2
1847	9.3	9.2	12.0	7.0	6.9	7.0
1848	8.0	8.2	13.6	5.9	6.0	7.5
1849	5.7	5.9	8.4	3.4	3.6	3.7
1850	14.0	14.1	20.6	15.3	15.5	15.9
1851	-13.6	-13.4	-12.3	15.5	15.6	13.3
1852	6.3	6.1	5.6	5.9	5.8	4.9
1853	-1.7	-1.0	-0.9	-9.7	-7.2	-5.6
1854	13.8	12.5	15.7	14.0	12.4	13.6
1855	15.6	15.9	18.0	25.0	25.3	27.0
1856	7.4	8.2	8.5	10.2	11.1	11.0
1857	6.6	6.9	8.4	6.9	7.1	8.4
1858	7.1	6.4	8.1	7.5	6.7	8.1
1859	-3.7	-2.4	-2.7	-4.0	-2.6	-2.9
1860	11.6	11.2	15.7	12.3	11.8	15.9
1861	13.0	12.2	19.1	14.0	13.0	19.8
1862	14.2	14.3	24.5	15.1	15.2	25.5
1863	16.1	16.4	25.3	18.5	18.8	29.0
1864	15.6	15.9	17.1	15.8	16.2	17.5
1865	11.9	12.1	11.6	12.0	12.3	11.9
1866	11.4	11.7	9.6	11.8	12.0	10.1
1867	-1.9	-1.6	-1.3	-1.3	-1.1	-0.9
1868	4.6	4.7	6.2	-0.3	-0.3	-0.4
1869	-0.5	0.0	0.1	0.1	0.7	1.2
1870	9.6	9.7	15.0	10.3	10.4	15.8
1871	10.9	11.0	14.4	12.1	12.3	16.0
1872	15.3	15.4	14.8	15.7	15.9	15.3
1873	13.2	13.3	12.2	13.5	13.6	12.6
1874	4.6	4.7	4.5	5.2	5.3	5.1
1875	-3.8	-3.7	-3.5	-4.4	-4.2	-4.0

1876	-2.1	-2.0	-2.7	-3.4	-3.3	-4.4
1877	5.9	6.1	8.9	4.4	4.5	6.5
1878	8.1	8.1	11.7	6.7	6.8	9.5
1879	4.8	5.0	6.3	1.6	1.8	2.1
1880	5.6	5.7	7.0	2.0	2.3	2.5
1881	8.3	8.4	10.9	9.3	9.5	11.0
1882	3.2	3.5	4.4	3.1	3.4	3.9
1883	4.3	4.8	6.5	4.4	5.0	6.0
1884	3.1	3.4	5.0	3.7	4.0	5.2
1885	-5.0	-4.8	-7.2	-9.8	-9.6	-12.2
1886	6.8	7.0	13.3	3.9	4.1	6.4
1887	4.6	4.6	8.7	4.0	4.0	6.1
1888	6.7	6.7	9.3	8.0	7.9	8.8
1889	7.2	6.7	7.3	7.8	7.1	6.3
1890	1.8	2.3	2.2	0.3	1.1	0.9
1891	5.1	5.0	5.6	2.0	2.4	2.1
1892	4.3	4.4	6.1	0.3	1.1	1.2
1893	5.6	5.5	7.9	7.2	6.7	7.1
1894	3.3	3.6	4.9	-1.3	0.1	0.1
1895	4.6	4.9	7.1	2.3	3.2	3.0
1896	6.7	6.5	9.0	7.4	7.0	6.3
1897	4.0	4.2	6.2	2.4	2.9	2.5
1898	3.7	3.7	5.2	1.1	1.5	1.3
1899	4.5	4.3	5.9	3.5	3.4	2.8
1900	2.8	3.2	4.5	1.3	2.5	2.0
1901	0.7	1.3	1.9	-8.4	-3.3	-2.7
1902	1.0	1.8	3.0	-10.6	-3.8	-3.5
1903	0.8	1.6	2.8	-8.1	-2.5	-2.2
1904	0.6	1.3	2.5	-2.4	0.1	0.1
1905	2.7	2.9	5.8	6.6	5.9	7.3

Notes: 1. Profit after tax (PAT) as percent of equity capital including reserves (E). 2. Profit before interest and tax (PBIT) as percent of equity and debt capital (E&D). 3. PBIT as percent of market value of equity and debt capital (MV). 4. As (1) except based upon standardised depreciation.
5. As (2) except based upon standardised depreciation. 6. As (3) except based upon standardised depreciation. In (4) - (6) the use of standardised depreciation affects annual profits and, cumulatively, the reserve component of equity capital.

Source: UCL, RMSPCA, 13-15, 26.

Patterns of Ownership and Finance in the Greek Deep-Sea Steamship Fleet, 1880-1914[1]

Gelina Harlaftis

After independence, a new age dawned for the Greek merchant marine. From almost 60,000 tons in 1838, the carrying capacity reached nearly 530,000 tons in 1913, an increase of almost nine-fold. In fact, one of the most impressive characteristics of the nineteenth-century Greek economy was the growth of shipping. Still, there was little relationship between domestic output and the cargoes carried by the fleet. Since Greek exports were fairly unimportant, the fleet was progressively internationalized, depending mainly on bulk cargoes, such as grain, cotton and wool, from the eastern Mediterranean and the Black Sea to western and northern Europe through commercial and maritime networks consolidated by Greek merchants and shipowners after the 1830s. It thus became an "international" tramp fleet meeting marginal transport demands in the cross-trades in an increasingly integrated international economy.

During the last third of the century, the Greek commercial and maritime network spread from Taganrog and Batoum to Marseille, London and Rotterdam, at the same time reducing its commercial activities and specialising more in shipowning. Two phases can be distinguished, identified broadly by the origins of the major shipowners: the more commercial "Chiot" period (1830s-1860s), established by men from the island of Chios, and the more maritime "Ionian" era (1870s-1900s).[2] The Ionian network was largely responsible for the transition from sail to steam.

---

[1]I would like to thank Professor Lewis R. Fischer and Dr. Simon Ville for their editorial assistance and Professor Edward Sloan for his useful comments.

[2]Gelina Harlaftis, *A History of Greek-Owned Shipping. The Making of an International Tramp Fleet in the Nineteenth and Twentieth Centuries* (London, 1993), chapters 2 and 3.

Research in Maritime History, No. 6 (June 1994), 139-165.

Steam superseded sail in the Greek fleet by 1903 (see figure 1). A dearth of international comparisons has allowed the mistaken notion to persist that Greeks were slow to adopt the new mode of propulsion.[3] Yet as late as 1880 no nation owned more steam than sail tonnage; indeed, seventy-three percent of the carrying capacity of the British fleet still lay below the decks of sailing vessels. In the 1880s steam surpassed sail in Britain, Germany, Spain and Belgium, while the transition occurred in the 1890s in Italy, Holland and Denmark, and between 1900 and 1910 in the USA, Norway, Sweden, Russia and Greece. By 1910, the Greek fleet was sixty-nine percent steam, compared with fifty-six percent for the USA and fifty-nine percent for Norway. Greece's transition was thus roughly contemporary with other countries.[4]

Figure 1
From Sail to Steam, 1875-1914

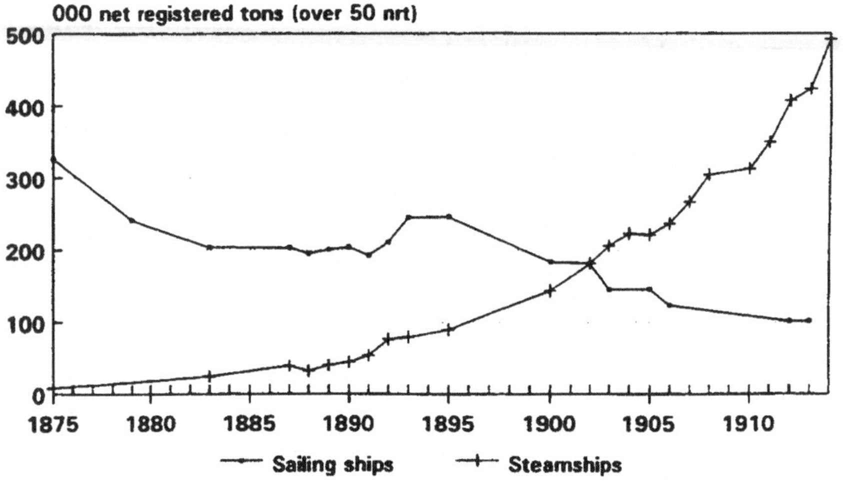

Source: G. Harlaftis, *History of Greek Shipping* (London, 1995), table 4.1.

---

[3]G. Dertilis, *The Greek Economy and Industrial Revolution, 1830-1910* (Athens, 1984), 32-33; M. Synarelli, *Roads and Ports in Greece, 1830-80* (Athens, 1989), 128; V. Kardassis, *From Sail to Steam. The Greek Merchant Marine, 1850-1914* (Athens, 1993), 174.

[4]Lewis R. Fischer and Helge W. Nordvik, "Maritime Transport and the Integration of the North Atlantic Economy, 1850-1914," in Wolfram Fischer, R. Marvin McInnis and Jürgen Schneider (eds.), *The Emergence of a World Economy 1500-1914* (Wiesbaden, 1986), table 4.

Table 1
Greek Shipping Offices in London, 1900-1914

	1900			1905		1910		1914		
	Ships	Nrt	% Total	Ships	Nrt	Ships	Nrt	Ships	Grt	% Total
A. Ionian Islands	9	13764	42%	3	5263	8	14328	29	79424	35%
Vagliano Bros.	4	6231		-		-		-		
Mango and Doresa	5	7533		3	5263	-		-		
Margo and Co.						4	6495	-		
Doresa C.						4	7833	7	19757	
Lykiardopulo and Co.								7	14440	
A. Frangopoulo								7	23652	
Theofilatos D.J.								1	622	
Vergottis								3	8978	
Ambatiello Bros.								4	11975	
B. Andros	4	6780	21%	8	14208	19	28159	46	88155	38%
S.G. Embiricos	4	6780		5	9095	6	11573	10	32140	
C.L. Embiricos				3	5013	3	5013	4	10892	
A.A. Embiricos						10	11573	13	45123	
Embiricos P. and L.N.								1	2751	
C. Chios	5	8416	25%	9	16509	20	35534	21	57501	25%
Michalinos	4	6581		4	7396	14	23787	10	22329	
Scaramanga Bros.	1	1835		3	5926	4	7642	8	24241	
Sechiari				2	3187	2	4105	3	10931	
D. Other	3	4041	12%	2	2678	7	3366	2	4752	2%
Galbraith and Pembroke	2	2839		1	1476	2	2839	1	2429	
Wigham and Richardson						5	527	1	2323	
	21	31799	100%		38558	54	81387	98	229832	100%

Source: Lloyd's Register of Shipping, 1900, 1905, 1910, 1914.

Table 2
Age Structure of Greek Acquisitions of Steamers, 1890-1910

Years	1890-1895		1895-1900		1900-1905		1905-1910	
	No.	Nrt	No.	Nrt	No.	Nrt	No.	Nrt
0-5	28	25275	14	17968	28	47265	18	31554
6-10	14	10850	14	17025	13	20325	14	21813
11-15	29	18953	11	12809	32	40564	24	24131
16-20	11	5489	18	15766	7	8504	42	55620
21-25	6	3589	8	6326	21	16019	25	22394
26 and Over	16	5706	10	5181	24	11123	83	43898
Unknown	-	-	5	5587	23	22303		
Total	104	69862	80	80662	148	166103	206	199410
Average Date of Build	1882 (8-13 yrs)		1885 (10-15 yrs)		1889 (11-16 yrs)		1886 (19-24 yrs)	

Source: Derived from *Lloyd's Register of Shipping*, 1895, 1900, 1905, 1910.

Two stages can be distinguished in the transition. The first, from the mid-1880s to the mid-1890s, was characterised by the dominance of the Ionian network, which owned all Greek tonnage operated from the Black Sea, Ottoman Empire and western Europe (see figure 2). By 1895 this group owned seventy-six percent, and in 1900 sixty-three percent, of Greek steam tonnage. These early steamship owners bought relatively new vessels: thirty-six percent of steam tonnage bought between 1890 and 1895 was less than five years-old. The Ionian network spawned the first large twentieth-century shipowning families. Knowledge of trade, an abundance of capital and connections in London enabled their descendants to be among the most successful shipowners in the first two decades of the twentieth century.

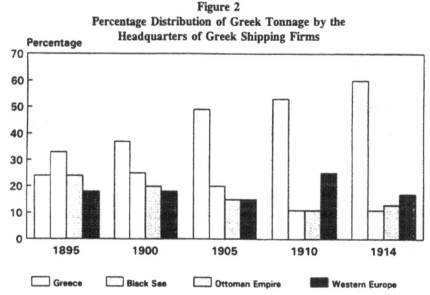

Figure 2
Percentage Distribution of Greek Tonnage by the Headquarters of Greek Shipping Firms

Source: Harlaftis, *History of Greek Shipping*, appendix IV.

The second stage, from about 1900 to the outbreak of World War I, involved the creation of a "new order" in Greek shipping, characterised by the consolidation of ownership in Piraeus and London. While in part this occurred because some owners from the Danube and Constantinople transferred their assets, a substantial number of medium and small owners also entered the profession. Figure 2 depicts the main headquarters of shipping firms. The operation of steamers from Black Sea ports plunged from thirty-six percent in 1895 to eleven percent in

1914, while Constantinople's share over the same period dropped from twenty-three to thirteen percent. At the same time, the proportion of steam tonnage operating from Piraeus rose from twenty-five to sixty percent. At the other end of the Greek-controlled maritime network, the share of steam tonnage operating from London and Marseille fluctuated, decreasing from eighteen percent in 1895 to fifteen percent in 1905, only to rise to twenty-five percent in 1910 before falling again to seventeen percent in 1914. The relative dips in 1905 and 1914 were only temporary, resulting from the entrance in Piraeus of many small owners who did not open new shipping offices – or link themselves with existing ones – in London. On the eve of World War I and beyond, Piraeus and London were the main centres from which Greek shipowners operated.

New developments in international shipping and trade meant that specialisation in ship ownership no longer implied dependence on a particular trade but rather attachment to a major international centre. Othon Stathatos, D.A. Stathatos, C. Stathatos, A.N. Theofilatos, N.D. Lykiardopoulos, G.M. Embirikos, and A.M. Vagliano moved their headquarters to London; Embirikos A.A. and Embirikos Bros. (from the Danube) and Michalinos and Ambatiellos and Mango (from Constantinople) also moved to London, while Theofilatos D.J. shifted from the Danube to Rotterdam and London. Until the 1890s Vagliano Bros. was the only Greek shipping office in London, but by 1900 there were five and in 1914, thirteen (see table 1).

The purchase of a large number of steamers during the first fifteen years of the new century enticed tramp owners to the main centres for chartering, insurance and fuel, and gave them immediate access to sales and purchase markets. The main groups came from the Ionian islands, as well as ftom Andros, Chios and Kassos. Island and kinship ties remained the most important conduits through which expansion was conducted, even in the interwar period. It is not surprising that in 1900 and 1914 Ionians possessed the most Greek-owned tonnage operated from London. Ionian merchants and shipowners were instrumental in the transition and a number specialised in shipping even after the decline of the commercial network. The Andriots, limited to the Embiricos, the most powerful family during the first two decades of the twentieth century, were also descended from prominent members of the Ionian network in the late nineteenth century.

The expansion of the Piraeus shipping market was due to the arrival of many small owners of sailing tonnage after 1905 through the vehicle of co-ownerships. The sixty-two shipping companies in Piraeus in 1905 grew to 111 in 1910 and 140 by 1914.[5] Steam tonnage acquired between 1900 and 1910 more than doubled that procured in the 1890s (see table 2). A main reason for this expansion was that the strong freight market at the turn of the century was followed by a period of relatively low rates, which also meant depressed ship prices. It was during this period that prominent shipowners like Rethymnis, Pneumaticos and Kulukundis from Kassos – and Lemos, Pateras, Hadjipateras, Livanos, Andreadis, Los and Margaronis from Chios – bought their first steamers. The limited capital possessed by these new owners meant that the age structure of the steam fleet deteriorated after 1905. While thirty percent of tonnage acquired in the century's initial quinquennium was new, only sixteen percent was between 1905 and 1910. Moreover, forty percent of newly-acquired Greek steam tonnage in the second five-year period was between fifteen and twenty-five years of age. The average age of new acquisitions doubled between 1890 and 1910 (see table 2).

This background is essentially an introduction to the main focus of this essay: the patterns of ownership and finance that accompanied the acquisition of steam. Although during the first phase of the transition most ships were purchased by the large shipowners of the Ionian network, in the second phase small owners, many of whom formed single-ship companies, entered the industry. Moreover, the second era was increasingly characterized by co-ownerships, an institution that continued for many years and was instrumental in the success of the Greek fleet in the interwar period. The remainder of the paper will examine the main owners and their sources of finance. Co-ownerships will also be examined, as will the lack of ship mortgages prior to 1910.

In order to investigate the precise patterns of finance during the transition, it is necessary to examine the ship registries of the main Greek maritime centres. Scattered in the various Greek ports and islands, these documents contain detailed information on the ownership of every ship. The fact that many owners, whether resident in Taganrog, Braila, Constantinople, Marseille or London, registered their vessels either in their home island or Syros, the main Greek maritime centre, makes this information particularly valuable. Table 8 indicates the ports and regions where Greek-owned vessels were registered. It is evident that Syros and the other Aegean islands constituted the main centres until the last third of the nineteenth century. But there was an important change in the first

---

[5]*Lloyd's Register*, 1905, 1910 and 1914.

decade of the twentieth century with the rise of Piraeus. This essay reports on data from the Syros and Piraeus registries for the years 1880-1910. These 188 ships of about 190,000 net registered tons (nrt) represent thirty-five percent of all steamers and thirty-seven percent of the total tonnage purchased by Greeks during the period.[6]

Table 3
Investment Groups in the Greek-Owned Steamers,
Syros and Piraeus Ship Registries, 1880-1910

Investment Groups	No.	%	(a) Nrt
Merchants/Shipowners of South Russia	13	6	11880
Merchants/Shipowners of the Danube	10	10	18100
Merchants/Bankers of Constantinople	38	17	31260
Bank of Athens	22	16	30837
Merchants/Bankers of Syros	63	32	59980
Self-finance	34	15	28516
Other	8	4	8607
(b) Total number of Steamers on Syros and Piraeus Registries	188	100%	189180
(b) / (c)	35%		37%
(c) Total acquisitions of the Greek steamship fleet 1880-1910	538		516037

Note: Includes owners of fifty percent or more of a vessel only.

Sources: Syros, Ship Registries, 1880-1910; Piraeus, Ship Registries, 1900-1910.

---

[6]The Syros ship registries in Hermoupolis contain information from 1880 to 1910, while those for Piraeus do not begin until 1900. The Department of Maritime Studies at the University of Piraeus is currently microfilming all existing registries from 1830 to 1939 for Syros, Andros, Chios, Santorini, Mykonos, Skiathos, Skopelos, Piraeus, Galaxidi, Patras, Cephalonia, Ithaca, Zakynthos and Corfu. The project also intends to computerize all the data. This project is the reason we were able to gain access to the Syros and Piraeus registries.

Table 4
Number of Shareholders in Greek Steamers
Registered in Syros and Piraeus, 1880-1910

Shareholders	1880-1889		1890-1899		1900-1910	
	Ships	Nrt	Ships	Nrt	Ships	Nrt
1	9	6295	31	20823	58	63992
2	2	1261	4	2170	18	20614
3-5	-	-	6	5628	29	31601
6-10	-	-	3	3935	3	1782
11-20	-	-	-	-	9	12308
21-30	-	-	-	-	5	6689
31-40	-	-	-	-	3	4767
41-50	-	-	-	-	-	-
51-60	-	-	-	-	-	-
61-70	-	-	-	-	1	1702
No Data	-	-	-	-	7	5613

Note: In the period 1900-1910 there is incomplete information for seven ships of 5613 nrt. For these vessels the registries list the name of the shipowner, the tonnage and other data, but excludes information on shareholders. This cannot be because the owners listed owned 100%, since in such cases the registrar wrote "100% owner" or "the whole ship." For this reason, the totals in this table are slightly different than in table 3.

Sources: See table 3.

As table 3 indicates, the capital for the Greek transition came from members of the Ionian network in south Russia, the Danube and Constantinople;[7] from the Bank of Athens, which was directly linked to the Ionian network; from bankers and merchants from Syros; and from the owners themselves. The Greeks of south Russia, the Danube and Constantinople were responsible for thirty-three percent of the steam tonnage registered at Syros and Piraeus between 1880 and 1910. This group included the earliest steam owners in the 1880s and 1890s, and their ships were mostly owned individually (see table 4). Nonetheless, a

---

[7]They were also situated in London and Marseille, but in order to facilitate the analysis I have divided them according to their branches in the Black Sea.

significant number of the masters who served on these ships eventually became part-owners; when the steamers became sufficiently old, masters, in conjunction with their families, were able to buy them. This is also why co-ownerships were rare prior to 1900 but the most common form of ownership thereafter.

Table 5
Ship Finance from the Bank of Athens for
the Entire Greek Fleet, 1900-1910

Dates	Number of Ships	Tons
1900	2	2170
1901-1905	3	3388
1906-1910	23	33351
Total Financed, 1900-1910	28	38809
Total Steamers Acquired, 1900-1910		365513
% Financed by Bank of Athens		11%

Source: *Lloyd's Register of Shipping*, 1900, 1905, 1910.

The Bank of Athens constituted the next important source of finance, accounting for sixteen percent of newly-acquired steam tonnage in the period 1880-1910 and eleven percent for the period 1900-1910 (table 5).[8] The bank was founded in 1894 by a group of investors who brought capital from abroad − Ep. Embirikos, Al. Lambrinudis, A. Kallergis, M. Iordanopoulos and N. Triantafillidis. By 1939 the institution had become the second most important commercial bank in Greece. In 1904, the shipowner Leonidas Zarifis from Constantinople joined the Board of Directors, as did his colleague, D. Eugenides, in

---

[8]The Bank appears as owner of vessels in *Lloyd's Register*, while those who received the financing were generally listed as managing owners.

1907.[9] Most of the ships were bought by the bank between 1906 and 1910, an era of low prices. Buying second-hand vessels during such periods became standard Greek strategy throughout the twentieth century. It was the expertise by members of the Board of Directors that led to the practice whereby the Bank bought second-hand steamers and then sold parts of them to Greek owners. In this way the Bank financed a large number of small shipowners entering the steam market for the first time.

Apart from the capital provided by members of the Ionian network resident abroad and the Bank of Athens, thirty-two percent of total steam tonnage registered at Syros and Piraeus were purchased by merchant/bankers from Syros. The most prominent included Avgerinos, Negroponte O. and Mavrogordatos, as well as the local factors Tsiropinas, Calvocoressis, Gangos, Ladopoulos, Vafiadakis, and Karellas. The Syros merchants also financed Chiots, Andriots and Kassians of which the shipowning families of Kulukundis, Andreadis, Los, Pithis and Vattis excelled. Until it was superseded by Piraeus at the end of the century, Syros was the main Greek maritime centre. Its large Chiot population, and the eventual establishment of the Chiot network, provided the financing and the expertise. Syros-financed steamships were especially important during the first fifteen years of the twentieth century.

The first steamship companies in the 1880s owned several ships that belonged to major merchant/shipowners of the Ionian network. Table 6 indicates the number of companies and ships as they appear in *Lloyd's Register* in 1885, when seventy percent of steamship owners had two to ten steamers and only thirty percent were single-ship companies. This suggests that it was wealthy capitalists who bought steamers during this period. Ten years later the picture had changed: while forty-three percent of concerns owned two to ten ships, single-ship companies had risen to fifty-seven percent. The expansion of single-ship companies in the 1890s can also be seen in other European fleets, such as the Spanish and the British. In the decade 1900-1910, however, the drop in freight rates and

---

[9]A. Lambrinudis was the first president. He came from Chios/Smyrna and had been a manager of the Ralli Brothers' branches in India. The general manager was A. Kallergis from Constantinople, while M. Iordanopoulos also came from Constantinople. The Bank opened branches in places such as London, Constantinople, Smyrna, Alexandria, and Khartoum. Established with a nominal capital of 10,000,000 drachmas, its real capitalization was 2,500,000. See *Panellinion Lefkoma Ethnikis Ekatontaetiridos, 1821-1921*, A' (Athens, 1921), 94-103.

the contraction of the market forced single-ship companies in the Spanish and British steamship fleets either to abandon the business or to merge with larger companies.[10] In the Greek fleet, however, the proportion of single-ship companies continued to rise, reaching seventy percent by 1914. It was during this era, of course, that Greek owners initiated the practice of "buying when everybody else sells."

Table 6
Degree of Concentration of Ships Owned by Greek Shipping Companies, 1885-1914

Number of Ships (size group)	Number of Companies	% Total of Companies in Each Size Group
1885		
6-10	1	10%
2-5	6	60
1	3	30
Total	10	100%
1895		
16-20	1	2%
10-15	1	2
6-10	6	12
2-5	14	27
1	30	57
Total	52	100%
1914		
16-20	1	0%
11-15	-	0
6-10	14	6
2-5	62	24
1	180	70
Total	256	100%

Sources: Derived from *Lloyd's Register of Shipping*, 1885, 1895, 1914.

---

[10]Jesús Valdaliso, "Spanish Shipowners in the British Mirror: Patterns of Investment, Ownership and Finance in the Bilbao Shipping Industry, 1879-1913," *International Journal of Maritime History*, V, No. 2 (December 1993).

Figure 3
Finance from Merchants in Southern Russia

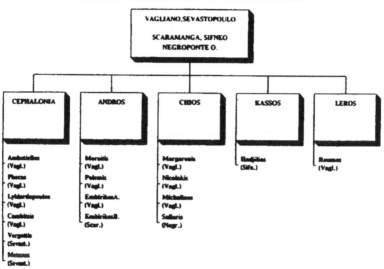

Source: Ship Registries, Syros and Piraeus; Andreas Lemos, *Modern Greek Seamen* (Athens, 1973).

It may be useful to note the extreme geographical concentration of the masters who were financed by members of the Ionian. These men came almost exclusively from Cephalonia, Ithaka, Andros, Chios and Kassos. The fact that Greek merchants/bankers in Constantinople, Taganrog, London or Marseille financed individuals from these five islands is proof not only of the islands' maritime traditions but also of the cohesion and common strategy of the Ionian network.[11]

Figure 3 portrays the shipowners financed by members of the Ionian network in southern Russia. Vagliano Bros., the network's most powerful commercial and shipowning house, financed twelve shipowners from Cephalonia, Chios and Andros and one from the small Aegean island of Leros. Sifneo Bros. from Lesbos employed the future shipowner Hadjilias. The Chiots Sevastopoulo, Scaramanga and Negroponte O. employed on their vessels the Cephalonians Vergottis and Metaxas, the Andriot N. Embiricos, and the Chiot Saliari Bros.

---

[11]There were other prominent maritime centres, like Galaxidi or Spetses, for example, where sailing shipowners were not financed by any member of the Ionian network and the fleet disappeared or decreased significantly.

Figure 4
Finance from Merchants of the Danube

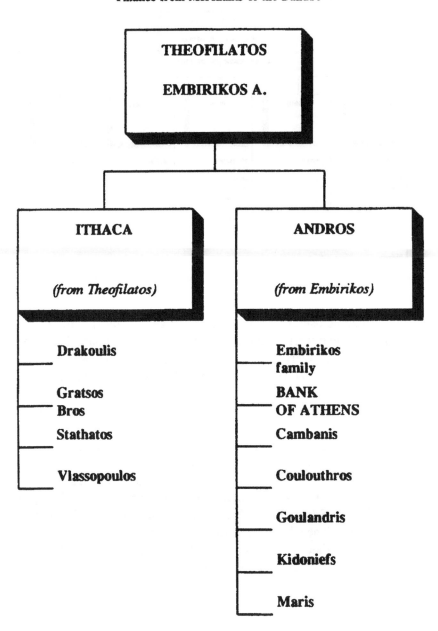

Figure 5
Finance from Merchants of CON/PLE

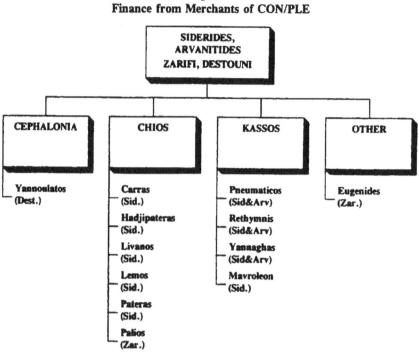

Source: As for Graph 3.

In figure 4 we can see the Danubian shipowner/merchants who financed exclusively compatriots or relatives. This was because the major Danube owners were themselves heavily involved in deep-sea shipowning. When Theofilatos, Stathatos and Embiricos transferred their activities to Piraeus and London at the turn of the century, they continued as shipowners. The Dracoulis brothers initially worked at the Theofilatos and Stathatos enterprises before starting their own firm (with their relatives, the Gratsos). The Embiricos family from Andros were the only important example of successful non-Ionians on the Danube. The Embiricos, apart from financing the entry into shipowning of many members of their large family, also recruited relatives from Andros, such as the Goulandris, Cambanis, Maris and Coulouthros. They became the most powerful Greek shipping family of the first third of the twentieth century. In addition, Epaminondas Embirikos was one of the founders of the Bank of Athens.

Figure 5 shows the shipowners financed by the merchant/ shipowners of Constantinople. Siderides and Arvanitides were merchants in Constantinople who imported oil from Batoum, while the Zarifis, grain merchants in Odessa, the Danube and later Marseille, became important bankers.[12] Spyridon Siderides, a Greek from Constantinople with Russian citizenship, was a representative for Russian petroleum in Constantinople and owned several steamers in the early twentieth century. Several Chiot masters benefited from his investments and eventually became leading shipowners themselves, including Livanos, Carras, Pateras, Hadjipateras and Lemos.[13] Cosmas Arvanitides also appears as a major Constantinople shipowner in the early years of the twentieth century. As an oil importer he combined commerce and shipping, and several of his masters – most notably the Kassians, Rethymnis and Pneumaticos – eventually became shipowners. Arvanitides continued as co-owner of the Rethymnis, Pneumaticos and Yannaghas ships during the interwar period. Leonidas Zarifis, an extremely successful banker in Constantinople, was also a shipowner. A. Palios was a master on Zarifis' ships, while Eugenios Eygenides, from the family of Zarifis' brother-in-law, became a leading shipowner. The Constantinople Greeks followed the pattern of the rest of the network in financing masters primarily from Cephalonia, Chios and Kassos.

Joint ownership characterised nineteenth-century Greek sailing vessels, a pattern that had long been common in Britain, Norway, France, Spain and elsewhere.[14] Similarly, strong geographic and kinship

---

[12]For more details on the banking activities of the Zarifis in Constantinople, see Harris Exertzoglou, *Adaptability and Policy of Greek Capital. Greek Bankers in Constantinople: The "Zarifis-Zafiropoulos" Office, 1871-1881* (Athens, 1989); Exertzoglou, "Greek Banking in Constantinople, 1850-1881" (Unpublished PhD thesis, University of London, 1986).

[13]The choice of Chiot masters was not accidental; Siderides' wife, Theofano, was a Chiot. Perhaps out of gratitude to his financier, Stavros Livanos, one of the five biggest Greek shipowners of the mid-twentieth century named his shipping firm "Theofano."

[14]Ralph Davis, *The Rise of the English Shipping Industry in the Seventeenth and Eighteenth Centuries* (London, 1962), 82-83; Sarah Palmer "Investors in London Shipping, 1820-1850," *Maritime History*, II (1973), 46-68; Helge Nordvik, "The Shipping Industries of the Scandinavian Countries, 1850-1914," in Lewis R. Fischer and Gerald E. Panting (eds.), *Change and Adaptation in Maritime History: The North Atlantic Fleets in the Nineteenth Century* (St. John's, 1985); R. Caty and E. Richard, *Armateurs*

ties – and merchant family networks – are not unique to nineteenth-century Greece. Indeed, co–ownership "continued to operate in Spain and Scandinavia throughout the 1860s and 1870s and also, contrary to previously held beliefs, in the coastal traffic and tramp shipping of England."[15]

Equally, family or place of origin played important roles in the structure of Norwegian or Atlantic Canada shipping firms until the beginning of the twentieth century.[16] As with Greek commercial and maritime networks, merchants constituted the main owners of sailing tonnage in most maritime nations. For example, at Bergen, Norway, in the mid-1860s "most men who provided the investment capital to the shipping industry were in fact merchants."[17] As well, "the merchant family remained the dominant form of ownership in the major ports of the [Canadian] Maritimes until the end of the nineteenth century."[18] Consequently, it should not be surprising that a large number of the shareholders of the first steamship companies in Bilbao, Marseille or Liverpool were also merchants.[19]

Shipping absorbed a large portion of human and financial resources in many Greek island communities and was frequently the main economic activity. The number of shares in each Greek ship was not set by any law but was usually divided into anywhere from two to twenty-

---

Marseilais au XIXe siècle (Marseille, 1986), 45-46; and Valdaliso, "Spanish Shipowners." As all these authors note, ownership was divided among a number of individuals, most typically merchants and mariners. Greek co–owners or partners were referred to as *argo parcineveli.*

[15]Valdaliso, "Spanish Shipowners."

[16]Nordvik, "Shipping Industries;" Eric W. Sager with Gerald E. Panting, *Maritime Capital: The Shipping Industry in Atlantic Canada, 1820-1914* (Montréal, 1990), chapters 4 and 7.

[17]Lewis R. Fischer and Helge W. Nordvik, "From Broager to Bergen: The Risks and Rewards of Peter Jebsen, Shipowner, 1864-1892," *Sjøfartshistorisk Årbok, 1985* (Bergen, 1986), 41.

[18]Sager with Panting, *Maritime Capital,* 147.

[19]Valdaliso, "Spanish Shipowners."

four parts.[20] Each share could be sold independently by its owner without the consent of the others, thus providing great flexibility. Joint ownership constituted a particular type of enterprise which, according to the modern Greek Private Legal Code, is not a company but a method of combined operation of a ship. It is considered a *sui generis* type of company that is not subject to rights or obligations itself (although joint shipowners are), and the manager represents the joint-shipowners rather than the joint-ship ownership. Following French commercial law, Greek law provided shipowners with limited liability for the deeds of the manager/master. The shipowner was discharged of any further liability by surrendering the ship and the freights to creditors, and even the liability of the co-owner or master was limited to the value of his participation in the ship.[21]

Traditionally, in Greek shipowning co-ownerships the partners were related, or at least came from the same island. Three reasons explain such co-ownerships in the Greek fleet: insufficient capital; the necessity to spread risks; and the need for an outlet for residual capital. Different commentators have put forward various interpretations of the relative importance of these factors in explaining the persistence of joint ownership through the nineteenth and twentieth centuries.[22] There were

---

[20]See G.A. Rallis, *Interpretation of the Greek Commercial Law. Vol. 2: About Maritime Trade* (Athens, 1863), 74. According to V. Kremmydas, prior to the founding of the Greek state the number of partners in ships usually ranged from two to sixteen. See Kremmydas, *Greek Merchant Shipping, 1776-1835* (2 vols., Athens, 1986), II, 20-25. Demetrios I. Polemis, *The Sailing Ships of Andros* (Andros, 1991), 44, draws his conclusions from a sample of 805 notarial documents on the purchase of shares of sailing vessels during the period 1830-1850. Polemis indicates that the number of shares on the big sailing vessels was usually around sixteen. The introduction of steam led to the convention of 100 shares as the usual division.

[21]Greece, Ministry of Marine Affairs, *Report about the Situation of the Greek Merchant Marine and the Government Measures that Should be Taken for Its Encouragement and Growth* (Syros, 1899), 53.

[22]Professor Kremmydas argues that the need to find an outlet for surplus capital was the most important reason for the development of joint ownership. His view is that "the predominance of the institution of this type of company must be interpreted as the behaviour of capital in a specific time of the Greek economy, and must be considered as a clear and conscious entrepreneurial practice implemented by a certain category of capitalists: it is about the expansionist character of capital in an internationally tried type of commercial company." See Kremmydas, *Greek Merchant Shipping*, II, 20-25.

three types of investors in Greek shipping. The first was the mariners, mainly masters whose job was to travel and administer a ship. The second comprises their relatives or co-islanders with small amounts of capital. The third included the large merchant capitalists who saw shipping as a profitable venture and a logical supplement to their business. For the first two types of investors, lack of capital seems to have been the main motivation for joint ship ownership – although risk at sea was by no means negligible – while for the third group maritime investments had the twin advantage of providing control over several ships and spreading risks. In Greek shipping, concentration of ownership led to the separation of merchants and shipowners in the last third of the nineteenth century; merchants who had previously invested in many vessels either disappeared or became shipowners. The first two types of investors remained, however, and the lack of capital led to the continuation of substantial joint ownerships in the form of single-ship companies. Unfortunately, little research has been done on the patterns of ownership of sailing vessels that would provide detailed information about the investors.

In order to examine the changes during the nineteenth century in patterns of ownership and the functions of shipping companies, we can distinguish three periods: the first covers the initial third of the century prior to the formation of the Greek state; the second extends to the 1860s; and the third spans the final part of the century. Before analyzing the main characteristics of each period, one further distinction is necessary. When Greek historians refer to domestically-owned shipping they seldom distinguish between coastal and deep-sea operations. This confusion deprives researchers of vital analytic tools and has led to misinterpretations about nineteenth-century Greek shipping.[23] In order to differentiate between the two sectors we will define coastal shipping

---

[23]A notorious example is Vassilis Kardassis, *Greek Shipping 1858-1914. From Sail to Steam* (Athens, 1993). Although he acknowledges in the introduction that the beginning of the transition was not contemporary with the establishment of the Greek Steamship Company, he spends one-third of the study analyzing the problems of this particular firm, which was almost totally engaged in coastal shipping and represented around one percent of total fleet tonnage. Another point that confuses deep-sea and coastal passenger trades is indicated by the argument that "in 1907 Greek coastal shipping shows a remarkable success. The Greek Transatlantic Company is established in March in Andros."

as trade carried out by vessels below 100 nrt in the area from Constantinople to Alexandria, Smyrna to Piraeus, and the Ionian seas.

A main characteristic of Greek-owned sailing vessels in the first third of the century was the combination of trade and transport. The owner of a ship in this period also owned the cargo. The master, who was vital to the success of the venture, was the manager and usually (but not always) the principal owner.[24] This structure meant that profits came not only from freights but also from mercantile activities. A commercial voyage began with the formation of *sermagia*, a mode of finance in which investors, who might be family, friends or even crew members, enabled the shipowner to purchase a cargo which the master could sell at the destination. These funds were invested for the duration of a voyage and hence represented something very different from investment in share capital. The investor in *sermagia* did not receive interest but rather a share of the profits.[25] *Sermagia* might be collected from a wide variety of capitalists, but half usually came from the ship's shareholders and the remainder from an extended kinship circle. The loss of a ship usually meant that the *sermagia* investors, as well as the shareholders, lost their money. Although marine insurance was not obligatory under Greek law, masters of deep-sea vessels that had outstanding loans had to insure their ships. The largest number of Greek vessels were insured by companies in Constantinople, Trieste and Odessa, although most took out only enough insurance to provide partial cover on the ship or its cargo.[26]

---

[24]According to Kremmydas, *Greek Merchant Shipping*, 54, even as early as this period the master was not usually the main owner of the ship.

[25]*Sermagia* is a Turkish word meaning capital in cash. On its meaning, see *Syros Shipping Conference of the 1st September 1902* (reprint, Athens, 1973), 152-153. According to Vassilis Kremmydas, *Hadjipanagiotis Archive* (Athens, 1973), 70-104, "*sermagia* is a company capital destined to cover the expenses of the cargo of the ship." *Sermagia* is used often in the nautical jargon to define a maritime loan. However, the difference between *sermagia* and a loan lies in the fact that the first aims at a share in the profits whereas the second at interest rates. See D. Gofas, "Maritime Loans, *sermagias* and *vlisidia*," *Analekta Naftikou Dikaiou* I (1988), 287-311.

[26]More about marine insurance and credit, especially about the local market of Syros can be found in Vassilis Kardassis, *Syros: Crossroads of the Eastern Mediterranean (1832-1857)* (Athens, 1987), chapter 4.

During the second period, the most important difference was that the ship became solely a carrier. Representative samples of charter-parties and other archival data indicate that few masters carried cargoes on their own account during this period, and *sermagia* continued to be used only in coastal shipping.[27] Now owners who needed funds relied upon short-term loans at high interest rates. In the 1840s, for example, interest ranged from two to two and one-half percent per month (twenty-four to thirty percent per year).[28] These high rates were justified by the high risks inherent in shipping. Moreover, the ship was seldom used as collateral, which meant that its loss effectively cancelled all loans. A random sample of such loans in the archive of the notary Andreas David during the summer 1846 suggests that they could be given either during shipbuilding or to provide working capital.[29]

Co-ownerships continued to dominate during the second period and masters remained managers, but for the most part they were not major owners. It is indicative of this trend that in twenty-five of the fifty-two ships owned in Andros in 1857, the master did not appear as a shareholder.[30] The formation of the Greek state in the 1830s brought

---

[27]A combination of merchanting and shipowning continued for small coastal ships up to the last third of the century, in many cases forming the basis for further expansion. An interesting example of the persistence of such practices is found in the autobiography of the founder of one of the twentieth-century Chiot shipowning families, Constantine I. Hadjipateras, who as late as 1879 used the 120-ton *Evangelistria* to work for his own account carrying and selling lumber and coal. I.A. Hadjipateras (ed.), *Autobiography of Constantine I. Hadjipateras* (London, 1963).

[28]Polemis, *Sailing Ships of Andros*, 51, presents equivalent data for the same period from Andros' notarial archives.

[29]Notarial archives are a valuable but overlooked source for Greek maritime history. For example, the Local Historical Archive on Syros has 31,505 acts endorsed by the notary Andreas David from 1832 to 1859, half of which it appears relate to shipping. Since the Syros Archive includes the private collections of another forty-six notaries — and since there are notarial archives for another fifteen important islands or ports – there is clearly an enormous amount of material. A computer programme to process this data will provide important insights into Greek and eastern Mediterranean maritime economic history. For more details on the Syros Archive, see Christos Loukos and Popi Polemi, *Guide to the Municipal Archive of Ermoupolis, 1821-1949* (Athens, 1987).

[30]Polemis, *Sailing Ships of Andros*, 74.

more formalised relations between the owners and masters. Contracts sworn before the local notary regulated this relationship.

In the last third of the century the growth of the fleet and its internationalization further changed the structure of shipowning. Management became even more detached from ownership. Processed data from the Archangelos ship registers indicate that in 1879 fewer than one-third (twenty-seven percent) of all ships above fifty tons had masters who were also owners (see table 7). Even in the coastal sector, only fifty-five percent of vessels under fifty tons had masters who also possessed shares. The 1870s marked both the peak and the beginning of the decline of the Greek sailing fleet: almost as soon as it peaked in 1875, the sail fleet began its irreversible decline.

The Greek deep-sea sailing vessels continued to operate up to 1914, albeit in diminishing numbers. The future clearly lay with steamers. Sailing masters and investors who wished to remain in the industry had to find ways to enter this capital-intensive sector. Demetrios Polemis, a shipowner and historian of Andros shipping, correctly notes that "the sailing ships did not make the steamships. However strange this may sound, the fact remains that the capital for the purchase of the steamships did not come from the sailing ship owners."[31]

One of the main problems of finding finance for Greek ships was the absence of any provision for maritime mortgages in the Greek legal system. Neither the state nor the main financial institution, the National Bank of Greece, pursued any policies that would have facilitated an earlier transition from sail to steam. The direct involvement of the state and the National Bank were confined to the creation of the Greek Steamship Company, which was founded to serve the coastal passenger and cargo trades. In addition, the state provided infrastructure by building quays, developing ports, and erecting lighthouses.[32] Other than that, its efforts to secure an effective instrument for ship loans for steamers were slow to materialize. A law to provide for ship mortgages was passed only after the transition from sail to steam had taken place.

---

[31]*Ibid.*, 105.

[32]The young Greek state under King Otto (1835-1856) also constructed the whole institutional framework within which Greek shipping functioned, creating the customs and port authorities; writing shipping laws; and negotiating bilateral trade treaties. For further details, see C. Papathanosopoulos, *Greek Merchant Marine, 1833-56* (Athens, 1983), chapter 1.

Table 7
Masters as Shipowners in Greek-Owned Shipping, 1879 (Nrt)

Port	Ships	% of total	tons	% of total	Ships	tons
Andros			1546	41%		3784
Cephalonia			2885	28		10260
Chios			2545	33		7679
Galaxidi			4297	33		13175
Milos			3009	56		5340
Piraeus			5471	30		18119
Santorini			1733	32		5386
Skiathos			1991	38		5162
Spetses			3417	26		12933
Syra			29743	31		94477
Zante			3288	20		15986
Other			15994	23		68838
Total	796	38%	75919	29%	2075	261139
Ships over 50 tons	390	30%	65291	27%	1301	241358
Ships under or equal to 50 tons	406	52%	10878	55%	774	19781

Note: Tonnage figures indicate the entire tonnage of the vessel.

From the late 1880s to 1910 there were heated debates over new laws to replace the obsolete maritime legal framework, which was unchanged from the 1830s.[33] One of the most important issues con-

---

[33]See the lengthy debate between Petros Chrysanthopoulos, a jurist and manager of the New Greek Steamship Company, who supported the implementation of the French legal system, and Epaminondas Embirikos, shipowner and MP who favoured the English legal system. For details, see Greece, Ministry of the Marine, *Report on the Situation*

cerned finance. The only type of finance that Greek law allowed was the shipping loan, or the "loan of necessity." Since the sailing fleet flourished under this system, few saw any reason to amend it. But the purchase of a steamer was quite different. As an asset of relatively low value, a sailing vessel normally required only small short-terms loans and hence its owners were not dissuaded by high interest rates. Steamers, as expensive assets, required large at low interest rates. Maritime mortgages, by limiting the creditor's risks, facilitated loans at cheaper rates.[34] As the sailing fleet contracted, and in an attempt to promote investment in steam, the Greek Parliament voted the law of 12 July 1890, which introduced maritime mortgages. But it was never promulgated. The main problem was that it legitimized the co-existence of both the shipping loans and maritime mortgages. Not until the law of 17 April 1910 were maritime mortgages legalized.

This twenty-year delay in legitimizing such an important instrument remains a puzzle, although it likely had to do with the economic interests of the merchants and bankers of Syros and their supporters. Syros was the main Greek maritime centre of the sailing ship era, and the principal financiers of vessels were its prosperous merchant/bankers. When the 1890 law was passed, eighty percent of the Greek fleet was still powered by sail, and ten years later the figure was still fifty-six percent. The Syros merchant/bankers thrived on the high interest rates that characterized short-term loans. It might have been that there was a conscious attempt by this group, whose economic power was buttressed by political connections, to delay the transition to steam. As table 3 indicates, this powerful group financed one-third of the steamers registered in Syros and Piraeus after the turn of the century. The law introducing mortgages passed only after one of its most prominent supporters, Epaminondas Embirikos, became Minister of Shipping. The

---

of the Greek Merchant Marine and Necessary Measures to be Taken for its Progress and Growth (Syros, 1899); and Greece, Ministry of the Marine, *Study of Articles 216 and 407 of the Commercial Code* (Athens, 1891). The leading figures in shipping met on 1 September 1902 at the Syros Shipping Conference, where they discussed extensively all the problems that had risen with the introduction of the new technology. The main subjects addressed were mortgages, the establishment of a shipping bank, insurance and the education of masters and engineers.

[34]G. Diovouniotis, "About Maritime Mortgage," in *Syros Shipping Conference of 1 September 1902*, 86-87.

expansion of the Greek fleet in the interwar period was largely based on the legal framework introduced by this law.

Table 8
Registration of Greek-Owned Vessels by Port, 1879-1914

Port/Island	1879	% total fleet	1895	% total fleet	1914	% total fleet
Aegean Islands	140330	54%	131227	37%	208828	32%
Syros	94477	36%	89680	25%	116269	18%
Andros	3784	2%	10802	3%	86678	13%
Mainland Ports	43291	16%	48606	14%	267788	41%
Piraeus	18119	7%	23395	7%	253036	39%
Ionian Islands	35044	13%	25025	6%	2304	0%
Ottoman Empire	17284	7%	84471	24%	90973	14%
Constan-tinople	5613	2%	40172	11%	60447	9%
Russia	-	-	8403	3%	21545	3%
Rumania	-	-	21594	6%	5816	1%
Western Europe	-	-	14244	4%	48995	7%
Other	25190	10	20427	6%	9241	2%
Total	261139	100%	353997	100%	655490	100%

Notes° "Western Europe" includes England, France and Italy. "Other" includes Egypt, Syria, Cyprus and Tunisia.

Sources: Archangelos Ship Register, 1879; *Lloyd's Register of Shipping*.

The lack of mortgages meant that until 1910 those who wanted to invest in shipping had to buy the ships in their own name. According to data from the Syros and Piraeus ship registries (see table 9), almost half of the steamship owners were bankers and merchants. Similarly, fifty-eight of newly-purchased steamers between 1900 and 1910 appear to have been owned individually (see table 4). Yet such a number was fictitious because banks are counted as individual owners. Shortly after the purchase, however, banks generally sold part of the ship to other partners. There is also a confusion as to who was a banker and who was a merchant; it is not uncommon for an individual to be listed as a merchant on one registry and a banker on another. Mariners appear to have purchased sixteen percent of steam tonnage; these were usually former owners of sailing vessels or steam masters purchasing such craft for the first time. Significantly, not a single owner in the Stros registries examined thus far has been called a "shipowner," although there are some examples of the use of this term in Piraeus in the early years of the twentieth century. These were usually previous masters of steamships who were already partners in at least one steamer or individuals who entered shipping directly into steam. The "other" category that accounted for one-fifth of Piraeus and Syros steamers between 1880 and 1910 includes owners who have no declared profession in the ship registries.

Table 9
Owners of Syros and Piraeus Steamships by Occupation, 1880-1910

Occupation	Ships	Nrt	% Total
Merchants	65	53387	28%
Banker/Banks	27	34531	18
Mariner	31	31093	16
Shipowner	17	21367	11
Joint-stock companies	19	13415	7
Other	29	35387	20
Total	188	189180	100

Note: All the tonnage of a vessel is assigned to the occupation owning the most shares.

Sources: See table 3.

This paper has investigated the patterns of ownership and finance in the Greek steam fleet during the critical years that spanned the transition from sail to steam. Although this shift, particularly in the last twenty years of the nineteenth century, was mainly the work of family networks operating outside of Greece, the patterns of ownership and finance continued practices that derived from the age of sail. Co-ownerships, composed of members of Aegean and Ionian island communities that primarily formed single-ship companies, constituted the main motive force in the growth of steam. Similar kinds of ownership and finance were also found in other nineteenth-century European and North American economies, albeit primarily in the sailing ship era. What was unique in the Greek case was the remarkable persistence of these characteristics.

Financial Weakness and Industrial Conflict in Italian Shipbuilding Between the Two World Wars[1]

Giuseppe Conti

In the interwar period Italian shipbuilders were financially weakened by conflicts among banks, iron and steel companies, and shipping firms, all of whom sought to control the yards and to reduce the industry's excess capacity. In this struggle for survival the most efficient yards were not always the winners. Until about 1923 "natural selection" was at work among the medium-sized shipbuilding companies not linked to the banks, but it did not resolve the problem. Nor did the many financial adjustments of the late 1920s aimed at averting the bankruptcy of large firms and the subsequent transfer of their losses to the banks. Before 1930 the big banks were unable to rationalize the industry. Although effective planning might have succeeded, it did not occur because the banks were more concerned with supremacy; in this struggle, the yards occupied a subordinate position. The creation of a sound maritime sector thus failed, and after the Great Slump the state replaced bank control, especially in shipbuilding, with IRI, a public holding company. While IRI restructured other sectors, it was less successful in shipbuilding.

An examination of the main Italian yards reveals two key features: the critical position of some twenty large shipbuilding companies, the weakest link in a production chain stretching from steel producers to shipowners; and a conflict between managers, keen to improve the quality and efficiency of ship production, and leading banks, which refused to surrender control to competitors in steel, engineering

[1]I am indebted to Gelina Harlaftis, Renato Giannetti, Anthony Slaven and the participants at the Glasgow Conference in August 1993 for their many comments on an earlier version of this paper. I am also enormously grateful to Professors Tommaso Fanfani and Lewis Fischer for a variety of suggestions. Final responsibility for any remaining errors rests with me.

Research in Maritime History, No. 6 (June 1994), 167-183.

or shipping. These traits explain the over-lending by banks associated with the two principal groups of shipyards. During the 1920s rival conglomerates headed by the two main mixed banks, Banca Commerciale and Credito Italiano, reorganised to try to achieve full integration. But such achievements were limited. In shipbuilding, each bank controlled a group of yards, but because they were incompletely integrated (while some were linked with engineering firms, ties with steel companies were only partial) the banks were compelled to provide funds to support their industrial strategies. Shipbuilding companies thus became sufficiently debt-ridden that they could not be allowed to fail.

Overcapacity, Competition and Specialisation, 1918 to the Mid-1920s

Italy emerged from the First World War as a maritime country.[2] In shipbuilding, the annexation of Trieste and Istria nearly doubled capacity to 250-320,000 gross tons per year. Output actually exceeded this figure in 1920, although such heights were never again reached (see table 1). But the considerable over-capacity caused fierce competition, which tended to focus on quality rather than costs, and the pursuit of power rather than sound finance. Indeed, the most solid yards owed their strength more to financial than organizational or productive power. Finance, rather than efficiency, enabled firms to remain afloat.

Technical progress was slow. The narrow domestic market, coupled with low wages, a protected iron and steel industry, and a traditional focus on design, diverted attention from efficiency to diversification, improved quality and labour-intensiveness.[3] Moreover, the economic fluctuations of the 1920s discouraged long-term investments. In general, shipbuilding was characterized by erratic levels of production and profits, albeit fairly stable debt ratios (see table 2).

---

[2]On the prewar period, see T. Fanfani, "The Troublesome Development of a Protected Industry: Italian Shipping from 1861 to 1914," in L.R. Fischer and H.W. Nordvik (eds.), *Shipping and Trade, 1750-1950: Essays in International Maritime Economic History* (Pontefract, 1990), 261-281.

[3]See I. Svennilson, *Growth and Stagnation in the European Economy* (Geneva, 1954); R. Giannetti, "The Success of the Italian Shipbuilding Industry Between the Wars: Market, Technology, Organization," *International Journal of Maritime History*, IV, No. 1 (June 1992), 143-154.

Table 1
Tonnage Built and Merchant Fleet, 1920-1939
(Gross tons)

Year	Tons Launched	Production of 19 Yards	Italian Merchant Tonnage	Increase in Merchant Tonnage	Italian Share of World Tonnage
1920	78640	344850	2242393	872296	3.9
1921	143193	122195	2650573	408180	4.3
1922	85834	80587	2866335	215762	4.5
1923	60000	88401	3033742	167407	4.7
1924	74000	74186	2832212	-201530	4.4
1925	126000	67363	3028661	196449	4.7
1926	250289	110618	3240630	211969	5.0
1927	93519	134841	3483383	242753	5.3
1928	66788	158746	3428817	-54566	5.1
1929	71834	83165	3284660	-144157	4.8
1930	96312	85661	3331226	46566	4.8
1931	167211	89310	3335673	4447	4.8
1932	49302	194838	3390572	54899	4.9
1933	18852	99026	3149807	-240765	4.6
1934	27363	18687	2928396	-221411	4.5
1935	32240	51475	2884406	-43990	4.4
1936	13914		3098159	213753	4.8
1937	42220		3212634	114475	4.8
1938	106243		3290484	77850	4.8
1939	135939		3448453	157969	5.0

Notes: The first column shows the gross tons launched according to rough data collected from maritime departments, a series not much different from those in *Lloyd's Register*. In the second column, the data are calculated from financial statements of nineteen main yards operative in 1935. The remaining columns are drawn from Lloyd's Register of Shipping.

Sources: Istat, *Sommario di statistiche storiche italiane 1861-1955* (Roma, 1958), 130; Archives of Banca Commerciale Italiana (ABCI), Sofindit file, 325/2; Lloyd's Register of Shipping, *Statistical Tables* (London, 1957).

As demand and output fell after 1920 the domestic position of shipbuilding declined more than other industries. Of all non-financial companies with equities of more than one million lira, shipbuilding firms had 4.8% of total assets in 1920 and 1.8% in 1927. On the other hand, engineering had 12.1% and 6.5%, respectively, while shipping companies accounted for 8.3% and 5.7%. The total for heavy industries fell in the same years from 25.9% to 14.4%.[4] Yet despite this re-allocation of capital from heavy to light industry, Italian shipbuilding enjoyed an enhanced position in world production, rising from 3.8% in 1921 to 6.5% of total world output by 1925, a share exceeded only by the United Kingdom and Germany.[5] Furthermore, shipbuilding employment increased from 17,590 to 20,919, and the Italian merchant fleet in 1927 comprised 5.3% of world tonnage compared to 3.4% in 1914.

The chief financial and industrial groups were headed by the two main mixed banks, Banca Commerciale Italiana and Credito Italiano, both of which sought to support and expand their clients, including shipbuilders.[6] After the war, the relationship between the banks and their industrial companies changed as the former became more dominant and acted primarily as the head of an industrial/financial conglomerate.[7] The banks changed Italian shipbuilding into a diversified and regionally distinct industry, with increasingly close banking links.

---

[4] Data on shipbuilders are drawn from Associazione fra le Società Italiane per azioni, *Notizie statistiche sulle principali società per azioni* (Milan, 1928). See also G. Tattara and G. Toniolo, "L'industria manifatturiera: cicli, politiche e mutamenti di struttura (1921-37)," in P. Ciocca and G. Toniolo (eds.), *L'economia italiana nel periodo fascista* (Bologna, 1976), 109-116.

[5] See the annual publication of Banca Commerciale Italiana, *Movimento economico dell'Italia* (Milan, 1926), 89, and (1927), 248.

[6] The phrase "mixed banks," which has been retained in Italian technical and banking terminology, characterizes the range of activity of some major banks which combined deposit banking with investment and issuing activities. These banks were Banca Commerciale and Credito Italiano, both set up with German capital in 1894 and 1895; Banco di Roma, established in 1880 and linked to the Vatican; and Banca Italiana di Sconto, which went bankrupt in 1921. See V. Zamagni, *The Economic History of Italy, 1860-1990* (Oxford, 1993).

[7] See P. Saraceno, "Nuovi assetti introdotti nel nostro sistema economico dalle misure richieste dalla grande crisi 1929-35," in G. Toniolo (ed.), *Industria e banca nella grande crisi (1929-1934)* (Milan, 1978), 5-17; P. Ciocca and G. Toniolo, "Industry and Finance in Italy, 1918-1940," *Journal of European Economic History*, XIII, No. 2 (1984), 113-136; G. Mori, *Il capitalismo industriale in Italia. Processo d'industrializzazione e storia d'Italia* (Rome, 1977), 141-215.

Table 2
Indebtedness and Performance of Main Shipbuilding Companies,
1919-1936 (Percentage)

Year	N Shipbuild-ing Firms	Debt Ratio	Return on Equities	Annual Increase in Debts	Annual Increase in Equity
1919	21	70.1	7.1		
1920	24	76.1	2.6	66.6	90.0
1921	24	79.1	-8.6	0.8	7.2
1922	26	79.8	-8.3	3.6	-6.3
1923	26	64.6	-0.5	-0.3	-46.4
1924	28	61.5	0.6	21.7	9.1
1925	29	70.9	0.6	6.6	63.6
1926	29	74.6	0.9	16.2	45.5
1927	27	67.6	-0.1	10.8	-22.7
1928	14	62.7	3.2	-39.4	-44.4
1929	13	73.1	-10.7	24.3	65.0
1930	14	76.6	0.3	16.7	63.4
1931	14	75.3	-1.7	-0.4	-8.6
1932	15	70.6	2.4	0.2	-17.4
1933	14	68.0	1.5	-0.5	-11.4
1934	14	59.8	2.6	0.5	-24.6
1935	15	66.6	4.3	-16.5	29.3
1936	15	70.6	7.4	5.2	43.8

Notes: The debt ratio is calculated as the ratio of total debts to total assets. The return on equities is measured by net income on net worth.

Sources: Calculated from Associazione fra le Società Italiane per azioni, *Notizie statistiche sulle principali società per azioni* (Milan, 1928, 1934, 1937).

The sector was comprised of about twenty large firms grouped into three clusters, each with its own structure, technological orientation and financial behaviour. First, there were the large companies of Genoa, La Spezia and Leghorn on the north Tyrrhenian Sea, which depended on military orders and were tied to national iron and steel producers either directly or through the banks. These yards were also linked with many Ligurian shipowners and Terni, a leading steel company that was part of the Banca Commerciale group. This region also included the Ansaldo shipyard which, after the fall of Banca Italiana di Sconto in 1921, came under the control of Credito Italiano (see table 3).

Table 3
Tonnage Built, 1920-1934
(Percentage of Total Tonnage Launched)

Ships	Trieste yards	Terni-BCI group	Ansaldo (Genoa)	Others	Total
Merchant					
-national	43.6	8.7	13.2	4.8	70.3
-foreign	9.7	Ns	0	0.1	9.3
Military					
-national	3.5	5.6	3.2	4.6	16.3
-foreign	0.1	1.7	0.3	1.0	3.1
Total Built	56.8	16.0	16.7	10.5	100

Notes: "Ns" indicates that the figure is insignificant. Total tonnage launched was 1,506,249 gross tons. The Terni-BCI group includes the shipbuilding companies linked to Banca Commerciale Italiana and to Terni at Leghorn, Muggiano (La Spezia), Foce (Genoa) and Sestri (Genoa). The Trieste yards include Cantiere Navale Triestino, Stabilimento Tecnico Triestino, Cantiere San Rocco, and Cantiere Navale Scoglio Olivi.

Sources: ABCI, Sofindit file, 325/2 (document A enclosed to dossier).

A second grouping comprised the large shipyards in Trieste and on the northeastern littoral of the Adriatic Sea which built merchant vessels and were integrated with many shipping companies. Links between the major builders and local shipowners, such as the Cosulich family, had existed since before the war. These yards maintained relative autonomy from the banks until the late 1920s through informal networks and legal trust devices carefully administered by local insurance companies, such as Assicurazioni Generali and Riunione Adriatica di Sicurtà. Only in 1928 did Banca Commerciale become involved when it took over the collapsing Banca Commerciale Triestina to prevent major shipowners from exploiting the situation and burdening the shipbuilding company with massive debts.

A third cluster of yards was comprised of small and medium-sized companies scattered mostly around the south of Italy. Some

Neapolitan yards were closed or demolished and the rest gradually abandoned new construction except for the Tosi yard at Bari, which specialized in submarines. Many diversified into repairs, careening, scrapping and harbour management, as well as into building small lagoon vessels, bridges, canopies, large cisterns, hangers, locomotives, and machine tools. This made the firms more flexible and strengthened their financial situation, but overall these firms were marginal.

In surveying the performance of shipyards a significant feature is the variable level of profits (see table 2). Only a few obtained a steady return. Among the better performers the Piaggio companies (Cantieri Navali Riuniti, Cantieri del Tirreno, and Ente Bacini) achieved profits slightly above the industry average from 1919 to 1936; moreover, they had no major debts. This was due to their technological flexibility, which allowed the construction of small and medium-sized ships (such as destroyers for foreign navies), the development of auxiliary activities (such as ship repairs), and the construction of locomotives, steamrollers, compressors, and all kinds of pumps. Integration and product diversification were the methods to reduce the production cycle and the time lag between shipowners' orders and receipt of final payments. These companies enjoyed a privileged relationship with Banca Commerciale, whose executive director was also vice-chairman of Cantieri Navali Riuniti. In addition, the Piaggios belonged to a voting trust of Banca Commerciale shares and to various linked holding companies.[8]

The performance of the principal firms was heavily influenced by the economic cycle and by government subsidies. The industry's recovery was sustained by military contracts and through the Acts of 1923 and 1926 which provided subsidies and various kinds of assistance for new construction. In 1923 the government subsidised hull and engine production and allowed materials to be imported duty-free, a policy which cost it some 200 million lira in three years. The 1926 Act put an end to duty-free imports but increased subsidies and aimed to stimulate technical progress in shipyards through a total expenditure of 513 million lira over twelve years.[9] To assist the shipbuilding and iron and steel

---

[8]Archives of Banca Commerciale Italiana (in future cited as ABCI), Sofindit files, 197/1, company report of 1931.

[9]See V.D. Flore, *L'industria di trasporti marittimi in Italia*. Vol. II: *L'azione dello Stato tra il 1860 e il 1965* (Rome, 1970); P. Fortini, *La marina mercantile nella depressione economica, nella ripresa e nella guerra (1930-1940)* (Milan, 1941).

industries, as well as to renew the fleet, a strategy of take-overs, mergers and specialization was initiated – much to the advantage of the big firms. The Genoese and western shipyards of the Terni and Odero groups obtained most of the naval orders. On the other hand, the Trieste yards increased the building of merchant ships (see Table 3). These yards produced fine examples of Italian engineering and naval design, such as the great passenger liners *Rex, Conte di Savoia*, and *Victoria*.[10]

Yet none of this improved the financial state of the larger firms, including the Terni and Trieste yards. The big firms, which usually over-borrowed, were burdened by a series of diseconomies due to inflexible work rules, a failing typical of assembly industries.[11] Overheads were affected by lags and delays, and inadequate inventory controls caused missed deadlines.[12] Such inefficiencies increased the cost of working capital at the various stages of vessel construction.

Financial and Industrial Problems in Northern Tyrrhenia

After 1926, the shipyards' situation worsened because of the "quota 90" policy, which re-valued the lira against sterling at ninety-two to one and led to harsh deflation. By 1928 the debt ratio of large companies rose because they were unable to reduce their borrowings as their equities declined (see table 2). The banks, on the other hand, could not abandon industrial financing. Banca Commerciale in particular was at the financial centre of productive linkages between the yards, the main steel firms and the armaments companies, including members of the Terni group. The shipbuilders Odero and Orlando had headed Terni's board until they were replaced by managers more prone to defend the overall interests of the Bank and its related firms. While Banca Commerciale (and its rival, Credito Italiano) had the interests of each of its firms in mind, it tried to

---

[10]See Fortini, *La marina*, 65, 142-143; V. Staccioli (ed.), *In cantiere. Tecnica, arte, lavoro. Ottant'anni di attività dello Stabilimento di Monfalcone* (Monfalcone, 1988), 74-98, 164-181.

[11]D.S. Landes, *The Unbound Prometheus. Technological Change and Industrial Development in Western Europe from 1750 to the Present* (Cambridge, 1969).

[12]G. Pedrocco, "Le origini della moderna navalmeccanica," *Annali Feltrinelli* (1979-1980), 951-972; G. Volpato, "Grande crisi e organizzazione scientifica del lavoro nell' industria italiana," in Toniolo (ed.), *Industria e banca*, 218; Staccioli, *In cantiere*, 164.

safeguard the portion of the economy with which it was associated. Pursuing closer inter-firm co-operation, the banks often agreed to invest in risky shares, relying on a bull market. During the latter years of the war and shortly thereafter, the banks had acquired a growing number of industrial shares and increasingly came to act as "head group banks." Only later did it become clear that the process was difficult to reverse.[13]

Economic difficulties and major losses occurred mainly in the construction of large ships. The cruiser *Trento*, launched by the Orlando shipyard in Leghorn, incurred huge losses: over twenty-seven million lira, or three times its equity in 1926.[14] Such a loss on a single order had enormous repercussions and the company was burdened by interest charges until 1929-1930. Most of the Terni yards, linked to Orlando and Banca Commerciale, were entangled in debt which jeopardized their survival. In 1927 this brought about the formation of Odero-Terni and in 1929, after the Orlando crisis, Odero-Terni-Orlando.[15] Financially, this operation compensated for losses elsewhere in the group, but it did not halt the growing debts until 1930. The group was not established according to a grand plan: there was little inter-firm co-ordination and the workshops remained unspecialized. The Leghorn yard's engineering department was inadequately equipped and its plants were not functional for certain types of construction. The Foce shipyard (ex-Odero) was demolished in 1931, and Sestri limited its activities to building motors, turbines and ship boilers. The Muggiano shipyard, which came under the control of the Terni group in 1923, was in better condition. It was one of the best organized and equipped yards in the region (and perhaps all

---

[13]P. Sraffa, "The Bank Crisis in Italy," *Economic Journal*, XXXII (1922), 178-187; R. Mattioli, "Problemi attuali del credito," *Bancaria* (1961), 1315-1322; G. Conti, "Finanza di impresa e capitale di rischio in Italia (1870-1939)," *Rivista di Storia Economica*, New Series, X, No. 3 (1993), 307-332.

[14]ABCI, Sofindit, 258/4, f. 29.

[15]Terni reorganized the controlled companies by transforming the Odero shipyards into partnerships. In 1926, Odero bought the Muggiano shipyard from Fiat, which had taken over Ansaldo-San Giorgio in 1923; see *Fiat 1915-1930. Verbali dei consigli di amministrazione* (2 vols., Milan, 1991), II, 646, 668, 675-677, 826. During the assembly of 16 November 1927, the company changed its name to Odero-Terni; see Associazione fra le Società Italiane per Azioni, *Notizie* (1928), 785; ABCI, Sofindit, 326/2, f. 45; F. Bonelli, *Lo sviluppo di una grande impresa in Italia. La Terni dal 1884 al 1962* (Turin, 1975), 173-175.

of Italy) and included plants for the production of hulls, cargo boats, artillery and, until 1926, large motors. Even so, Muggiano's activities progressively diminished in the 1920s. In 1924-1925, some cruisers and submarines were built, but these activities ended by 1928.

The rival Ansaldo group, the second Genoese conglomerate in shipbuilding, struggled after the financial crisis of 1921 and the loss of the Muggiano yard to Odero-Terni in 1923.[16] At the end of the 1920s, Ansaldo gravitated towards the Credito Italiano group. Its shipyards were technologically inefficient, which added extra expense. The Ansaldo yard, the largest in western Italy, was poorly located and its major slipways were cut off by the Genoa-Ventimiglia railroad, which caused major problems in launching. Moreover, engine installation had to be completed in the port of Genoa.[17] On the other hand, its machine tool department was technically and organizationally efficient and provided one-third of the yard's sales. Ansaldo was affected by the postwar upheaval and reverted to being primarily a marine engineering (rather than a shipbuilding) firm.[18] Since the group had dismantled its shipping operations after the war, it was unable to depend on such orders. Consequently, it came to concentrate on military craft and had to terminate production of medium-sized cargo ships.

Thus, along the north Tyrrhenian Sea there were serious problems in the industry. Ansaldo's shipyard operations remained essentially an annex of its engineering department and the Odero-Terni-Orlando shipyards continued to be out of proportion to the machine tool workshops. Both were integrated with iron and steel enterprises. The conflicting interests of Terni and Ansaldo hampered the reorganization programmes of the two groups, although each tried to assure a good number of naval orders for its yards and to purchase steel and motors

---

[16]After 1923 Ansaldo-San Giorgio was sold to Fiat while Muggiano, owned by Ansaldo-San Giorgio, became part of Odero-Terni. M. Doria, *L'Ansaldo. L'impresa e lo stato* (Milan, 1990), 156; V. Castronovo, *Giovanni Agnelli* (Turin, 1971), 322, 394-395, 429.

[17]ABCI, Sofindit, 258, 4, report of 15 January 1935, f. 8; and Guarneri report in ABCI, Sofindit, 325, 1, ff. 32-33.

[18]See the report of 15 January 1935 in ABCI, Sofindit, 258, 4, ff 9-10; P. Rugafiori, *Uomini macchine capitali: L'Ansaldo durante il fascismo 1922/1945* (Milan, 1981), 43-45; Doria, *L'Ansaldo*, 151-158, 167-168.

from its own firms. The new banking order had little impact on shipbuilding, since it only changed the legal status of firms to enable the conversion of loans into shares and to permit a bank's intervention in company decisions. The Orlando crisis was resolved by changing the Orlando partnership into a joint-stock company. The same happened to the Odero yards. But the debts were so high and the equities so weak that the final financial device was to set up a larger company, Odero-Terni-Orlando, in which the shipbuilding and other armaments companies merged, and to view allied companies as new shareholders through fictitious valuations of capital.

Agreements and Struggles between Shipowners and Banks in Trieste

The Banca Commerciale had eliminated its traditional competitors in Trieste after the war when it took over the financial role previously played by the Austrian banks.[19] Nonetheless, there were circumstances which prevented it from becoming the city's leading economic power. Immediately after the war, Banca Commerciale obtained a significant position in the third largest shipping company, Lloyd Triestino, using it as a bridgehead from which to enlarge its interests.[20] But the presence of influential local groups forced Banca Commerciale to form alliances. The Cosulich family, for example, controlled the shipping companies "Cosulich" and "Austro-Americana." In 1908 Callisto and Alberto Cosulich built a modern yard in Monfalcone (Trieste) to form the Cantiere Navale Triestino company, with shares owned by the Banca Commerciale Triestina and Wiener Bank Verein. At the same time, they negotiated an agreement to divide orders with other shipbuilders, such as Stabilimento Tecnico Triestino and Cantiere San Rocco. After the war, Cosulich support for the Kingdom allowed the family to make a painless passage from Austro-Hungarian to Italian citizenship.[21] At the beginning of the 1920s, "Cosulich" controlled the main shipbuilding

---

[19]G. Sapelli, *Trieste italiana. Mito e destino economico* (Milan, 1990), 76; B. Michel, *Banques et banquiers en Autriche au début du 20e siècle* (Paris, 1976), 257.

[20]G. Stefani and B. Astori, *Il Lloyd Triestino. Contributo alla storia italiana della navigazione* (Verona, 1938), 433-434.

[21]M. Barsali, "Cosulich, famiglia," *Dizionario biografico degli italiani* (Rome, 1984), XXX, 419-436.

company, Cantiere Navale Triestino, whose yard at Monfalcone was one of the largest and most modern in the Mediterranean.

Stabilimento Tecnico Triestino also had links with Trieste's industrial and shipowning families, as well as owning the San Marco shipyard and Fabbrica Macchine S. Andrea. Until 1919 it was linked to a steel/machine tool group in Linz, but it then passed under the control of the three main shipping companies, Lloyd Triestino, "Cosulich," and Navigazione Libera Triestina. The most important board members were Lloyd Triestino agents allied with Banca Commerciale Italiana. Stabilimento Tecnico Triestino's greatest advantage over Cantiere Navale Triestino lay in its engineering plant (Fabbrica Macchine S. Andrea), which constructed the diesels patented by Burmeister and Wain. Cantiere Navale Triestino had to buy these from Stabilimento Tecnico.

Stabilimento Tecnico initiated an intensive acquisitions programme after increasing its equity in 1920 from six to forty million lira. In 1923 it obtained half the shares of Cantiere San Rocco from Lloyd Triestino; two years later it acquired Officine Navali Triestine, and a fifty percent shareholding in Cantiere Navale Scoglio Olivi (Cantiere Navale Triestino owned the other half).[22] The latter also became a shareholder in the Tosi yard in Taranto.

The new controlling interests in Trieste shipyards (see table 3) determined the shift from military to merchant vessels. Linked shipping companies accounted for eighty percent of merchant vessels built in the Monfalcone and San Marco yards. This heavy reliance on tied orders limited attempts at technological improvements because the shipping companies ordered standardized ships which were then modified as necessary during construction. Nonetheless, the yards were able to obtain good prices and payment schedules, which helped to reduce the debt ratios, which had reached as high as ninety-three percent of equity for Cantiere Navale Triestino and seventy-three percent for Stabilimento Tecnico in the early 1920s. The Trieste yards were relatively independent of Italian iron and steel producers. This enabled them to obtain raw materials abroad,[23] especially from 1924 when the merchant fleet was renewed and business boomed. The yards started to augment their bank

---

[22]ABCI, Sofindit, 326, 4; and 52, ff. 168, 174.

[23]See ABCI, Sofindit, 52, 1, f. 195. For information on the ability of medium-sized European economies, Italy included, to buy steel abroad at a good price for their own shipyards, see Svennilson, *Growth*, 156; and R. Giannetti, "The Success."

borrowings and, until 1928, were able to maintain stable rates of return, albeit generally lower than the most profitable companies.

The shipbuilding crisis of 1928 had general causes such as the revaluation of the lira and the state of international shipping. The slump caught the shipping companies at a time when they were enjoying strong growth. Losses were heavy and all the companies under the control of the "Cosulich" and Brunner groups suffered when the Banca Commerciale Triestina, the banking arm of the local groups, crashed.[24]

The rivalry between the two yards increased in these years. The Trieste-based shipyards suffered losses of up to 44,000,000 lira in 1929,[25] in part due to serious engine problems in the transatlantic ships *Saturnia* and *Vulcania*, built by Cantiere Navale Triestino.[26] But Stabilimento Tecnico failed to obtain better results with the great liners *Conte Grande*, *Conte Savoia* and *Victoria*, which involved huge financial commitments at a time of sharp price and exchange rate fluctuations not covered by the contracts. Indeed, between 1927 and 1931 Cantiere Navale Triestino lost about 16.9 million lira because of exchange rate problems alone.[27] Stabilimento Tecnico, with an equity of sixty million lira in 1927, was in debt by 110 million lira. Interest charges alone consumed twelve million lira per year at an average rate of 11.5%.[28]

The situation eventually became even more complicated. While the post-1926 deflationary policy compelled the banks to curtail credit, the maritime crisis of 1928 led to their further involvement in shipping and shipbuilding. In February 1927, the Cosulich family, which was already heavily involved in shipbuilding, shipping and other industries, including textiles and commerce with Brunner, owned through "Cosulich" a majority interest in Lloyd Triestino. A large part of the shares

---

[24]See Sapelli, *Trieste*, 111-116, 118-127; N. Tridente, *La concentrazione bancaria dalla prima guerra mondiale ai giorni nostri* (Bari, 1955), 128-131.

[25]Stabilimento Tecnico Triestino alone suffered losses of 42.5 million lira; ABCI, Sofindit, 326, 1.

[26]The Burmeister and Wain motors had been furnished by the Fabbrica macchine S. Andrea. ABCI, Sofindit, 326, 1; 52, f. 96; and 258, 1, 3.

[27]ABCI, Sofindit, 325, 1 and 258, report of January 1935, 4, f. 60.

[28]See Di Veroli's 1928 report in ABCI, Sofindit, 52, ff. 127-128.

were likely bought from Banca Commerciale, which wanted to reduce its exposure.[29] Through Lloyd Triestino, "Cosulich" had access to enough shares to gain hegemony over much of Italian shipbuilding, including Cantiere Navale Triestino, Stabilimento Tecnico, Cantiere San Rocco, the "Arsenale" of Lloyd Triestino, Officine Meccaniche Metlicovitz, Officine Navali Triestine, and Cantiere Navale Scoglio Olivi.[30] In the worsening situation of 1928, the Cosulich brothers attempted to transfer work from Stabilimento Tecnico to Cantiere Navale Triestino and to burden the former with the group's losses. Already fearful of the creditworthiness of Stabilimento Tecnico, Banca Commerciale opposed this tactic, which threatened to dilute Stabilimento Tecnico's equity and drain it of the assets that guaranteed its loans. Banca Commerciale preferred to keep the two yards separate to control their respective financial flows and thus minimize risk. But in order to block the Cosulich family it was necessary to change management and arrange a merger to protect the *status quo*.[31] In 1930, Cantiere Navale Triestino and Stabilimento Tecnico merged to form Cantieri Riuniti dell'Adriatico. Banca Commerciale displaced the Cosulich brothers and obtained majority control after extending ownership to the electrical group of Volpi and Cini, Fiat (vehicles) and Ilva (iron and steel), which supplied the newly-merged firm.[32]

In this case the banks were driven to shoulder new industrial risks in order to control the financial arrangements produced by mergers and over-indebtedness. This happened in the Tyrrhenian and Trieste shipyards, where banks stepped in to quash mergers initiated by steel and shipping companies which, in the extreme, were aimed at burdening other companies with losses and forcing them into bankruptcy. Perhaps

---

[29]Sapelli, *Trieste*, 112; Barsali, "Cosulich," 43; Stefani and Astori, *Il Lloyd Triestino*, 527.

[30]See Di Veroli report in ABCI, Sofindit, 52, ff. 2-4, 152, 154, 174; and B. Astori, "La concentrazione della marina mercantile giuliana," *Economia*, VI (1928), 125.

[31]Stefani and Astori, *Il Lloyd Triestino*, 535; Barsali, "Cosulich," 428.

[32]See the compromise of 26 July 1930 and the text of the voting trust of 28 December 1931, in ABCI, Sofindit, 258, 1; and T. Fanfani, "Per una storia della cantieristica in Italia: dallo 'Squero San Marco' all'Italcantieri," *L'Industria*, IX (1988), 324.

one of the most neglected aspects of the Italian banking crisis of 1931 is its relationship to the plight of shipbuilding and shipping.[33]

Industrial Strategies and Financial Adjustments

The concentrations and mergers of the late 1920s did not bring about a substantial improvement in solvency. Ever since the revaluation policy, companies had burdened themselves with debt; losses in subsequent years further increased vulnerability. Around 1931, close to one billion lira were invested in the industry, excluding the military arsenals, with direct employment of over 30,000.[34] Total debts stood at 845 million lira in 1927 and 900 million in 1929, a figure representing more than three percent of total credits of all commercial banks to the private sector.

According to contemporaries, the shipbuilding crisis was the result of a vicious cycle caused by government industrial policy, which wavered between protectionism and subsidies. Extensive borrowing did little to harmonize the various sectors and contributed to the over-expansion of shipyards. This excess capacity in turn raised costs, further hindering Italy's ability to compete in foreign markets.[35] Government policy did little to create a solid financial footing for builders and debt became the essential element of survival and amalgamation. By the end of the 1920s, shipbuilding was decisively weakened and heavily in debt, a more-or-less direct consequence of efforts to compete for the construction of new vessels in previous years. Only a few medium-sized yards fared better by avoiding this competition and through specialization in engineering, repairs and the administration of harbour services. This stabilized them financially and created a better income flow.

Although the Italian shipbuilding industry was not exceptionally large, the main iron and steel, electrical, engineering and shipping companies fought to control it. The resulting conglomerates had opposing interests and seldom allowed the yards to go their own way, even after the crisis of the 1920s. Under these conditions, the firms suffered great

---

[33]P. Grifone, *Il capitale finanziario in Italia* (1945; reprint, Turin, 1971), 95.

[34]Banca Commerciale Italiana, *Movimento* (1932), 335.

[35]N. Albini, "Il problema dei cantieri navali," *La Riforma Sociale*, XXXIX (1932), 450-458; A. Cabiati, "Il problema attuale," *La Riforma Sociale*, XXXIX (1932), 459-466.

losses and were forced to disinvest, a process which sometimes had disastrous effects on local economies. Industrial and financial amalgamation in the 1920s had brought no significant reorganization of production, nor had it helped the financial plight of many shipyards.

With the crisis of the 1930s, the large banks became responsible for most of the shipbuilding industry. By 1934 IRI, in rescuing the major mixed banks, took over their industrial shares and began to control the main shipbuilders.[36] Except for the Piaggio shipyards, which remained private, almost the entire sector was thus in a position to move toward reorganization. But this was still undertaken on a company-to-company basis; IRI did not impose a co-ordinated approach to technical and industrial problems. After the Second World War, Finmeccanica – an engineering subsidiary of IRI – owned shipbuilding shares worth more than ninety-nine billion lira, representing about forty-three percent of IRI's investments at the end of 1950. The firms were divided among Ansaldo (with its yards in Genoa, Muggiano and Leghorn), Cantieri Riuniti dell'Adriatico (of Monfalcone and Trieste), and Navalmeccanica (Castellammare), with an annual manufacturing capacity of 250,000 gross tons. In spite of these arrangements, many problems remained unresolved: besides reductions in orders compared to foreign firms, Italian yards suffered from high costs for raw materials, semi-finished goods, machine tools and equipment. Progress in standardization remained slow. Despite common ownership, purchasing remained decentralized and offices, technical personnel and management were duplicated. Shipyards belonging to the same company used different construction methods and some suffered from wasteful discontinuities in production. Competition between the various components of the Finmeccanica empire remained unchecked.[37] In general, IRI's operations did little to bring about significant reorganization. The yards remained unspecialized and their manufacturing capacity was divided. According to Saraceno, an IRI manager, problems persisted because attempts at

---

[36]Ministero dell'Industria e del Commercio, *L'Istituto per la Ricostruzione Industriale*, I: *Studi e documenti* (Turin, 1955), 174.

[37]Ministero dell'Industria e del Commercio, *L'Istituto*, II: *Progetti di riordinamento*, 428-432, 442.

rationalization met with opposition over the allotment of military and merchant orders. This limited specialization and sapped profits.[38]

Even so, government intervention through IRI had one salutary effect: it severed the relationships between the iron and steel firms, shipowners and engineering companies, which had viewed the shipyards as valuable (though weak) elements in their rival dealings. The struggles between banks and their respective business interests exacerbated the problems faced by shipbuilders in the interwar years, adversely affecting rationalization. Perhaps more than any other single factor, it was this inability to restructure output that made the interwar decades a period of financial distress for Italian shipbuilding.

---

[38]Ministero dell'Industria e del Commercio, *L'Istituto*, III: *Origini, ordinamenti e attività* (Turin, 1956), 45, 251-255; L. Avagliano, *Stato e imprenditori in Italia. Le origini dell'IRI* (Salerno, 1980).

Responding to the Global Market in Boom and Recession: Japanese Shipping and Shipbuilding Industries, 1945-1980

Yukio Yamashita

Introduction

At the end of World War II, Japanese shipping and shipbuilding had to start almost from scratch because both had been destroyed by the war. Although damage to shipbuilding was less serious, it could be claimed with some justification that both rose virtually from the ashes. The devastation gave Japan's maritime industries the opportunity to develop afresh, bringing about what came to be called the "late development effect,"[1] which was enhanced by the postwar expansion of international trade. The period also saw the development of close co-operation between companies, the stabilization of labour-management relations, the injection of financial aid from the government, the introduction and development of the latest technology, and the creation of a national consensus that supported the restoration of maritime industries. The result was a concentration of activity which propelled both shipping and shipbuilding to international leadership. In terms of tonnage constructed, Japan had become the world leader by 1956, while the country achieved the same stature in 1969 in terms of tonnage owned (see tables 1 and 6).

But this unprecedented achievement also spelled the end of the "late development effect." After the 1960s Japan, which had until then been striving to catch up with more advanced countries, found itself in the lead. The change is most clearly characterized by a decline in the international competitiveness of Japanese shipping, mainly because of increases in labour costs. Shipping firms in advanced countries, which

---

[1]Ronald Dore, *British Factory – Japanese Factory: The Origins of National Diversity in Industrial Relations* (London, 1973), chapter 15.

Research in Maritime History, No. 6 (June 1994), 185-202.

relied heavily on inexpensive seamen from developing countries and used "flags of convenience,"[2] were gaining strength in the world market. In addition, the shipping fleets of developing countries, while continuing to fly the national flag, were rapidly becoming powerful competitors.

Table 1
Japanese Ship Ownership, 1945-1972

Year	number of ships owned	tonnage 000 (gross tons)	yearly rate of growth %	proportion to world total %
1945	1,499	1,871		2.2
1955	1,770	3,735		3.7
1960	3,124	6,931		5.3
1963	4,819	9,977	12.5	6.8
1964	5,401	10,813	8.4	7.1
1965	5,836	11,971	10.7	7.5
1966	6,105	14,723	23.0	8.6
1967	5,409	16,883	14.7	9.3
1968	6,877	19,587	16.0	10.0
1969	7,665	23,987	22.4	11.3
1970	8,402	27,004	12.6	11.9
1971	8,551	30,509	13.0	12.3
1972	9,433	34,929	14.5	13.0

Source: Japan Shipowner's Association, *Survey of Maritime Statistics* (Tokyo, 1973), 64-65.

Just when the Japanese maritime industries were confronting these problems, the oil crisis erupted, partly precipitated by the third Mideast war. As a result, the world economy entered a prolonged depression. With the oil crisis and the depression, the problems facing the Japanese maritime sector became all the more apparent. Inflation resulting rapidly pushed up seamen's wages and other costs, while a decrease in cargoes brought about a worldwide oversupply of shipping. All these factors propelled Japanese shipping and shipbuilding into a new era. To examine how they responded to the new environment is the objective of this essay.

[2]If shipowners register their vessels under another nation's flag for pragmatic reasons, such as lower costs, the new flag is referred to as a "flag of convenience."

Shipping and Trade during the Postwar Era

In April 1950, control over Japanese marine transport was transferred
from the government, in the form of the Shipping Administration
Committee, to the private sector. This marked the beginning of
independence for Japanese shipping. Fortunately, at the same time
Japan's trade achieved significant growth (see table 2).

Table 2
Japan's Trade During the Postwar Period
($US 000)

Year	Exports	Imports
1950	820,005	974,339
1951	1,354,520	1,995,639
1952	1,272,915	2,028,193
1953	1,274,843	3,409,637
1954	1,629,236	2,399,464
1955	2,010,600	2,471,430
1956	2,500,636	3,229,734
1957	2,828,018	4,283,586
1958	2,876,560	3,033,125
1959	3,456,492	3,599,491
1960	4,054,537	4,491,132

Source: Japan, Ministry of International Trade and Industry (MITI), *Commercial White Paper* (Tokyo, 1950-1960), attached material, annual statistics.

There was a major change in the proportion of Japan's exports
that went to Asia. In 1938, the region accounted for 72.5% of exports,
but after the war the focus shifted away from non-industrialized nations,
the category which included most Asian nations. By 1959 industrialized
countries took 52.3% of exports, while the share of non-industrial
nations fell to 47.7% (see table 3).[3]

These changes in markets were accompanied by shifts in the
composition of exports. Before the war, Japanese exports comprised
mainly light industrial products, especially textiles. But after the war, and
particularly from the late 1950s, heavy industrial products such as steel,

---

[3]Liberia is classified as advanced in table 3 because it registers under its own flag ships owned by advanced industrialized countries.

machinery, ships and fertilizers assumed a larger proportion. This trend further accelerated in the 1960s and 1970s (see figure 1). Heavy industrial products reached 74.6% in 1971, while light industrial products, including non-metal and textile goods, made up 13.1% of exports (adding food and other items only raises the figure to 25.2%). This indicates a major change in the structure of Japanese exports.[4]

Table 3
Changes in Structure of the Japanese Export Market (%)

Market			Year		
	1938	1948	1951	1958	1959
Total	100.0	100.0	100.0	100.0	100.0
Industrialized countries	27.4	37.1	26.3	49.1	52.3
North America	17.8	26.6	15.7	29.5	36.1
Western Europe	9.6	10.5	10.4	11.4	10.2
Liberia	-	-	0.1	8.2	6.1
Non-industrialized countries	72.5	62.9	73.7	50.9	47.7
South America	2.2	0.5	5.9	4.0	4.1
East and Southeast Asia	59.7	48.5	49.0	32.8	29.4
Others	10.6	13.8	18.9	14.1	14.2

Note: These are percentages of trade values. Figures for North America include Central America. Figures for Liberia indicate exports of ships.

Source: Japan, MITI, *Commercial White Paper* (Tokyo, 1960), 74.

Imports During the Postwar Period

Table 2 shows that imports exceeded exports throughout the 1950s. This means that Japan's trade balance was still in deficit fifteen years after the coming of peace. Since Japan lacks natural resources, imports and exports are symbiotic: the latter could not have expanded without increasing the former. Table 4 depicts the composition of Japanese

---

[4]The shift to heavy industries led Japan to transfer the principal operations of its light industries to developing countries. This has forged a new relationship between Japan and the less-developing countries based on the division of labour and parallel trade.

imports. It shows that between the mid-1950s and mid-1960s the share of food declined while metal raw materials (iron ore) and mineral fuels (oil) increased and textiles decreased. The former reflected an increase in agricultural production and hence in self-sufficiency, while the latter indicated the shift to heavy industries.

Table 4
Changes in Proportions of Imports, 1955-1964

Products	1955	1959	1964
Total	100.0	100.0	100.0
Foods	25.3	13.8	17.5
Textile raw materials	24.3	18.2	11.0
Metal raw materials	7.5	13.8	12.2
Other raw materials	-	-	15.8
Mineral fuels	11.7	15.5	17.7
Chemicals	3.2	6.1	5.8
Machinery	5.5	9.8	10.4
Others	22.5	22.8	9.6

Source: Japan, Finance Department, Bureau of Tariffs, *General View on Foreign Trades* (Tokyo, 1955-1965); Japan, MITI, *The History of Policies on International Trade and Industry*, Vol. 16 (Tokyo, 1992), 240-241.

Over the postwar period, the countries from which Japan imports, as well as their proportions of total trade, closely resembles the destination of exports. If we examine the 1963 figures, for example, we can see that the proportions for North America and Asia are high – 35.6% and 29.3%, respectively – and are close to export figures (36.1% and 29.4%). The proportion of imports from the Communist bloc, including China, remained low (4.1%), but it was gradually increasing.[5]

Changes in Global Demand and the Japanese Response

The factors that promoted the swift development of Japanese trade and shipping after World War II demonstrate the "late development effect," which involved government support as well as expansion in world trade. What is particularly significant is that Japanese trade and industry,

[5]Japan, Ministry of International Trade and Industry (MITI), *Commercial White Paper* (Tokyo, 1964), 89.

including the vital shipping sector, were well adapted to the new pattern of global demand after 1945.

Looking again at exports, the Japanese response to shifts in global demand was characterized by a rapid rise in the value of exports and changes in the nature of goods exported (see figure 1). But how significant was this response for the international market? Table 5 examines exports from the Organization for Economic Cooperation and Development (OECD) and four major industrialized countries in the 1960s. When we compare export growth rates for individual nations with those for the OECD (the latter of which is a surrogate for "advanced countries"), we see some interesting characteristics.

The categories in the table include many items, such as textiles, paper, and wood and metal products; miscellaneous products include scientific and optical equipment. Japan showed remarkable growth in exports of miscellaneous products, machinery and chemicals. Its export growth rates exceeded the OECD average (8.8% in the first half of the decade and 11.3% in the second half). The growth rates for Britain and the United States were both relatively low, perhaps because both had almost reached their upper limits of current expansion. West Germany and Japan experienced faster growth. Chemicals contributed significantly to Germany's export performance, while Japan depended more on machinery, including transport and electrical equipment and high-precision machinery.

While Japan was meeting the needs of the new international market and enjoying vigorous economic growth, the nation's shipping industry was upgrading its vessels and increasing their number. In November 1969, the government announced new shipping policies, including a plan to build vessels totalling more than twenty million tons. This plan was scheduled for completion by the mid-1970s; by 1972, the government had achieved a total of 10.21 million tons, about half the target. A high proportion of the vessels built during this period were large ships, including specialized carriers and container ships. Around the world there had been an increase in the construction of container ships since 1966, and in September 1968 Japan's first container ship went into operation. Over the following ten years, the number of container ships built grew rapidly.[6]

---

[6]Maritime Industry Research Institute (MIRI), *Progress of Ocean Container Transport* (Tokyo, 1978).

Figure 1
Changing Values of Exports ($ thousands)

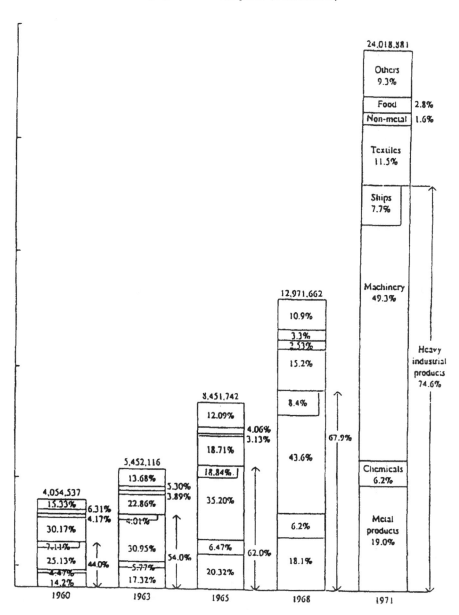

Source: Japan External Trade Organisation, *Overseas Market White Paper* (Tokyo, 1972), 34.

Table 5
Composition of Exports of Industrial Products from OECD and Major Industrialized Countries

	OECD			United States			Britain			West Germany			Japan		
	(1)	(2)	(3)	(1)	(2)	(3)	(1)	(2)	(3)	(1)	(2)	(3)	(1)	(2)	(3)
Total															
1960	78,809	100	8.8	20,300	100	5.9	9,902	100	6.0	11,415	100	9.4	4,054	100	15.8
1965	119,990	100	11.3	27,003	100	8.5	13,227	100	6.3	17,892	100	12.9	8,452	100	17.3
1969	184,434	100		37,444	100		16,894	100		29,051	100		15,990	100	
Total Industrial Products															
1960	56,170	71.3	9.3	10,129	64.0	5.9	8,398	84.8	5.9	10,129	88.7	9.4	3,602	88.8	16.7
1965	87,346	72.8	13.2	17,288	64.0	11.6	11,179	84.5	7.0	15,905	88.9	12.3	7,778	92.0	17.9
1969	143,310	77.7		26,780	71.5		14,617	86.5		26,221	90.3		14,971	93.6	
Chemical Industrial Products															
1960	6,325	8.0	10.5	1,720	8.5	6.9	886	8.9	6.8	1,261	11.1	10.5	169	4.2	30.8
1965	10,400	8.7	12.5	2,402	8.9	8.9	1,230	9.3	7.5	2,077	11.6	14.7	547	6.5	16.7
1969	16,645	9.0		3,383	9.0		1,644	9.7		3,590	12.4		1,016	6.4	
Mixed Products															
1960	20,685	26.3	8.4	2,982	14.7	1.8	2,605	26.3	5.4	2,955	25.9	6.2	1,854	45.7	13.0
1965	28,534	23.8	10.6	3,258	12.1	8.7	3,390	25.6	6.5	3,987	22.3	12.7	3,421	40.5	12.4
1969	42,750	23.2		4,555	12.2		4,360	25.8		6,434	22.2		5,463	34.2	
Transport and Other Machinery															
1960	23,362	29.6	10.6	6,952	34.3	7.6	4,266	43.08	5.4	4,949	40.5	10.8	928	22.9	23.3
1965	38,632	30.0	14.7	10,016	37.1	13.1	5,560	42.04	8.4	8,269	46.2	12.8	2,643	31.3	49.0
1969	66,767	36.2		16,380	43.8		7,090	42.0		13,375	46.0		6,195	38.6	
Miscellaneous Products															
1960	5,798	7.4	11.0	1,341	6.6	3.8	641	6.4	9.3	964	8.5	10.3	651	16.1	12.6

	OECD			United States			Britain			West Germany			Japan		
	(1)	(2)	(3)	(1)	(2)	(3)	(1)	(2)	(3)	(1)	(2)	(3)	(1)	(2)	(3)
1965	9,780	8.2	15.1	1,612	6.0	11.2	999	7.6	11.1	1,572	8.8	15.7	1,167	13.8	18.8
1969	17,148	9.3		2,462	6.6		1,523	9.0		2,822	9.7		2,327	14.6	

Notes: Column 1 depicts exports in US dollars; Column 2 reflects the percentage of total exports; Column 3 is the mean annual growth rate. The bottom four product groups (chemical industrial products, mixed products, transport and other machinery, and miscellaneous products) are subsets of "total industrial products."

Sources: Japan External Trade Organization, *Overseas Market White Paper*, (Tokyo, 1972) 37, and Ministry of International Trade and Industry, *Commercial White Paper* (Tokyo, 1973), 159.

Recovery and Progress in Shipbuilding: The Export Boom

Shipbuilding suffered less than shipping during the war and made an earlier recovery by adding postwar technologies. This enabled it to produce high-quality ships, thus contributing to the development of the Japanese merchant fleet.[7] Yet up to the mid-1950s the shipping industry could not absorb all the new output, despite the support it received from government in the form of a special shipbuilding plan and interest subsidies.[8] Hence, shipbuilders were obliged to export ships to maintain their capacity. The boom in ship exports occurred in four phases: 1954-1957, 1962-1964, 1965-1970 and 1972-1973. Overall, this expedited the development of postwar Japanese shipbuilding. In the process, Japan became the world leader (in tonnage) in 1956, a position it has maintained ever since (see table 6). This underlines the significance of ship exports in the reconstruction of Japanese shipbuilding in the postwar era.

Background to the Boom in Ship Exports

When we look at the genesis of the boom, we can see that government introduced a number of measures to promote exports, including subsidies (also provided by the Export Bank of Japan) and joint financing. Moreover, there was a recovery in demand for shipping and the Suez crisis of 1956. Japanese shipbuilders were also fortunate in having a good deal of slack capacity, which enabled them to respond quickly to overseas demand. The industry also significantly restructured and rationalized its operations. Although Japanese yards continued to use prewar technologies, rationalization was promoted by incorporating new technologies, such as electric welding and block building. By 1955 ship prices had declined because the industry consumed twenty percent less material and had cut its processes by thirty-five percent compared with 1949.[9]

---

[7] Yukio Yamashita, "Inheritance of Technologies in the Japanese Shipbuilding Industry from Prewar to Postwar Periods," in K. Nakagawa (ed.), *Historical Study of Corporate Management* (Tokyo, 1990).

[8] This is a system under which government determines the tonnage to be built each year and extends low-interest loans to shipowners purchasing ships built under this plan.

[9] Japan Ship Exporting Association, *Twenty Years of the Post-War Shipbuilding Industry* (Tokyo, 1966), 62-63.

Table 6
Japanese Shipbuilding, 1949-1980

Year	Number of Ships	Gross Tons	%
1949	70	117,995	3.8
1950	76	232,434	7.1
1951	87	430,987	12.1
1952	97	513,024	12.2
1953	122	731,631	14.8
1954	180	433,002	7.9
1955	158	561,390	11.3
1956	297	1,538,247	24.5
1957	420	2,309,275	28.4
1958	452	2,234,086	24.7
1959	503	1,727,533	19.9
1960	653	1,838,666	21.9
1961	627	1,719,419	21.3
1962	564	2,072,569	25.3
1963	699	2,269,373	25.1
1964	699	3,763,932	38.7
1965	699	4,885,605	41.5
1966	733	6,494,613	46.0
1967	905	7,217,375	47.6
1968	1118	8,349,212	49.6
1969	1113	9,167,930	48.9
1970	1037	10,099,965	48.1
1971	992	11,132,359	45.6
1972	885	12,857,119	48.1
1973	1080	14,750,831	48.5
1974	1045	16,894,017	50.4
1975	930	16,991,230	49.7
1976	912	15,867,828	46.8
1977	1107	11,707,635	42.5
1978	1046	6,307,155	34.7
1979	993	4,696,996	32.9
1980	943	6,094,142	46.5

Note: % denotes Japan's tonnage as a proportion of the world total.

Source: *Lloyd's Register of Shipping* (London, 1965, 1982), statistical tables.

From about 1958 shipping slumped in the aftermath of the Suez crisis. Cheaper and larger vessels that would offer economies in construction and operation were now demanded by shipowners, and the ability of Japanese shipbuilders to respond in terms of both price and quality brought about the second boom in ship exports.[10] The industry received a flood of orders, particularly for large tankers and dry bulk carriers. Moreover, it also earned growing recognition, which led to further orders. Competition between shipbuilders was severe and there was even talk of "prosperity without profits" to maintain low prices.

The third boom, like the first, coincided with conflict, in this case the third Mideast War. With the Suez Canal closed, Japanese shipbuilders received orders for enormous ships, especially supertankers. This boom was also fuelled by renewed expansion in global trade.

After the third boom subsided, shipbuilding lost ¥400 billion through exchange rate fluctuations triggered by emergency measures taken by the US to protect the dollar in August 1971 and by the shift to floating exchange rates in 1973. Anticipating an appreciation of the yen, overseas shipowners placed massive orders with Japanese builders, thus sparking the fourth boom. In 1974 the industry established a record by building 1045 ships of 16,894,017 tons, or 50.4% of global tonnage built that year (see table 6).

Response of the Shipping and Shipbuilding Industries to Recession

Having made such spectacular strides, the Japanese shipping and shipbuilding industries had to confront considerable difficulties after the outbreak of the fourth Mideast war in October 1973, which precipitated an oil crisis and a long recession. The growth in global production fell from 4.5% over the period 1970-1973 to 2.4% in 1975. Japanese mining production declined by nineteen percent from October-November 1973 to January-March 1975. While there were signs of a recovery in 1976, the Iranian revolution in 1979 led to a second oil crisis, and the world entered another recession extending into the 1980s.[11]

---

[10]Factors contributing to low ship prices included the recovery of the steel industry and the resultant fall in prices. Japanese steel production increased 280 percent from 31.5 million tons in 1963 to 119.3 million tons ten years later. See Japan Iron and Steel Federation, *Survey of Iron and Steel Statistics* (Tokyo, 1974).

[11]Japan Trade Promoting Association, *Overseas White Paper* (Tokyo, 1980), 9-10.

Response of the Shipping Industry

There are two aspects to the shipping industry's reaction to the recessions of the late 1970s. In the first place, it succeeded in meeting the increasingly advanced demands of the global market, as it did during the economic boom. Second, in an effort to combat spiralling costs, the industry increased its dependence on foreign ships.

Adaptation To New Product Demand

In the 1960s the Japanese economy shifted towards heavy industry. As the production of machinery became increasingly important, at the expense of such industries as steel and shipbuilding, Japanese exports became increasingly high in value-added and information-intensive, a trend reinforced by the first oil crisis (see table 7). In particular, items such as semiconductors, automobiles, televisions and radios, as well as machinery, electric and chemical plants, and the engineering technologies essential to these plants, grew dramatically. Japan enjoyed an especially good reputation for its plants and technologies, and was therefore well positioned to respond to a growing demand.[12]

Being particularly dependent on foreign energy, Japan felt the impact of the oil crisis acutely. The impact hastened rationalization and increased the move toward sophistication in many industries, including shipping, thereby enabling Japan to adjust swiftly during the recession of the 1970s. As well, the close relationship between shipping and other industries facilitated such responses. The shipping industry was able to meet the transport needs of a wide spectrum of traders, not only in terms of types and classes of ships but also in terms of shifts overseas, thanks to its systematic and efficient operations. Structural flexibility and the Japanese management style also played key roles in enabling the industry to co-operate closely with related sectors and exporters.[13]

---

[12]Japan, Finance Department, Bureau of Tariffs, *General View on Foreign Trades* (Tokyo, 1974), 4-12; Japan, MITI, *Commercial White Paper* (Tokyo, 1981), 207-208.

[13]MIRI, *Japan's Sea Transport by Regular Oceangoing Ships* (Tokyo, 1981), 27-28; Nihon Yusen Ltd., *Trend of Industries of Japan, Structural Change and Response by Japanese Shipping Industry* (Tokyo, 1983), 27-31; K. Nakagawa, "Organized Entrepreneurship in the Process of Japan's Industrialization," *Business History Review (Japan)*, II, No. 3 (1967).

Table 7
Japan's Exports

	1979		1980		
	Amount	Increase Over Previous Year	Amount	Increase Over Previous Year	Share
	($ Mill)	(%)	($ Mill)	(%)	(%)
Food Items	1,207	15.3	1,588	31.6	1.2
Textile and Textile Products	4,908	0.8	6,296	28.3	4.9
Chemical Products	6,100	19.6	6,767	10.9	5.2
Non-metal Mineral Products	1,547	12.2	1,863	20.4	1.4
Metals and Metal Products	18,379	14.6	21,319	16.0	16.4
Machinery	63,182	1.1	81,481	29.0	62.8
Others	7,708	16.9	10,494	36.1	8.1

Source: Japan External Trade Organization, *Overseas Market White Paper* (Tokyo, 1981), 27.

Increased Dependence on Foreign Ships

Rising costs, especially of labour, became a huge burden in the late 1960s when Japanese shipping was on the verge of global dominance. Competitiveness was impaired not only by high wages but also by the spare crew system, which is unique to the Japanese fleet.[14] In order to avoid becoming uncompetitive, Japan began to use foreign ships, manned by alien crews at lower rates of pay. The proportion of Japanese-built ships among the world's commercial fleets fell. This trend accelerated as inflation worsened following the oil crisis of 1973 (see table 8).

---

[14]Reserve seamen as spare crew included those on stand-by, paid holiday, leave due to illness as well as those working on shore. Salary was paid to all these people.

Table 8

Change in Volume of Japanese Trade and in Volume Transported by Japanese Ships

Year	Exports (M/T)			Imports (M/T)		
	Trade Volume	Transported by Japanese ships	Loading Ratio by Japanese ships	Trade Volume	Transported by Japanese ships	Loading Ratio by Japanese ships
1930	7,620	4,505	59.1	22,020	11,681	53.0
1935	13,704	8,908	65.0	32,916	18,104	55.0
1940	14,640	10,535	72.0	33,216	21,605	65.0
1946	1,104	1,033	93.6	1,476	298	20.2
1950	3,130	543	17.3	10,503	2,813	26.8
1953	4,957	1,868	37.7	31,289	13,466	43.0
1954	5,717	2,476	43.3	33,526	15,611	46.7
1955	7,712	3,357	43.5	36,713	19,116	52.1
1956	8,814	3,948	44.8	46,474	22,094	47.5
1957	8,445	4,157	49.2	58,723	25,148	42.8
1958	9,280	5,254	56.6	49,119	28,174	57.4
1959	10,080	5,505	54.6	64,959	34,967	53.8
1960	11,054	5,793	52.4	87,617	41,581	47.5
1961	11,117	5,965	53.7	115,254	47,969	41.6
1962	13,189	6,911	52.4	120,673	55,043	45.6
1963	15,955	7,908	49.6	144,583	67,873	46.9
1964	17,640	8,906	50.5	173,827	77,317	44.5
1965	23,376	8,795	37.6	199,383	86,738	43.5
1966	24,847	9,201	37.0	229,826	105,430	45.9
1967	24,935	9,335	37.4	284,922	134,019	47.0
1968	30,416	11,086	36.4	330,411	157,454	47.7
1969	36,834	14,300	38.8	387,728	186,507	48.1
1970	40,041	15,441	38.6	467,832	208,501	44.6

Year	Exports (M/T) Trade Volume	Transported by Japanese ships	Loading Ratio by Japanese ships	Imports (M/T) Trade Volume	Transported by Japanese ships	Loading Ratio by Japanese ships
1971	50,117	17,118	34.2	489,187	220,353	45.0
1972	49,577	14,233	28.7	512,882	215,009	41.9
1973	51,243	13,633	26.6	601,188	262,463	43.7
1974	63,634	15,147	23.8	612,526	248,809	40.6
1975	61,074	14,222	23.3	554,561	252,790	45.6
1976	71,047	14,623	20.6	576,513	269,856	46.8
1977	73,060	15,277	20.1	592,709	262,959	44.4
1978	73,478	15,301	20.8	567,460	235,912	41.6
1979	76,060	15,838	20.8	618,486	239,809	38.8
1980	76,494	15,685	20.5	605,635	236,636	37.4

Source: Japan Shipowners' Association. *Survey of Maritime Statistics* (Tokyo, 1982), 170.

Although its merchant ships stood to lose by this change, Japan's dependence on foreign craft gradually increased for several reasons. First, labour costs were lower. Second, the number of ships could be fairly well adjusted to respond to economic fluctuations. Third, because charges were always quoted in foreign currencies, these ships maximized the appreciation of the yen, which happened twice in the postwar era. Most important, when Japan's economy was growing rapidly, ships, especially liners, were often in short supply and the deficiency was overcome with foreign ships.[15] For these reasons, Japanese firms were obliged to increase their number of foreign ships. It was a technique that proved effective against recession and growing competition.

The Shipbuilding Industry: From Crest to Trough

The impact of the oil crisis on shipbuilding was more serious because it followed a boom in ship exports. Orders for new ships, particularly large tankers, fell considerably. In 1973, the industry built thirty-four million tons, of which tankers comprised eighty-two percent; by 1978 construction had slumped to only three million tons. In addition, cancellations reached between eighty and ninety percent of orders for 1975 and 1976.[16] The industry had slipped from a crest into a trough. Orders declined not only for tankers but also for bulkers and other specialized vessels. Since there was a worldwide oversupply of ships, the international market was inelastic, although shipbuilders did attempt to increase market share by cutting ship prices, as they had done in the 1960s.[17]

Diversification of the Shipbuilding Industry

Under the circumstances, shipbuilders had two options: to contract or diversify. For example, Mitsubishi, which had concentrated on shipbuild-

---

[15]Tomohei Chida and Peter N. Davies. *The Japanese Shipping and Shipbuilding Industries* (London, 1990), chapter 6; Yukio Yamashita, *The Shipping and Shipbuilding Industries and their International Markets* (Tokyo, 1993), 77-83, 178-185.

[16]Maritime Industry Research Institute, *Sequel to the History of the Contribution to the Post-War Japanese Shipping Industry* (Tokyo, 1985,), 13, 192-193.

[17]Shigeru Yoshida, *Demand Trend of the Industries which Purchase Ships. Nikkan Kaiji Tsushinsha* (Tokyo, 1977), 165-166.

ing for many years, shifted its focus to machinery, transferring its attention to the development and export of equipment and industrial plants. It did not curtail its shipbuilding operations, but it did divert the division's emphasis toward new types of ships, such as LNG and LPG carriers and more energy-efficient vessels. Mitsubishi also moved into the construction of crude oil transshipment stations, put increased energy into developing new markets in Japan and abroad, and tried to strengthen its domestic marketing network and sales system.[18] In other words, Mitsubishi diversified into a wide variety of operations. In the process, it created a corporate structure that responded effectively to economic fluctuations. The Mitsubishi story was repeated for other shipbuilders.[19]

Conclusion

This essay has examined the reactions of Japanese shipping and ship-building to postwar booms and recessions. Their behaviour during the latter is of special interest since both reached turning points during downturns. Shipping responded by developing efficient ships manned by smaller crews, overhauling seamen's employment to suit the new breed of vessel, and increasing the use of container ships. Rationalization and modernization were as extensive as in shipbuilding.

But the outlook remained sombre during the protracted recession. In 1980 the Shipping and Shipbuilding Rationalization Examining Committee, a government organization set up to modernize maritime industries, expressed concern that the ratio of foreign ships in the Japanese fleet had reached almost fifty percent. The committee expressed its hope that Japan could modernize its ocean-going operations through a combination of advanced technology and human resources.[20] If both succeed, the recession will have proven an ill wind that blew some good.

---

[18]Mitsubishi Heavy Industries Ltd., *By Sea, Land and Space – History of Mitsubishi Heavy Industries, Ltd.* (Tokyo, 1990).

[19]Ishikawajima – Harima Heavy Industries Ltd., *Its History – Development and Materials* (Tokyo, 1992); Hitachizosn Ltd., *Centennial History of Hitachi Shipbuilding Industries* (Tokyo, 1985).

[20]Japan Shipowners' Association, *Changes in Oceangoing Sea Transport Policies: Question from the Government to the Shipping and Shipbuilding Rationalization Council and Its Report and Proposition* (Tokyo, 1983), 62-63.

Shipping and Trade of Chinese Junks
in Southeast Asia, 1730-1830: A Survey

Kuo-tung Ch'en

The junks that plied Southeast Asian waters between 1730 and 1830 can be divided into two Chinese and Siamese/Cochin-Chinese groups. This paper focuses primarily on Chinese junks and examines ownership, organisation, numbers, size, cost, manning, trade routes, goods and customs controls.

During the Ch'ing dynasty, Chinese nationals were allowed to trade abroad, except in 1661-1683 and 1717-1726. From 1727 to 1735, during the Yung-cheng Emperor's rule, only twenty to thirty junks per year sailed from Kwangtung and Fukien. But from 1735, when Emperor Ch'ien-lung's reign began, the trade began to flourish. As early as 1742, the numbers had risen to about 100. The apex of Chinese junk shipping to Southeast Asia was in the 1780s and 1790s. Thereafter, according to official Chinese sources, the numbers trading to Southeast Asia began to decline (although Western sources do not confirm this).

Ownership and Organisation in Chinese Shipping

Junk owners were usually from Kwangtung and Fukien, two provinces on China's southeast coast. In Fukien, the prefectures of Chang-chou and Ch'uan-chou were famous for sea-going junks.[1] Their counterpart in Kwangtung was Ch'eng-hai County in Ch'ao-chou prefecture.[2] Junk ownership was more important in Fukien than Kwangtung, for the

---

[1]Kuo-tung Ch'en, "Maritime Trade of Amoy during the Mid-Ch'ing Period, 1727-1833" (in Chinese), in *Collected Essays on the History of the Maritime Development of China*, IV (Taipei, 1991), 85.

[2]Sarasin Viraphol, *Tribute and Profit: Sino-Siamese Trade, 1652-1853* (Cambridge, MA, 1977), 214.

Research in Maritime History, No. 6 (June 1994), 203-214.

Fukienese had long traditions of seafaring.[3] Patterns of ownership
varied. Individuals might sometimes own a junk outright, but more
frequently several persons would pool their money. Moreover, owners
might invest concurrently in a number of junks, prudent practice since
the absence of marine insurance meant that owners had to assume high
risks and investment in a number of craft clearly spread those perils.
Precisely whom the owners were is often difficult to ascertain. Chinese
documents as a rule state only that they were "well-to-do civilians of
Chang-chou and Ch'uan-chou," without giving further details.[4] Who the
"well-to-do" were must therefore be a matter of conjecture, but from
what is known of Fukien and Kwangtung, capital is likely to have been
drawn from landed gentry or officials or, alternatively, from other
commercial sectors, such as the salt monopoly or trade-related businesses.[5] Such suppositions are bolstered by the fact that in a traditional
society like Ch'ing China, government service and commerce were the
only ways to amass fortunes. Those who wanted to increase their wealth
invested in activities they deemed secure and profitable. In addition,
there were no restraints on junk ownership. An example of such
entrepreneurship is the famous merchant house of T'ung-wen Hang
whose proprietors, Puan Khequa I (1714-1788) and Puan Khequa II
(1755-1820), served chiefly as brokers between Chinese and foreign
merchants in Canton. Yet they also invested in the Southeast Asian trade
by dispatching junks with their own cargoes. In addition, they owned
several rental warehouses and a store that sold British woollens.[6]
Whether or not the Puan Khequas actually owned junks is unclear, but
their activities clearly indicate that there were no barriers to entry for
Chinese merchants interested in shipping and overseas trade.

---

[3]Wang Gungwu, "Merchants without Empire: The Hokkien Sojourning Communities," in James D. Tracey (ed.), *The Rise of Merchant Empires: Long-Distance Trade
in the Early Modern World, 1350-1750* (Cambridge, 1990).

[4]Ch'en, "Maritime Trade of Amoy," 85.

[5]Kuo-tung Ch'en, *The Insolvency of the Chinese Hong Merchants, 1760-1843* (Taipei,
1990), 154.

[6]Kuo-tung Ch'en, "Puan Yu-tu (Puan Khequa II): A Successful Hong Merchant" (in
Chinese), in *Collected Essays on the Maritime Development of China*, V (Taipei, 1993),
245-300.

Figure 1
The Trading World of Chinese Junks During the Eighteenth Century

Source: Map is based on Geoffrey Barraclough ed., *The Times Atlas of World History* (London: Times Books, 1982), 177 and 279; ports of call are based on Kuo-tung Ch'en (1992) 63-65.

Junk owners seldom operated alone. Instead, they consigned their craft to brokers known as *ch'uan-hang*. Merchants rented space through a *ch'uan-hang* and entrusted their goods to a supercargo. Junks were typically manned by a commander, several officers and a crew. Those bound for Southeast Asia naturally took advantage of seasonal conditions, particularly the monsoons. In consequence, they usually left China during the winter and spring, and returned home in the summer and fall.[7]

The Size, Costs and Numbers of Junks

Chinese sources suggest that junks in the Southeast Asian trades ranged between 2000 and 8000 piculs (120–480 tons).[8] Data from the *Singapore Chronicle* shows that the eight vessels entering Singapore in 1828-1829 were between 250 and 400 tons burthen. The next year, nine junks averaged 333 tons, while in 1830-1831 eighteen ranged from 100 to 500 tons.[9] It is often assumed that smaller junks were on the order of fifteen metres long by 4.8 metres wide, while larger ones averaged twenty-two by 6.6 metres; depths were usually close to widths.[10] But these dimensions are drawn from tax records and appear to be grossly underestimated. A 5000-picul junk was in fact likely about 62.5 metres in length, 10.5 metres in width and nine metres in draught. For a junk of 2000 piculs, dimensions were about thirty-five by 7.5 by nine metres.[11]

The cost of building a junk varied according to time and place. For a larger junk built near Amoy about 1700, the cost was about 8000 taels (3 taels = £1). A smaller junk of 2000-3000 piculs cost about 2000 taels. But over time Amoy became relatively expensive.[12] Commanders

---

[7]*Palace Memorials, Yung-cheng Period* (32 vols., Taipei, 1979), I, 815; III, 777; IX, 626-627 (in Chinese).

[8]Ch'en, "Maritime Trade of Amoy," 61-100.

[9]John Phipps, *A Practical Treatise on the China and Eastern Trade* (Calcutta, 1835), 281-282.

[10]Ch'en, "Maritime Trade of Amoy," 67-74.

[11]O.H. Bedford, "Chinese Junks," *China Journal*, XXVIII (June 1938), 264-267.

[12]Ch'en, "Maritime Trade of Amoy," 69-70.

testified that in 1830 an 8000-picul junk could be built in Siam for 7400 Spanish dollars (5328 taels) and at Chang-lin in the Ch'eng-hai area for 16,000 dollars (11,520 taels), while in Amoy charges ran as high as 21,000 dollars (15,120 taels). In comparison, the costs in Amoy almost doubled between 1700 and the 1830s.[13] The reason building was more expensive in Amoy – and in China generally – was that some items, such as fir for keels and masts, were scarce.[14] Partly due to costs and Chinese prohibitions on building larger craft, many junks trading to Southeast Asia were built in Siam. Junks built abroad were usually quite large, sometimes up to 15,000 piculs (900 tons).[15]

Numbers of Junks

According to Chinese evidence, about twenty Fukienese junks traded to Southeast Asia between 1727 and 1735, forty in the 1760s, and about seventy in the late eighteenth century. After 1800, the numbers began to decrease.[16] For Kwangtung, the figures were slightly lower. More than twenty junks returned from Southeast Asia in 1731 (giving provincial officials "much pleasure"), a level that was maintained in succeeding years.[17] Later there was a slight increase: a 1773 report stated that between thirty and forty were in the trade.[18] Although no detailed data on Cantonese junks are available, in the early nineteenth century small junks from Kwangtung, especially Hainan and the Pearl River estuary,

---

[13]Phipps, *A Practical Treatise*, 205.

[14]*The Gazetteer of Amoy* (Taipei, 1961), 165 (in Chinese).

[15]Phipps, *A Practical Treatise*, 204: Tien Ju-k'ang, *Chinese Junks in South East Asia between the 17th and Mid-19th Centuries* (in Chinese) (Shanghai, 1957), 33-37.

[16]Ch'en, "Maritime Trade of Amoy," 74.

[17]*Palace Memorials, Ch'ien-lung Period* (75 vols., Taipei, 1984), XXIII, 134, 247-248, 589-590 (in Chinese).

[18]*Ibid.*, 88-90.

traded to Southeast Asia. The 100 from Hainan averaged 2500 piculs (150 tons), while there were twenty or more from the Pearl estuary.[19]

According to testimony to a British parliamentary enquiry, 202 junks were active in Southeast Asian maritime trade around 1830, eighty-nine of which traded with Siam and twenty with Cochin China. Since it is likely that most were owned by Siamese, Cochin-Chinese or overseas Chinese, the number owned by resident Chinese must have been less than 100, excluding the smaller junks from Hainan.[20] The same source suggests that between 1750 and 1830 the number of Chinese junks remained constant, although there is some evidence that more small junks participated in the trade.[21] The difference between British and Chinese sources may be due to inefficiencies in Chinese registration and the avoidance of regulations and taxes by junk operators.

Customs Controls and Shipping Routes

All junks trading to Southeast Asia had to secure permits from the Maritime Customs Administration. Moreover, all imports and exports were subject to duties. The *ch'uan-hang* served as guarantors for the junks and were liable for violations by officers or crew. The brokers who specialised in Southeast Asian trade were called *yang-hang* (ocean ship-brokers). In Amoy there were six in 1764, eight in 1796, but only one in 1813; the *yang-hang* completely disappeared by 1821.[22] In Canton, there were at least four in 1760 and three about 1795, but none there-after.[23] The demise of the *yang-hang* may have been associated with corruption and inefficiency in the Customs. It appears that to avoid financial demands from the officials, many junks in the Southeast Asian trade pretended to be engaged in coastal commerce, where duties were

---

[19]Phipps, *A Practical Treatise*, 203-204; Kuo Ting-i (ed.), *Addenda to the Collected Papers Relating to the Management of Foreign Affairs 1820-1851* (Taipei, 1966), 318-319 (in Chinese).

[20]Phipps, *A Practical Treatise*, 203.

[21]*Gazetteer of Amoy*, 180.

[22]Ch'en, "Maritime Trade of Amoy," 92.

[23]*Gazetteer of Kwangtung Maritime Customs* (Taipei [c. 1838]), 25/11a-14a.

far lower. The merchants were so successful in trading clandestinely and bribing officials that they no longer needed the *yang-hang*, who were replaced by *shang-hang*, brokers specializing in coastal trades.[24]

Chinese junks traded to the Philippines, East Indies, Indo-China, and the east coast of Malaya during this period (see figure 1). Before the 1780s trade with Batavia thrived, but from the late 1820s the new port of Singapore was favoured.[25] Three routes were utilized by Chinese junks in the eighteenth and nineteenth centuries. The first passed by the Paracel Islands to the Philippines and Borneo. The second followed the coast past Hainan, Vietnam, Cambodia and Siam to Malaya. The third was a deep-sea voyage, passing the Paracel and Spratly Islands bound for Malaya.[26] This last course disproves suggestions that insufficient navigational knowledge forced the Chinese to use only coastal routes.

The Manning of Junks

Most officers and crew of Chinese junks were from Fukien or nearby Ch'eng-hai County. The Fukienese had long played maritime roles.[27] Indeed, their reputation was so well known that in 1782, when the English East India Company recruited sailors at Canton, it chose fifteen Ch'uan-chou seamen who were considered "a great acquisition."[28] Chinese documents also reveal that many Siamese junks hired Chinese from Fukien and Ch'eng-hai.[29] Such examples suggest that the Fukien-

---

[24]Ch'en, "Maritime Trade of Amoy," 92-93; Phipps, *A Practical Treatise*, 206.

[25]C.J.A. Jörg, *Porcelain and the Dutch China Trade* (The Hague, 1982), 19-38; Leonard Blussé, *Strange Company: Chinese Settlers, Mestizo Women and the Dutch in Batavia* (Dordrecht, 1986), 123; Phipps, *A Practical Treatise*, 283.

[26]Yu Ssu-wei, "Canton's Trade with South-east Asia in the Early Part of the Ch'ing Dynasty," *Bulletin of the Sun Yat-sen University*, No. 2 (1983), 73-83 (in Chinese).

[27]Huang Fo-i, *A Gazetteer of the Wards of Canton* (Canton 1948), 5/5b-6a/3ab (in Chinese).

[28]India Office, Library and Records (IOLR), East India Company (EIC), Factory Records: China and Japan, G/12/72, 83, 1781/04/28.

[29]*Gazetteer of Kwangtung Maritime Customs*, 21/34a-35a; Viraphol, *Tribute and Profit*, 189-190, 246.

ese likely comprised a majority of the crews. According to Chinese sources, a 2000-3000 picul junk (120-180 tons) was manned by about 100 sailors, while larger craft required many more.[30] But these figures seem high. John Phipps, a contemporary British commentator, noted that a 350-400 ton junk was manned by eighty to 100 seamen and "that the same number was sufficient to man five European ships of similar tonnage."[31] This incongruity in the records might be explained by the fact that the Chinese data likely included passengers and even emigrants.[32]

The functional division of labour is discussed in a book entitled *T'ai-hai Shi-ch'a Lu*, which is now available in English translation. In general, junks had crew structures similar to those on European sailing vessels. The one exception was the presence on every junk of a *hsiang-kung* (incense burner), whose duty was to burn incense and paper money in the morning and evening in honour of the Goddess of the Sea and to pray for a safe journey. A parallel might be the chaplains employed on the East India Company's larger vessels.[33] Officers and crew on Chinese junks were not usually paid a salary but rather received an allocation of space in which to carry merchandise. The vested interest thus created was particularly significant because junks were constantly liable to pirates and European privateers.[34] At the outset of the nineteenth century, Chinese waters were especially pirate-infested.[35] Indeed, things were so bad that junks occasionally used European ships as escorts. An example occurred in 1796 when a Chinese junk bound for Penang made arrangements with a Bombay-based cruiser, *Intrepid* (Captain Selby), to escort it through the Malacca Strait. Although the

---

[30]Ch'en, "Maritime Trade of Amoy," 74.

[31]Phipps, *A Practical Treatise*, 282.

[32]IOLR, EIC, G/12/84, 47, 1786/12/23; G/12/110, 31, 1795/06/20; Phipps, *A Practical Treatise*, 283.

[33]Laurence G. Thompson, "The Junk Passage Across the Taiwan Strait: Two Early Chinese Accounts," *Harvard Journal of Asiatic Studies*, XXVIII (1968), 184-185.

[34]Phipps, *A Practical Treatise*, 205.

[35]Dian H. Murray, *Pirates of the South China Coast, 1790-1810* (Stanford, 1987).

naquidah (junk's commander) paid 400 Spanish dollars for this service, when the junk came under attack from pirates Captain Selby demanded a further 200 dollars, an action later condemned by the Superintendent at Penang as "infamous."[36] The incident reveals the dangers faced by Ch'ing junks in Southeast Asian seas and may account for the stagnation and possible decline of Chinese shipping in the early nineteenth century.

Merchants and Merchandise

Merchants who sailed on junks usually owned neither the vessel nor the cargo. Instead, their position was similar to the supercargoes on East Indiamen: they were hired by the owners of the cargoes and expected to use their discretion in its sale and the purchase of goods for the return leg. In short, the supercargo had charge of the mercandise and its sale. He also shared responsibility in case of shipwreck.[37]

The merchandise carried by Chinese junks to Southeast Asia was for both Chinese emigrants and the natives. Before 1784, when the Dutch East India Company was still functioning effectively, Batavia was an entrepôt for the transshipment of tea from China to Europe, and it appears that many junks conveyed tea to the port. In 1782, for example, when Britain was at war with the United Provinces, Captain McClary of the Royal Navy seized a Chinese junk bound for Batavia. Its owner, Chowqua, a *hong* merchant (a merchant licensed to deal with Europeans and Americans), applied for assistance to Bradshaw, an official of the English East India Company, declaring that the cargo was his and not the property of the Dutch. He also presented Bradshaw with a cargo list, which serves as a good example of the variety and value of goods carried by a Chinese junk in the Batavian trade. Table 1 reveals that tea comprised seventy percent of the value or volume of the cargo. This was clearly for re-export, as all the listed types were favoured in Europe. But the trade with Batavia dwindled after 1784 when Dutch commerce to Europe was curtailed.[38] In consequence, tea no longer comprised a

---

[36]IOLR, EIC, G/12/113, 100-103, 1796/09/08.

[37]Great Britain, Foreign Office (FO), 233/189, no. 220.

[38]Hoh-cheung Mui and Lorna H. Mui, *The Management of Monopoly: A Study of the East India Company's Conduct of Its Trade, 1784-1833* (Vancouver, 1984).

major part of the junk cargoes. Thereafter, goods shipped in Chinese junks were increasingly consumed in Southeast Asia.

Table 1
Composition and Value of the Cargo of an
Outward-Bound Junk in 1782

Items	Volume	Units (piculs)	Unit Price (taels)	Total Price (taels)
Tutenague		700	6	4,200
Pekoe (tea)	76	55.48	28	1,553,440
Hyson (tea)	53	35.51	50	1,775,500
Chulan (tea)	12	9.60	100	960,000
Skins (tea)	28	15.60	18.415	287,280
Souchon (tea)	199	149.25	28	4,179,000
Campoi (tea)	38	23.56	20	471,200
Congo (tea)	302	241.60	17	4,107,200
Bohea (tea)	521	911.75	14	12,764,500
Cassia	82	24.60	15	369,000
Rhubarb	13	20.80	50	1,040,000
Chinaware	35	---	---	4,550,000
Sugar Candy and Sweet Oranges	121	---	---	121,000
Preserved Plums	1	---	---	20,000
Total Value				36,398,120

Note: Volume is measured in chests except for cassia (bags), and chinaware, sugar candy and preserved plums (tubs).

Sources: India Office Library and Records, East India Company, Factory Records: China and Japan, G/12/76, 85, 9 September 1782.

The import cargoes of both the Amoy and Canton junks were similar; both brought the same articles, year after year, with little or no variation. From Amoy they were composed chiefly of earthenware, tiles, granite slabs, paper umbrellas, vermicelli, dried fruit, joss sticks and paper, tobacco, and a few miscellaneous products. In total, these articles were worth $30,000–60,000. The cargoes from Canton consisted of the same items, along with silk, satin, camphor, sugar candy, and tea. The value of the Canton cargoes was about the same as from Amoy.[39]

In addition to merchandise there was also a significant trade in emigrants, notably farmers and skilled labourers, to Southeast Asia during the late eighteenth and early nineteenth centuries. There was a large demand for Chinese labour in British settlements, such as Benkulen, Trincomalee and Penang,[40] and there were even unrealised proposals to ship Chinese to Australia, which E.G. Wakefield favoured, noting their "admirable qualities as settlers in a waste country."[41]

Return cargoes usually carried Southeast Asian products, notably betelnuts, *bêche de mer*, birds' nests, Bornean camphor, China root (smilax), cubebs, rattan, tin and peppers.[42] Betelnuts, which have been little discussed by scholars, deserve special attention. That they were imported on a large scale is shown by the actions of Puiqua, a Cantonese *hong* merchant, who once purchased a huge consignment worth 65,000 Spanish dollars from a Macao trader.[43] This view is reinforced by an 1834 report in the *Prince of Wales's Island Gazette*, which estimated average annual exports to China at between 75,000 and 80,000 piculs.[44]

Conclusion

This survey of the shipping and trade of Chinese junks with Southeast Asia reveals that while there may have been some fluctuations in the level of activity, the trade did not undergo any significant changes between 1730 and 1830. This may seem surprising, for international

---

[39]Phipps, *A Practical Treatise*, 205.

[40]Gerald S. Graham, *Great Britain in the Indian Ocean: A Study of Maritime Enterprise, 1810-1850* (Oxford, 1967), 316; IOLR, EIC, G/12/113, 100-103, 1796/09/08; G/12/14, 21-22, 1796/12/01.

[41]Bernard Semmel, *The Rise and Fall of Free Trade Imperialism: Classical Political Economy, The Empire of Free Trade and Imperialism, 1750-1850* (Cambridge, 1970), 83.

[42]Phipps, *A Practical Treatise*, 320-325.

[43]IOLR, EIC, G/12/118, 48-49, 1797/07/08.

[44]Phipps, *A Practical Treatise*, 320.

trading in this area changed considerably in these years, as British traders came to dominate the "country trade" (intra-Asian trade). Yet junk traders do not appear to have competed.[45] Indeed, there are even a few cases in which Chinese merchants used foreign shipping to conduct their sea-going trade. For example, in 1782 a British country ship, *Nonsuch*, brought more than 1600 chests of opium to Canton and sold them to a newly-enrolled *hong* merchant named Sinqua. When he subsequently found it difficult to sell the drug in Canton, he acquired a foreign vessel at Macao and unsuccessfully shipped the bulk of his cargo to the Malay coast.[46] It must be admitted, however, that Sinqua's case was unusual: the opium trade was illegal – hence his use of a foreign vessel – and during this period Chinese merchants generally relied on native shipping.

It would seem that the junk trade and the British "country trade" had their own spheres and that occasionally the two were complementary. In 1781-1782, for instance, when British ships brought insufficient pepper to meet Chinese demand, junks imported enough to fill the gap, thereby demonstrating that merchants from Kwangtung or Fukien could respond to profitable opportunities.[47] It also suggests that the supply of junk shipping was elastic, primarily because coasters, which differed little in size or manning requirements from those in the Southeast Asian trade, could move into long-distance ventures when required. But again, this case was probably an exception. Overall, it appears that junks did a steady business serving Chinese markets on the mainland and overseas, and thus did not compete with British country traders.

---

[45] Serafin D. Quiason, *English "Country Trade" with the Philippines, 1644-1765* (Quezon, 1966).

[46] IOLR, EIC, G/12/76, July 1782, 62; G/12/76, 14 October 1782; G/12/76, 127-129, 29 October 1782; G/12/76, 30 October 1782.

[47] IOLR, EIC, G/12/73, 139-140, 1782.

Printed and bound by CPI Group (UK) Ltd, Croydon, CR0 4YY

16/04/2025

14658578-0004